Replicas of a Female Prometheus

North American Studies in Nineteenth-Century German Literature

Jeffrey L. Sammons
General Editor

Vol. 27

PETER LANG
New York • Washington, D.C./Baltimore • Bern
Frankfurt am Main • Berlin • Brussels • Vienna • Oxford

Lisabeth M. Hock

Replicas of a Female Prometheus

The Textual Personae of Bettina von Arnim

PETER LANG
New York • Washington, D.C./Baltimore • Bern
Frankfurt am Main • Berlin • Brussels • Vienna • Oxford

Library of Congress Cataloging-in-Publication Data

Hock, Lisabeth M.
Replicas of a female Prometheus: the textual personae
of Bettina von Arnim / Lisabeth M. Hock.
p. cm. — (North American studies in nineteenth-century
German literature; vol. 27)
Includes bibliographical references and index.
1. Arnim, Bettina von, 1785–1859. 2. Authors, German—19th century—
Biography. 3. Feminism and literature. I. Title. II. Series.
PT1808.A4 H59   838'.709—dc21   00-020929
ISBN 0-8204-4962-8
ISSN 0891-4095

Die Deutsche Bibliothek-CIP-Einheitsaufnahme

Hock, Lisabeth M.:
Replicas of a female Prometheus: the textual personae
of Bettina von Arnim / Lisabeth M. Hock.
–New York; Washington, D.C./Baltimore; Bern;
Frankfurt am Main; Berlin; Brussels; Vienna; Oxford: Lang.
(North American studies in nineteenth-century
German literature; Vol. 27)
ISBN 0-8204-4962-8

The paper in this book meets the guidelines for permanence and durability
of the Committee on Production Guidelines for Book Longevity
of the Council of Library Resources.

© 2001 Peter Lang Publishing, Inc., New York

All rights reserved.
Reprint or reproduction, even partially, in all forms such as microfilm,
xerography, microfiche, microcard, and offset strictly prohibited.

Printed in the United States of America

to my parents

Contents

Acknowledgments..ix
List of Abbreviations...xi
Preface: Mirror Images of Bettina/Bettine xiii

INTRODUCTION..1
Dichtung und Wahrheit:
Life as Text

ONE 21
The Child Speaks:
Goethe's Briefwechsel mit einem Kinde (1835)

TWO 53
Youth and Ideal Friendship:
Die Günderode (1840)

THREE..87
Behind the Mask of a Mentor:
Dies Buch gehört dem König (1843)

FOUR..125
Child Turns Woman:
Clemens Brentano's Frühlingskranz (1844)

FIVE..157
"Motherhood" and the Perils of Autonomy:
Ilius Pamphilius und die Ambrosia (1847)

SIX...181
The Genius Speaks:
Gespräche mit Dämonen (1852)

CONCLUSION 211

Notes 215
Works Cited..235
Index 251

Acknowledgments

This project would not have been possible without the extensive support and assistance of numerous individuals and institutions. The editor of this series, Jeffrey Sammons, provided encouragement and invaluable suggestions. I thank the College of Wooster for a faculty development stipend that facilitated the completion of this project. Wooster student John Zesiger assisted with the final proof-reading and preparation of the typescript. The Washington University German Department offered consistent and generous support, including a direct exchange scholarship to Berlin and a dissertation fellowship. My deepest gratitude goes to Professor Lynne Tatlock for her inspiration and friendship.

I thank the helpful staffs of many libraries and archives: the Sterling and Beinecke Libraries of Yale University, the Washington University Library and especially that library's interlibrary loan department, the *Staatsbibliothek* in Berlin, the library of the German Department at the *Freie Universität* in Berlin, the *Deutsches Literaturarchiv* in Marbach, the *Goethe- und Schiller-Archiv* in Weimar, and the *Freies Deutsches Hochstift* in Frankfurt. I am indebted to Hartwig Schultz of the *Freies Deutsches Hochstift* for providing generous access to materials while the archive was officially closed for renovation and for an invitation to participate in a lovely symposium on Bettina von Arnim in Wiepersdorf.

My parents, Rometta and Eugene Hock, have believed in me through the inevitable ups and downs of working on an extended project. My high school German teacher, Trudy Rumple, continues to inspire me with her love of ideas. Finally, I thank Mark Burde for his linguistic and editorial input, and most of all, for our time together.

ABBREVIATIONS

GB/Briefwechsel: Bettine von Arnim. *Goethe's Briefwechsel mit einem Kinde.* Ed. Walter Schmitz and Sibylle von Steinsdorff. *Werke und Briefe.* Vol. 2. Frankfurt/Main: Deutscher Klassiker Verlag, 1992.

G/Günderode: Bettine von Arnim. *Die Günderode. Werke und Briefe.* Vol. 1. Ed. Walter Schmitz. Frankfurt/Main: Deutscher Klassiker Verlag, 1986.

DB/Dies Buch: Bettine von Arnim. *Dies Buch gehört dem König. Werke und Briefe.* Vol. 3. Ed. Wolfgang Bunzel, Ulrike Landfester, Walter Schmitz, and Sibylle von Steinsdorff. Frankfurt/Main: Deutscher Klassiker Verlag, 1995.

CBF/Frühlingskranz: Bettine von Arnim. *Clemens Brentano's Frühlingskranz. Werke und Briefe.* Vol. 1. Ed. Walter Schmitz. Frankfurt/Main: Deutscher Klassiker Verlag, 1986.

IPA/Ambrosia: Bettine von Arnim, *Ilius Pamphilius und die Ambrosia, Werke und Briefe.* Vol. 2. Ed. Gustav Konrad. Frechen: Bartmann Verlag, 1959.

D/Dämonen: Bettine von Arnim. *Gespräche mit Dämonen. Werke und Briefe.* Ed. Gustav Konrad. Vol. 3. Frechen: Bartmann Verlag, 1963.

PREFACE

Mirror Images of Bettina/Bettine

> *Du deuchst mir der Lehm zu sein, den ein Gott bildend mit Füßen tritt.*
> Günderode to Bettine
> Bettina von Arnim, *Die Günderode*

During her lifetime, Bettina von Arnim (1785–1859) made no secret of her interest in achieving immortality. In her letters and literary texts, she and the figures that served as her stand-ins repeatedly expressed a desire to distill a permanent essence out of their own lives as well as out of the lives of their real and fictional interlocutors. Yet despite this wish for eternal life, the reader familiar with Arnim's texts can imagine her dismay were she to discover that her immortality had won her a late-twentieth-century place on the German five-mark bill. Perhaps, if she were to see this denomination, she would jump up and down in a rage as she was purported to have done upon seeing Karl Steinhäuser's rendition of her Goethe monument. Or she might scold the designer of the bill just as the Bettine of *Clemens Brentano's Frühlingskranz* reprimanded her brother in response to his attempts to idealize her: "Du siehst im Zauberspiegel die Bettine, wie sie sein könnte, aber nicht ist!" (*CBF* 275). Just as Clemens tried to mold Bettine into a suitable form of inspiration for himself, thereby disregarding the person she believed herself to be, the five-mark bill presents an image that, while it may appeal to the modern eye, presumably bears less than an exact resemblance to the countenance of the historical Bettina von Arnim. Indeed, one might posit that it expresses more about how the present wishes to see and remember Arnim.

If we examine this most recent visual representation of Bettina von Arnim more closely, we find it offers a reflection not of one but of two magic mirrors. Its original source is a miniature painted by an unknown artist in 1809. This well-known portrait depicts a young and rather homely girl. Her straggly hair frames a pudgy face with small, almond-shaped eyes. Although Bettina von Arnim was twenty-four when she sat for the portrait, the figure in the painting appears to be much younger: she sits hunched over, wrapped in a pale yellow shawl as if to hide all hints of the woman she is to become. Calling to mind the role most frequently associated with Arnim—that of the child—she gazes dreamily into the distance, more concerned with her own thoughts than with the painter in front of her. Since the miniature bears close resemblance to other portraits of Arnim—the sketches of Ludwig Grimm come to mind—the viewer is tempted to presume that it approaches a relatively undistorted depiction of its subject. But does it? The viewer might also question the filters through which the unknown painter viewed her. Was he (or she) attracted to her? Irritated or puzzled by her? Indifferent? Such questions undermine our faith in the accuracy of the portrait.

Accurate or not, this miniature served as the model for a painting by one of Arnim's grandsons, the painter Achim von Arnim-Bärwalde. The Bettine of his rendition seems a few years older, on the verge of womanhood, an effect achieved through the elongation of the figure. She sits upright and holds her head more demurely cocked than in the miniature. Her complexion seems clearer, her "Italian eyes" rounder, larger, and more inviting to the viewer. Why the changes? Perhaps the grandson felt that the original was not flattering enough. Perhaps, conflating the author Arnim with her literary stylizations, he sought an image that approximated the literary Bettine's description of her appearance following an illness: "ich sah im Spiegel; schwärzer waren die Augen wie je, die Züge hatten sich unendlich verfeinert, die Nase so schmal und fein, der Mund geschwungen, eine äußerst weiße Farbe; ich freute mich und sah mit Genuß meine Gestalt" (*GB* 70). Further on in this passage, Bettine expresses the wish that her outward appearance represent an internal *Verklärung*. Perhaps Arnim-Bärwalde intended his portrait as a visual transfiguration, as an apotheosis transforming the image of a disheveled girl into that of admired relative and writer. Again, as viewers we are left guessing what his motivations might have been.

Although Arnim-Bärwalde may have wished to capture a specific image of his grandmother, the image has refused to remain fixed. Just as the miniature served as the model for Arnim-Bärwalde's portrait, Arnim-Bärwalde's painting inspired the 1989 rendering of Bettine on the five-mark bill of the most recent and final series of German mark notes (which will give way to the *euro* in 2002). Here we find a more stylized figure printed on the most diminutive of the paper denominations. Her curls have been transformed to evoke a gentle softness and orderliness; her eyes and face form near-perfect ovals to which the artist has drawn our attention by cropping the picture at the neck. Furthermore, in an ironic twist this twentieth-century portrait depicts Bettine in mirrored reverse of the earlier paintings, thus serving as a magic mirror in the most literal sense of the word. This image owes its existence to its two predecessors, but it alters even further the appearance of the woman who sat for the original painting while at the same time preserving an image of the author as eternally young.

If one examines the textual reception of Bettina von Arnim as historical and literary figure and as writer, one finds parallels to this pictorial mirroring. Yet while one can follow the lineage of the image on the five-mark bill back through two previous depictions, the genealogy of the many textual and cultural images of Bettina von Arnim presently in circulation proves far more difficult to trace. This in itself indicates that, from a present-day perspective, Arnim's attempts to achieve immortality were not in vain. Her life, her writing, and the myths and anecdotes that grew out of both provided magic mirrors in which various writers could see themselves reflected. These reflections, in turn, became material for authors and scholars to knead into their own constructions of Bettine, a development foretold by the figure Günderode in Arnim's second published work when she described her friend Bettine not as an artist but as clay ready to be shaped by a Prometheus-like god. Yet, despite this immortality, Arnim might also exclaim upon seeing any one of these figures, "Das soll *meine* Bettine sein?"

The writers who have integrated Bettine figures into their literary texts are manifold, and their depictions of Bettine have changed over time.

During Arnim's lifetime, she was depicted both as child and as political activist. Clemens Brentano transforms his sister into the childlike Annonciata in *Godwi* (1801). In Balzac's *Modeste Mignon* (1844) and in Fanny Lewald's *Adele* (1855), *Goethe's Briefwechsel mit einem Kinde* represents a negative example of a young girl's book of manners. In contrast, a number of mid-nineteenth-century publications reveal a more positive depiction of Bettine as political activist: Karl Gutzkow's *Wally, die Zweiflerin* (1835), Theodor Mundt's *Carmela oder die Wiedertaufe* (1844), Louise Aston's *Revolution und Counterrevolution* (1849), and Karl Ludwig Häberlin's *Reaktionäre und Demokraten* (1850). These texts are the product of a time when Young Germans, Young Hegelians, and other intellectuals read Arnim's first three major texts with enthusiasm and gathered in her salon to discuss their political and literary ideas. In the latter part of the nineteenth century both the author and her literary Bettines become a source of personal inspiration in Malwida von Meysenbug's *Memoiren einer Idealisten* (1875) and in Hedwig Dohm's autobiographical novel *Schicksale einer Seele* (1899). Once again emphasizing Bettine's youth, spontaneity, and innocence, Rilke depicts her as the ideal lover in *Die Aufzeichnungen des Malte Laurids Brigge* (1910). Since 1970, Arnim and her literary Bettines have become players in the so-called gender wars. The author Arnim becomes a model for women's emancipation in Sarah Kirsch's Wiepersdorf poem cycle (1977) and in Christa Wolf's two texts *Kein Ort. Nirgends* (1979) and "Nun ja! Das nächste Leben geht aber heute an" (1981). As "Bettine" she becomes a more ambivalent voice for equality of the sexes in Günter Grass's *Der Butt* (1977). In contrast, in Karl Mickel's *Halsgericht. Erster Teil: Bettina. Oper* (1986) and in Milan Kundera's *Immortality* (1991) she comes to represent the threat posed to men by a woman striving for autonomy. When examined together these texts illuminate various aspects of the lives of Arnim and her literary Bettines. Individually they are reductive, however, insofar as these renderings of Bettine—as child, as lover, as activist, as assertive woman—develop out of each author's glance into his or her own magic mirror.

Literary and cultural scholars, of course, engage in their own form of mirroring and fashioning, thereby themselves reshaping the objects of their investigation. There have been four peak periods of scholarly and popular interest in Arnim's work: 1) the years between the publication of *Briefwechsel* and *Frühlingskranz* during which Arnim was often received more as a cult figure than as a writer; 2) the two decades following the publication of Ricarda Huch's literary history *Die Romantik* (1899, 1902) in which Huch assessed Arnim as the embodiment of German romantic ideas; 3) the 1950s and 1960s, during which time East German scholars such as Gertrud Meyer-Hepner and Ursula Püschel emphasized Arnim as political activist; and 4) the 1970s and 1980s, in the wake of the texts by Kirsch and Wolf and new interest in women writers, as feminist scholars directed considerable attention toward Arnim. Recent dissertations by Daley, Hock, Janssen, Krimmer, Lemke, and Schwaneflugel indicate that scholarly interest in Arnim continued through the 1990s.

Especially since the 1970s, Arnim scholarship has become increasingly nuanced. The Metzler volume by Konstanze Bäumer and Hartwig Schultz provides a welcome overview of the author's life and work and offers a fine example of just how far Arnim scholarship has progressed. Yet even the most recent work on Arnim remains selective. While *Briefwechsel, Günderode,* and *Frühlingskranz* have received extensive treatment, comparatively little scholarship is available on the author's more overtly political texts. The two most recent scholarly editions of her oeuvre, though providing valuable studies of the works they include, inadvertently contribute to this trend. The Deutscher Klassiker Verlag edition includes only excerpts from *Ilius Pamphilius und die Ambrosia* and excludes *Gespräche mit Dämonen* altogether; the manuscript for the third volume of the Aufbau edition, which includes *Dämonen,* is complete but regrettably has not been published.

As a result of factors that may have been out of the editors' hands, these editions—with their authority as collected works—reinforce the commonly held impression that Arnim's earlier works are more worthy of consideration than her later publications. While the literary quality and interpretive fecundity of Arnim's later texts may be open to debate, the scholarly emphasis on Arnim's earlier works (together with literary reception that attributes a limited number of roles and meanings to "Bettine") ignores the fact that in her six published texts Arnim wrote the story of a life that ran parallel to her own, namely an account of the collective life of her Bettine personae. By truncating this life, we deprive ourselves of knowledge not only of a literary character but also of the author herself.

During the time I have spent reading and researching Arnim's texts, I have come to view the author's life and her writing as a continuous narrative and to regard the texts she decided to publish as an amalgam of autobiography and developmental fiction that she both derived from and (re-)incorporated into her personal biography. I include here not only the books generally assumed to be Arnim's autobiographical trilogy—*Briefwechsel*, *Günderode*, and *Frühlingskranz*—but also *Ambrosia* and the two "king's books." By integrating her private letters into many of her texts and by making herself the model for her protagonists, the writer Arnim positioned herself in close relationship to what I will refer to as her literary personae. I borrow this term from Cheryl Walker, who defines the persona as "a mask that may be related simultaneously to the biographical data available about the author and to other cultural and literary voices" (114). Walker notes further that "the mask may well be at odds with some information we have about the author. However, the significance of the persona goes beyond its congruence with or divergence from typical authorial moods and meditations" (114). Arnim's Bettine personae include not only her Bettine figures, but also Frau Rath Goethe, Ambrosia, and a daemon, among others. She created roles for them (often by accepting, rejecting, or redefining roles that had been assigned to her) with the intention that these roles would reflect back onto her. The individual process of writing and the public process of reception became part of what Teresa de Lauretis would call Arnim's "experience." This experience informed both Arnim's public actions and the roles she created for the protagonists in subsequent texts. I thus consider the "Bettine" of *Briefwechsel* a precursor both to the politically active Arnim of the 1840s and to protagonists of Arnim's subsequent texts.

In the following chapters I will discuss Arnim's texts in the order in which they were written and focus on readings of the individual texts, the intertextual links between them, and the relationship of the author to her Bettine personae. I will refer to the author as "Bettina von Arnim" or simply as "Arnim" and to both the textual figures in her novel-length works and the mythical figures that grew out of these works as "Bettine." I will maintain a similar distinction between the writer Karoline von

Günderode and the Caroline von Günderode who appears in Arnim's texts, and between Catharina Elisabeth Goethe and the Frau Rath figure of *Briefwechsel* and *Dies Buch*. In the first two instances, the differences between the spellings are admittedly subtle. Yet as Patricia Anne Simpson has noted, the "almost imperceptible difference" between Bettine and Bettina, and between Günderode and Günderrode, indicates the extent to which Arnim blurred the line between historical persons and her literary creations (249).

In Chapter One I demonstrate how, while defying strict generic categorization, Arnim's texts appropriate generic aspects of autobiography, the letter-form, and the *Bildungsroman* in a manner that lends them, when viewed as a whole, the quality of an extended developmental text. I then employ feminist theories of positionality to propose a new model for conceptualizing the relationship between Arnim's life and her writing. Chapters Two through Seven offer a sustained reading of Arnim's six major works: *Goethe's Briefwechsel mit einem Kinde* (1835), *Die Günderode* (1840), *Dies Buch gehört dem König* (1843), *Clemens Brentano's Frühlingskranz* (1844), *Ilius Pamphilius und die Ambrosia* (1847), and *Gespräche mit Dämonen* (1852). Focusing on the roles that Arnim assigned to her literary namesakes, I argue that, while one cannot and should not conflate Arnim with her literary personae, the roles Arnim played in her public life were informed by the roles she assigned to these characters, roles that included child, friend, lover, mother, writer, and genius. Conversely, I will demonstrate how Arnim's increasing public stature over the course of the 1840s strongly influenced the transformation of her literary namesakes from childlike and youthful figures who focused primarily on the development of the self into figures who concerned themselves first and foremost with the relationship between a ruler and his subjects. Through this analysis I will show how Arnim's support of a constitutional monarchy in her later political writings reveals an attempt to apply the model for interpersonal interaction (*romantische Geselligkeit*) that she foregrounds in her first two works to the relationship between a king, a state, and the citizens of that state. I conclude that this model would not have been possible without the strong sense of self that Arnim developed through her Bettine personae.

In attempting to answer the question "Who was Bettina von Arnim?"

one finds validation for Foucault's claim: "What is found at the historical beginning of things is not the inviolable identity of their origin; it is the dissension of other things. It is disparity" ("Nietzsche, Genealogy and History" 142). We have no way of determining with absolute precision who the historical Bettina von Arnim was, because in tracing her genealogy, we encounter numerous mirrors reflecting off of one another. As in a hall of mirrors, some produce less distorted images than others, but none brings us to an origin, to an absolute truth. This is as true for Arnim's own textual production as it is for others' depictions and analyses of her. My task here is to examine the texts that served as the bases for—or were ignored in—the production of many of these subsequent depictions, that is, to look at the images Arnim saw in her own mirror(s) and the replicas of herself that she shaped at different points during her writing career. In so doing, I hope not to arrive at a truth statement about the life of the historical individual, but rather to complicate and deepen our understanding of both Bettina von Arnim and the literary personae she chose to create in her own image.

INTRODUCTION

Dichtung und Wahrheit: Life as Text

The Development of a Life

It has long been acknowledged that, when Bettina von Arnim decided to revise and publish her correspondences with Goethe, Karoline von Günderrode, Clemens Brentano, and Philipp Nathusius, and when she incorporated her life experiences, political views, and correspondence with Friedrich Wilhelm IV of Prussia into *Dies Buch gehört dem König* and *Gespräche mit Dämonen*, she made no attempt to narrate her life the way it really was. If anything, she intentionally created a world in her own image and manipulated her central characters to play specific roles within that world. Despite this commonly held understanding of how Arnim transformed life experiences in her writing, attempts to navigate the distance between Bettina von Arnim as a historical individual and the textual personae she produced have been fraught with difficulty, often resulting in reductive readings of both the author and her texts. This reduction includes the neat division of Arnim's life into periods of creative productivity and periods of stagnation: the formative period of her youth and young adulthood during which she corresponded with Goethe, Günderrode, and her brother Clemens (1785–1811); the years of her marriage to Achim von Arnim (1811–31) during which she devoted her energies to her roles as wife and mother, and according to popular lore, had no time for writing; and the period following Achim von Arnim's death during which she came into her own as a writer (1831–1859).[1] Such a division facilitates an awareness of the distance between Arnim's original correspondence and the texts into which she later integrates many of her letters, but it tends to elide the fact that Arnim's letter and dialogue books constitute the product of a lifetime of recursive writing.[2]

Like other women writing in the late eighteenth and early nineteenth centuries—Arnim's grandmother Sophie von La Roche, Caroline Schlegel-Schelling, and Rahel Varnhagen come to mind here—epistolary exchange provided the young Bettina Brentano with a means to develop her sense of self. She began the process of writing her life as a young woman, and upon examination of her early letters, one encounters a Bettina Brentano who already employs the written text to define herself and to express her desires. She writes to Claudine Piautaz in 1806, for example:

> Diese Einsamkeit reizt mich sehr, und ich fange an zu glauben, daß ich gar nicht für das Gesellschaftliche geboren bin, ich kann hier meiner Phantasie nachgeben, ohne mich zu erhitzen, durch den Widerspruch meiner Umgebung; ich fühle mich so glücklich durch die Freiheit, die mir doppelt durch die herrliche Gegend wird, in deren Mitte ich wohne.[3]

Here Bettina Brentano gives free reign to her imagination, rejecting the hectic pace of social life while at the same time utilizing social exchange as a vehicle for exploring her own feelings. Like her grandmother and unlike Caroline Schlegel-Schelling or Rahel Varnhagen, Arnim eventually publishes her texts; later in life she integrates the letter from which this passage is excerpted into *Günderode*. Yet this early document provides a sense of budding self-sufficiency and a need for freedom, those qualities often associated with the Bettine personae of Arnim's texts.

Arnim's years of marriage set the parameters for what is traditionally designated as her "second life." Ingeborg Drewitz writes in her influential biography that Arnim put her expectations and capabilities on hold from the time she was married in 1811 until Achim von Arnim's death in 1831 (86). Raising seven children and sustaining a commuter marriage that spanned the eighty kilometers from Berlin to Wiepersdorf where her husband spent most of his time managing the family estate certainly consumed much of Arnim's time. Dagmar von Gersdorff notes that Arnim spent a significant amount of energy just making sure her children stayed alive: "wie eine Naturheilkundige [behandelte Bettine] die Krankheiten der

Kinder so klug...daß keines starb, während bei anderen Familien der Kindertod umging" (171). Furthermore, especially in the last ten years of their marriage, Bettina and Achim grew apart. She spent increasing amounts of time in Berlin and entered into what Gersdorff describes as *Romanzen*, first with the student Philipp Hössli and then with the military officer Karl Ludwig von Wildermeth. As Gersdorff writes of the romantic pair "Bettina and Achim:"

> In gewißer Weise hatte sich ihre Ehe in einer unglücklichen Verkettung von inneren und äußeren Unverträglichkeiten tragisch entwickelt. Früher waren sie verbunden durch gemeinsames Arbeiten, Dichten und Erzählen, durch das Sammeln von Volksliedern, durch Musik und Theater. Was war geblieben? Die wirtschaftliche Interessengemeinschaft einer kinderreichen Familie. (186)

An often-cited passage would thus appear to substantiate Drewitz's claim about Arnim's lack of productivity during her marriage. She wrote to her brother-in-law Friedrich Savigny in 1823: "Ich habe die zwölf Jahre meines Ehestands leiblich und geistigerweise auf der Marterbank zugebracht...Mein Perspektiv ist das End aller Dinge."[4]

Arnim's difficulties and frustrations notwithstanding, her documented activities corroborate neither Drewitz's assertion nor Christa Wolf's claim that, during her marriage, Arnim's letters lay locked in a drawer, serving only as "die Zeugnisse ihres ersten Lebens" ("Nun ja!" 320). On the contrary, Arnim remained a prolific letter-writer throughout her marriage, and she retold and reshaped the stories of her youth (and especially accounts of her relationship with Goethe) both orally and in letters.[5] Evidence of Arnim's active story-telling can be found in an entry that Mala Montgomery-Silverstolpe, a Swedish traveler who spent extensive time in Berlin, recorded in her diary on December 1, 1825:

> Am Nachmittag machte ich mit Lindblad bei Frau Arnim Visite. Wir fanden Bettina schreibend. Adolf setzte sich auf ihren Wunsch an das Piano forte, und sie las mir den Brief vor, den sie eben schrieb—ich weiß nicht, an wen. Arme Bettina! Ich verstehe sie vielleicht besser, als sie glaubt, obgleich ich in ihrer Lage, als Gattin und Mutter von sechs Kindern, wohl genug für mein Herz und meinen Tätigkeitsdrang hätte. Aber größere Gaben bedingen wohl auch größere Bedürfnisse, Gefahren und Verlockungen. Ihre "Liebesbegegnisse" mit Goethe sind eigen! (157)

In this passage and throughout her diary, Montgomery-Silverstolpe provides a sketch of Arnim honing her skills as a writer, doing her best in the face of disapproval and innumerable obstacles to juggle family responsibilities with her need for creative expression.[6]

Arnim often did, however, feel confined during the years of her marriage. In one of the first works to consider in depth the influence of Arnim's marriage upon her artistic production, Bäumer and Schultz chart the development of Arnim as an artist between the years 1810 and 1835. They note that, although aware of a strong need to assert her own voice, the Arnim of this period had not yet settled on an adequate means of expression (57). Throughout her marriage Arnim gave voice to her creativity in letter-writing, story-telling, painting, music, and especially social interaction. Her talents were not locked away in a drawer, but she experienced significant difficulty giving them shape and direction, a difficulty that she eventually thematized and valorized in her published texts.

From 1831 on, her husband deceased and her children almost grown, Arnim found the time to write for publication. Although her extended family did not particularly approve of her work, the decision to publish was certainly made easier because she did not have to contend with a disapproving husband, or as was the case for Fanny Lewald, a disapproving father.[7] She began by examining her earlier correspondence with Goethe. She edited, added to and deleted from these letters, incorporated other letters, and eventually shaped this amalgam into *Briefwechsel*. More works followed soon thereafter. Often her work on one text coincided with work on another. She began to reflect on her relationship with Karoline von Günderrode in the first section of *Briefwechsel*. While writing *Günderode*, she entered into correspondence with two students, Philip Nathusius and Julius Döring, with the intention of publishing their letters. Although her conception changed over time, these letters served as the basis for *Ambrosia*. In addition, she began *Frühlingskranz* during the period she was working on *Dies Buch*. As in the earlier periods of her life, she also continued her correspondence with numerous individuals, and this exchange influenced her published texts.[8] The diaries of Karl August von Varnhagen indicate that Arnim remained as intellectually active as her waning health permitted until her death on January 28, 1859.[9]

Poetry or Truth?

Arnim spent much of her life—including the years of her marriage—writing her life. For this reason, her interpersonal and epistolary exchanges up to and even beyond 1832 must be considered preliminary stages of her published works. This raises the question, posed already in Arnim's lifetime, whether those works should be read as autobiography or as fiction.

Arnim sprinkled autobiographical anecdotes throughout her works. In *Briefwechsel*, *Günderode*, and *Frühlingskranz*, the reader finds accounts of the protagonist's parents, her brother Peter, her status as her father's favorite child, and the death of her mother. The figure who tells of these people and events, who recounts to Clemens her memories of their first encounter, who writes to Günderode of her work on *Des Knaben Wunderhorn*, and who reconstructs for Goethe tales of her experiences in a convent, calls herself "Bettine." Original correspondences indicate that these accounts parallel the experiences of the author as a young girl. In addition to interactions with individuals, another formative experience in the life of Bettina Brentano was her introduction, initially through her brother Clemens, to the ideas of German romanticism, and these ideas make their way alongside the anecdotes into her later writing.

Arnim's texts also allow the reader to become acquainted with her as an adult. The following passage from *Ambrosia* describes the protagonist's tireless activity during the 1830s:

> [Lieber Pamphil,]
> Gehst du nach Neapel?—Willst Du Empfehlungen nach Weimar?...Alles ist fort wegen der Cholera. Unser Versandter in Rom ist in Potsdam, wird mir am Donnerstag Empfehlungsbriefe schicken für Dich. Alles stirbt wie die Fliegen... ich bin allein im Haus mit der traurigen furchtsamen schwarzgekleideten Schwester der armen an der Auszehrung verschiedenen Russin, diese legt sich ins Bett und will auch sterben; nun braucht nur die Polizei auch noch zu sterben, dann bin ich König von Berlin. Bei Dir bin ich auch schon König, denn wie mich deucht, widersprichst Du mir nicht mehr. Bald bin ich zustande mit meinem großen Werk der Unmöglichkeit mit meiner Übersetzung, besonders sind die Sonette ganz unmöglich vortrefflich geworden. (*IPA* 506)

Through Ambrosia's mention of her ability to make contacts for Pamphilius, the author Arnim alludes to the social status she has achieved by 1840. In addition, this passage makes reference to Arnim's idealized love-relationship with Nathusius, to her volunteer work during the recurring cholera outbreaks in Berlin,[10] and to her English translation of *Briefwechsel*, published in 1837 to earn money for her Goethe Monument.[11]

Arnim also wove into her texts her increasing concern for political and social causes. *Dies Buch* and *Dämonen* constitute a critical response to both her interactions with Friedrich Wilhelm IV of Prussia and the political situation in Prussia preceding and following the uprisings of 1848.[12] Just as the young Bettina Brentano was influenced by German romanticism, the adult Bettina von Arnim followed the debates of Young Hegelians and Young Germans and incorporated many of their liberal and radical ideas into her texts. Moreover, although Arnim was not officially engaged in the German women's movement, the ideas of women's emancipation were in the air, and they present themselves in her texts alongside ideas of a more general human emancipation. Arnim's body of work reveals that, as she grew older, she became increasingly involved in the social issues of her time; she never gave up her hope that her literary works would influence those who had the political power to make changes in the lives of the common people. Indeed, one cannot imagine the works of Bettina von Arnim without the active life that provided the material for them.

Because Arnim's textual production developed out of her life experiences and because a close relationship existed between her writing and those experiences, many reviewers and scholars have chosen to read her texts for autobiographical content. These readings generally fall into two categories that, borrowing from Biddy Martin's study of Lou Andreas-Salomé (26), I will refer to as the "referential model" and the "textual model" of (auto)biography and representation. Whereas referential accounts read Arnim's texts as a series of "exhaustive and accurate representations of the truth" (26) about Arnim's life, analyses based on a textual model steer away from reading in search of verifiable facts. Instead, they study the texts to gain a sense of who Arnim was while at the same time allowing for and even encouraging multiple and conflicting readings of the author and her figures. Furthermore, textual accounts generally strive to distinguish between Arnim's "original" correspondence and her published texts.

It will come as no surprise that early reception of Arnim is replete with referential readings of her texts. Many reviewers of *Briefwechsel*, among them Ludwig Börne and Willibald Alexis, considered the text a historical document and made no attempt to distinguish between Arnim and her literary Bettine. This was, perhaps, understandable in light of the fact that Arnim's original correspondence with Goethe had not yet been published. Yet even after Loeper's 1879 publication of fourteen of Goethe's original letters revealed the extent to which Arnim had, in *Briefwechsel*, altered Goethe's correspondence, the conflation of Arnim with her textual personae continued.[13]

In more recent scholarship, this referential reading has been employed to foreground Arnim's interest in and activity on behalf of oppressed groups such as minorities and women. For example, scholars from Ludwig Geiger at the turn of the century to Helmut Hirsch in the present have cited *Briefwechsel*, *Günderode*, and *Frühlingskranz* as evidence for Arnim's interest in the rights of Jews.[14] Their studies have served both as a response to anti-Semitism and as an attempt to idealize Bettina von Arnim. More recently, however, Bäumer, Hoock-Demarle, and I have noted that, while Arnim's literary Bettines may have supported the rights of the Jewish Veilchens and Ephraims she encountered, the attitudes of the author were far more ambivalent and often contradictory.[15]

With its aim to highlight the heretofore undervalued contributions of women to history and culture, feminist scholarship has also offered referential readings of Arnim's texts as autobiography. These studies harmonize the author with her literary personae in order to present Arnim as an example of an exceptionally self-determined woman living in a historical context in which women's possibilities for self-determination were limited. Against the backdrop of this approach, *Günderode* becomes the most authentic of Arnim's texts because of its emphasis on female friendship.[16] Like the studies of Arnim's relations to Jews, feminist studies of the emancipatory potential in Arnim's texts have provided invaluable contributions to scholarship, significantly revising less political approaches to her texts. Nevertheless, by focusing on Arnim as a role model for political behavior, they tend to overlook the complexities of and contradictions in Arnim's life and letters. Further, they tend to attribute the thoughts and actions of Arnim's more idealized Bettine personae to the author while ignoring more problematic figures such as Ambrosia. While a definite link exists between literary production and concrete action, they cannot be regarded as one and the same, and doing so distorts our understanding of both the ways in which the historical Arnim *was* politically active and the ways in which her social circumstances and personal choices restricted her actions.

Alongside referential readings one finds textual approaches to Arnim's texts as autobiography. Reviews and studies that fall under this category resist the temptation to read Arnim's texts as verifiably true. Rather, they provide the reader with a portrait of what they consider to be Arnim's inner or ideal self. While these readings allow for more differentiated accounts of the relationship of Arnim to her literary production, they still posit a unified self, consistent throughout all texts, that is—at least psychologically—taken to be identical with Arnim. This approach was followed in early biographical overviews by Gustav von Loeper, Moriz Carriere, and Reinhold Steig who, although aware of the discrepancies between Arnim's life and the life of her literary characters, insisted that those characters were true to the "spirit" of Arnim.[17] In more recent scholarship, Christa Bürger describes Arnim's epistolary novels as the attempt of a woman, "schreibend dem eigenen Leben die Form der Geschichte zu geben, um es so sich allererst aneignen zu können."[18] In this manner, Bürger, too, argues that Arnim's texts reveal a higher truth about the author than that which can be revealed by verifiable facts. Although the sympathetic accounts of Carriere and Bürger have contributed to interest in and resulting scholarship on Arnim, they tend to idealize the author and to erase the fine line between her life and her texts.

Despite the many readings of Arnim's texts as to some degree or another (auto)biographical, much in them resists both referential and textual readings. First and foremost, their structure frustrates attempts to read them as traditional autobiography.[19] While the contents often encourage an identification of the author with her Bettine personae, Arnim disrupts this tendency by dispersing accounts of her life throughout her writing without making any attempt to establish a coherent chronology, and by assigning random dates even to those entries based on original letters. Furthermore, Arnim wrote *Briefwechsel*, *Günderode*, and *Frühlingskranz* in inverse order of the correspondence on which they are based, and these texts can be read as part of a larger developmental novel only when read in the order in which they were written.

The selectivity with which Arnim integrated biographical material into her published texts further thwarts the identification of the author with her literary Bettines. To varying degrees, Arnim revised, rewrote, added to, and deleted from her original letters in order to create her letter and dialogue books. The process was unquestionably a creative one, but what Arnim left out of her texts is as intriguing as what she fabricated. Although her published correspondence with Achim von Arnim fills two volumes, for example, Bettina von Arnim's life as wife, *Gutsfrau*, and mother of seven children finds no mention in the texts I will discuss here. Perhaps she felt unable or unwilling to include the banality of her daily life in a published text. Perhaps she was so intimately involved with her husband and children that she could not gain the distance necessary to stylize them as she did her other literary figures. Perhaps the prosaic and difficult nature of everyday life as wife and mother prohibited her from doing so. Or perhaps she accepted the early nineteenth-century convention dictating that accounts of the domestic sphere were not worthy of serious attention. Whatever the motivation, much of Arnim's life did not make its way into her published texts so that, while some sections may be autobiographical, the texts as a whole by no means provide a comprehensive account of Arnim's biography.

The awareness that Arnim both omitted from and added to her original source material has led to readings of her published texts as fictional rather than as autobiographical works. Some early reviewers, especially those committed to establishing a leading position for Goethe within the German literary canon, went so far as to stigmatize Arnim as an outright liar. In an article that appeared anonymously before the publication of Arnim's original correspondence with Goethe, the author employs the adjective *Bettinisch* to describe a style of writing that, in his view, "in keinem Wort Glauben [verdient]."[20] This and similar readings were influenced more by the authors' desire to defend Goethe's reputation than by any attempt to theorize the relationship of Arnim to her texts.

More recent studies of Arnim's epistolary and political texts distance themselves from this type of character critique to provide a more sophisticated account. In her study of Arnim's poetics, Ursula Liebertz-Grün focuses on the following aspects:

> die Formarbeit der Autorin, ihre Schreibstrategien und literarischen Techniken, ihr souveränes Spiel mit der literarischen Tradition, mit den Helden und Heldinnen der literarischen Szene, mit der Zensurbehörde und den Erwartungshaltungen des Publikums, die kunstvoll-komplizierte Komposition, die Strukturelemente und Aufbauprinzipien ihrer Texte, die literarische Qualität ihrer Werke und die ihnen zugrundeliegende Poetik. (*Ordnung im Chaos* 2)

Liebertz-Grün's study has helped to shift the emphasis in scholarship away from the cult of Arnim's personality and towards her texts. Nonetheless, the sole emphasis on the poetic elements of the texts comes with its own problems. Whereas reading Arnim's texts as autobiography ignores possible motivations Arnim may have had for changing her story as well as such issues as form and aesthetics, placing the sole emphasis on the poetic aspects of her texts leads to the tendency to disregard how Arnim incorporated her experience into them.

Bettina von Arnim wrote throughout her life, thus rendering the caesurae between her "three lives" less than clearly discernable. Accordingly, the distinction between Arnim's private correspondence and her publications remains blurred to this very day. Further, neither the autobiographical nor the fictional approach is ultimately adequate to an analysis of Arnim's writing style. The perennial question arises yet again: How does one classify *das unklassifizierbar Bettinische*?

The Relationship between Life and Text

Because Arnim's texts elude strict genre categorization it becomes necessary to take a multi-faceted approach both to her writing and to Arnim herself as author and historical subject. To this end, feminist revisions of the categories of autobiography and the female *Bildungsroman*, as well as Janet Altman's analysis of epistolary writing, will prove useful for framing my readings of Arnim's texts without forcing them into rigid generic categories. In addition, feminist theories of subjectivity will aid in examining the complex relationship of the author to the texts she decided to publish. Only such a differentiated approach is adequate to understanding the roles that Arnim assigned to her protagonists and the manner in which these roles change and develop from one text to the next.

The feminist work on genre and subjectivity most important for my analysis has been heavily influenced both by developments within feminism itself and by poststructuralist theories that, though they pay scant attention to issues of gender, have radically challenged perceptions of the human subject and readings of the texts once assumed produced by that subject. Critics including M. M. Bakhtin, Julia Kristeva, Roland Barthes, Louis Althusser, and Michel Foucault have helped to dismantle notions of both the autonomous human subject and the literary (or other) text as a product of that subject while pointing instead to the manner in which discourses and ideology shape the individual, his or her society, and the artifacts produced by individuals and societies. In addition to these critics' theories of intertextuality and discourse, reception theory and reader-response criticism have posited the role of the reader as producer of the text. Wolfgang Iser and Hans Robert Jauss have argued that the reader(s) of a text helped to constitute its meaning, a notion taken up by Stanley Fish in his discussion of the role of interpretative communities in determining the meanings of texts.

These approaches to reading texts and to understanding the roles of the author and the reader have challenged the hegemony of the notions of Subject and Author. This, in turn, has opened the door to numerous developments in the field of literary studies: the breakdown of the traditional literary canon, the weakening if not the dissolution of the boundaries between high and low art, a broader understanding of the parameters of various genres, and the study of the discourses that have informed various texts at various times. These developments have proven useful in the study of women writers and women protagonists; they have also undermined attempts to attribute agency to either the female subject or the female author. Critics including Katherine Goodman, Biddy Martin, and Michèle Barrett have argued that, in refusing to attribute agency to the human subject, and in seeing discourse as the source of all meaning, poststructuralist theories of the subject deny agency to those to whom agency has traditionally not been attributed: women, minorities, the poor, gays and lesbians.[21] As Martin notes, despite their attraction these theories "constitute a certain danger, given the institutional privileges enjoyed by those who can afford to disavow 'identity' and its 'limits' over and against those for whom such disavowals reproduce their invisibility" ("Lesbian Identity" 78). As a result of this dilemma some scholars have attempted, through theories of genre and subjectivity, to bridge the distance between agency and discourse. It is within this context that I will situate my reading of Arnim's texts.

As one might expect, the genre of autobiography provides an optimal site for exploring the tension between determined subjectivity and the agency of the subject. Felicity Nussbaum argues in *The Autobiographical Subject* for maintaining the notion of female subjectivity against claims for the absolute power of discourse. But she also insists that one must avoid the claims of "biologism and essentialism that trivialize the issues of gender and segregate them from problems of class and race" (129). Applying this approach to the study of autobiography, she proposes grounding studies of women's voices "in particular and local instances of autobiographical writing within a systematic theory, provisionally held and subject to critique" (132).

Katherine Goodman adapts a similar approach in her study of autobiographies by nineteenth-century German women, *Dis/Closures*. She cites Barthes and Foucault as having helped to dismantle the traditional German and North American models of autobiography with their shared emphasis on a unified self, models that more often than not excluded the experiences and autobiographies of many women. At the same time, rather than accepting that there is no clearly demarcated self—with this claim's implication that the individual cannot escape the constraints of discourse—Goodman favors the concept of a fragmented self, which leaves room for notions of "historical change,...individual innovation, and difference" (*Dis/Closures* x).

Applying this approach to the work of Bettina von Arnim, Goodman describes *Briefwechsel, Günderode*, and *Frühlingskranz* as works of "radical autobiography," that is, as texts rooted not only in Arnim's childhood, but also in the time in which they were written and in Arnim's notion of her ideal self. According to Goodman, Arnim retells in her letter books one (not the only possible) fragmented story of her life, in which the past continues to inform and be shaped by the present. Goodman argues further that the epistolary form of these texts points to the construction of the self through others. Thus, although she argues that Arnim creates herself in her works, Goodman does not posit Arnim as the sole source of her identity but rather as a product of conscious and subconscious interaction with the world around her.

Bäumer's categorization of Arnim's oeuvre as a *kontinuierliche Partnerautobiographie* adds another dimension to Goodman's approach. For Bäumer, Arnim's texts represent a continuous (auto)biography that arose first and foremost out of her conversations and epistolary communication with others, a genesis that Bäumer regards as unique in literary history (Bäumer and Schultz 155). Bäumer contends that each of Arnim's texts is a product of dialogues past and present; while many similar themes run through her text, they are altered by Arnim's contacts with various individuals. According to Bäumer, this continuation constitutes women's writing as Hélène Cixous formulates the concept in *Die unendliche Zirkulation des Begehrens*. Like Cixous, Bäumer attributes "fließende, ausufernde, überströmende" qualities to women's writing, and here I take issue with her. Describing Arnim's work as exemplary of women's writing essentializes the categories of "woman" and "women's writing" in the manner criticized by Nussbaum. This, in turn, denies the great variations in women's writing not only in the nineteenth century but throughout the history of German letters; it also denies the very uniqueness of Arnim's writing, which Bäumer herself emphasized throughout her work on Arnim. This criticism notwithstanding, Bäumer's designation of a new generic category for Arnim's texts provides a productive tool for reading them.

Despite the strengths of their arguments, neither Goodman nor Bäumer takes into account the fictional aspect of Arnim's writing. Because her texts oscillate between autobiography and fiction, conceptions of the female developmental novel also afford a useful framework for reading them. In their collection of essays, *The Voyage In. Fictions of Female Development*, the editors Elizabeth Abel, Marianne Hirsch, and Elizabeth Langland apply to their readings of women's novels the model of the

Bildungsroman, which—like autobiography—emphasizes the development of the individual into a mature person who, in traditional reception of the genre, has been perceived as having a unified and clearly demarcated self. Whereas the goal for the (male) protagonist of the traditional *Bildungsroman* is the acceptance of an adult role within a social community, the editors of this volume argue that female developmental novels substitute inner concentration for action. Rather than moving into and through the physical world in order to explore one's social milieu (that is, rather than setting forth on a *Bildungsreise*), female protagonists tend to turn inward, focusing not on clearly marked external events and actions but rather on their subjective responses to a world whose boundaries are much narrower than those of their male counterparts. This is the tendency in Arnim's texts, whose protagonists include a child standing in the "Shadow of Olympus"[22] and a daemon whispering to a king, remaining on the fringes of the public sphere while at the same time hoping to influence the shape of a new society.

Abel, Hirsch, and Langland propose two models for the female developmental novel: the novel of awakening and that of apprenticeship. While the novel of apprenticeship shows a gradual, linear development from childhood to adulthood and places emphasis on those internal transformations that contribute to this process, the novel of awakening presents one key event—often but not always related to sexual maturation—as leading to this transition. To an extent, Arnim's texts fit into both categories. *Briefwechsel* could be described as a text of awakening insofar as the protagonist arrives at a sense of who she is through often erotically defined interaction with Goethe. This becomes especially apparent in the final section. The emphasis on epistolarity and dialogicity in Arnim's novels also supports a categorization of *Briefwechsel*, *Günderode*, and *Frühlingskranz* as novels of apprenticeship. Unlike Wilhelm Meister, however, the Bettines of these texts do not learn so much through their travels as through interlocutors whom they need in order to discover their own identity. This is one reason for reading Arnim's texts as a continuous whole, for this development continues not only within each text but also from one text to the next.

One significant difference between Arnim's texts and many of those discussed in *Fictions of Female Development* is that the female developmental novel often ends with either the death or the madness of its protagonist. This was not the case for Arnim or her Bettine personae. Arnim may have avoided the fate of so many of her real and fictional contemporaries—Günderode comes first to mind—because she was able to establish in her texts a realm of action, albeit one that was imaginary and largely internalized. Indeed, in her final texts, we see Arnim not in the role of apprentice but rather in that of teacher trying to pass on to others the education she has attained.

The epistolary and dialogic structure of Arnim's texts serves as another central generic aspect that underscores both the construction of subjectivity through interaction with one's environment and the resulting fragmentation of subjectivity. Bäumer and Goodman have noted that the forms of letter exchange and conversation help to convey a key tenet held by both Arnim and her protagonists, namely the belief that knowledge of one's self and the world stems directly from interaction with others. Janet Altman's wide-ranging study of "the use of the letter's formal properties to create meaning" (*Epistolarity* 4) provides a lens through which to view this interaction and its implications for the subjectivity of Arnim's protagonists.

Altman presents six theories of how epistolary form exerts pressure on meaning: 1) The letter serves as both a bridge and a barrier between interlocutors (186); 2) confidence is an essential part of epistolary exchange (186); 3) both writing and reading, intimacy and the need for an audience, constitute epistolarity (186); 4) "letter narrative depends on reciprocality of writer-addressee" and creates an illusion of the present (187); 5) letter writing is both a closed form (each individual letter comes to a conclusion) and an open one (each letter anticipates the continuation of the exchange) (187); 6) "The letter's duality as a self-contained artistic unity and as a unit within a larger configuration make it an apt instrument for fragmentary, elliptical writing and juxtaposition of contrasting discrete units, yet at the same time the very fragmentation inherent in the letter form encourages the creation of a compensating coherence and continuity on new levels" (187). All six of these paradoxical theses are applicable in differing degrees to Arnim's texts; they reflect not only the complexity of interpersonal interaction, but also the tension between the writer and the written text.

Arnim's texts demand reading through various lenses—radical autobiography, *kontinuierliche Partnerautobiographie*, the female developmental novel, and epistolary writing—while at the same time resisting strict generic categorization. These categories are useful insofar as they facilitate a reading of the development of Arnim's protagonists within each of her texts and from one text to another. They do not, however, entirely account for changes in these protagonists or in their relationship to the author Bettina von Arnim. Goodman's insightful study deals with only three of Arnim's works and Bäumer's reliance on Cixous's essentializing approach to women's writing does not adequately support her argument for a continuous partner-autobiography. In order to account both for those points where author and figure may plausibly overlap and for those where a historically verifiable distance exists between them, and in order to analyze the relationship of Arnim's textual personae to the author, it is useful to turn away from questions of genre and toward feminist theories of subjectivity and positionality.

Responding to the destabilization of the subject as witnessed in poststructuralist writings and to its problematic implications for feminist theory, some feminist scholars have posited—as did Goodman—the concept of the fragmented subject. Teresa de Lauretis has offered one of the most useful contributions in this area. In *Technologies of Gender* she argues for a feminist theory of gender that "points to a conception of the subject as multiple, rather than divided or unified, and as excessive or heteronomous vis-à-vis the state ideological apparati and the sociocultural technologies of gender" (ix). Such a theory necessarily relies on the categories of the subject and of woman, but it problematizes them by arguing for differences among individual subjects and within individual women.

This understanding of the fragmented subject has the advantage of incorporating Foucauldian theories of the shaping of subjectivity by discourse(s). It also questions Foucault by noting that his concept of discourse creates two problems for feminist scholars. First, it denies the subject (and thus women) any form of agency, and secondly, it provides no account for how change comes about. Lauretis addresses these lacunae in *Alice*

Dichtung und Wahrheit: *Life as Text*

Doesn't.[23] Lauretis proposes the term "experience" to "designate the process by which, for all social beings, subjectivity is constructed." Borrowing from the semiotic theories of Charles Sanders Peirce and Umberto Eco, she employs the term:

> in the general sense of a *process* by which, for all social beings, subjectivity is constructed. Through that process one places oneself or is placed in social reality, and so perceives and comprehends as subjective (referring to, even originating in oneself) those relations—material, economic, and interpersonal—which are in fact social and, in a larger perspective, historical. The process is continuous, its achievement unending or daily renewed. (159)

This definition opens the door to the agency of the subject without insisting that all women and individuals have the same possibilities for exercising agency. The process of experience affords *some* women the possibility of placing themselves in a social reality; others' experiences deprive them of the opportunity to choose how and where they place themselves within that reality.

According to Lauretis, the category of experience accounts for the manner in which discourses are inscribed onto individuals while at the same time allowing for individual appropriation of those discourses, and most importantly, for change:

> For each person, therefore, subjectivity is an ongoing construction, not a fixed point of departure or arrival from which one then interacts with the world. On the contrary, it is the effect of that interaction—which I call experience; and thus it is produced not by external ideas, values, or material causes, but by one's personal, subjective, engagement in the practices, discourses, and institutions that lend significance (value, meaning, and affect) to the events of the world. (159)

Subjectivity is not static, nor is it a reflection of one's "inner-self" or of the discourses inscribed on that self. Rather, it is a result of subjective interaction with one's experiences and environment. As Frederiksen and Goodman note, the German language offers two words for experience, one of which accounts for this subjective interaction:

> In German there are two words for "experience" (*Erlebnis* and *Erfahrung*), and the distinction merits our consideration. It is one that is actively upheld, even today. In a recent interview Christa Wolf made the distinction as clearly as it can be made. When Wolf was asked what was biographical in her texts, Bettina Brentano-von Arnim might well have provided the same response. Wolf differen-

tiated between "the material that life brings you, often forces on you" ("den Stoff, den das Leben einem zugeführt, oft aufgezwungen hat") and "that mysterious process, which cannot be marveled at enough, which makes an *Erlebnis* into an *Erfahrung*," ("jenen geheimnisvollen, nicht genug zu bestaunenden Vorgang, der aus einem Erlebnis erst eine Erfahrung macht.")[24]

In the case of Arnim, the writer appropriated the experiences of her life, and through reflection, a term also important for Lauretis, transformed them into *Erfahrungen*.

Both Linda Alcoff and Leslie Adelson have drawn on Lauretis's theories of the subject to formulate their conceptions of positionality. Supporting neither a purely essentialist nor a purely discursive understanding of the category "woman," Alcoff describes positionality as consisting of two main points. She argues first that the concept of woman— she refers not to individual women but to a category of gender designation—"is a relational term, identifiable only within a (constantly moving) context" (434). In order to understand "woman," then, one must look to the historical context in which women are defined.

Secondly, Alcoff argues "that the position that women find themselves in can be actively utilized (rather than transcended) as a location for the construction of meaning, a place from where meaning is constructed, rather than simply the place where a meaning can be discovered" (434). Here she uses the concept of identity politics as developed in the Combahee River Collective's "A Black Feminist Statement" to argue that women have more options than passively accepting their position within their historical context. They can (she does not insist that they all do) also utilize this position to construct their own meaning. She then employs Lauretis's concept of experience to argue that women are subjected to their experience but can also utilize it to form new subject positions.

As indicated above, certain conditions facilitate agency to a greater extent for some women and groups of women than for others. Leslie Adelson addresses this issue in *Making Bodies Making History*. Crediting Lauretis for her unique contribution to feminist theory, Adelson notes that "by accounting for the embodied and inscribed positionalities of social experience, Lauretis is able to treat women conceptually as both constructed and construct-ing, that is, as agents in their own construction" (59). Adelson uses Lauretis's concept of experience to emphasize the role of materiality and the significance of women's bodies in determining subjectivity. This emphasis, she argues, is lacking in Alcoff's understanding of positionality.

Although Adelson's reading of Alcoff is at points ungenerous, one cannot ignore her criticisms. On the one hand, she questions Alcoff's understanding of identity politics, which, according to Adelson, reduces materiality "to a matter of taking (choosing) a political stand" (62). Adelson implies that this possibility may not be open to all women. Further Adelson notes that, although Alcoff seems to want to account for differences between women that arise, for example, along the lines of race, class, and national identity, she nevertheless makes the generalization that women occupy a position lacking in power and mobility and requiring political change (62). Adelson points out that not all women occupy this position and that some women do possess power while others may not be interested in pursuing political change. Out of this criticism arises Adelson's definition of positionality:

> Positionality does not demarcate a *place*, nor does it consist of choice alone (although it does entail standpoint). Rather, it characterizes a set of specific social and discursive relations in a given historical moment. These relations concern and also produce gender, race, class, sexuality, ethnicity, and other practices through which power is constructed, exercised, and resisted or challenged. (63–64).

Adelson's emphasis on the dual nature of positionality (it accounts both for the construction of woman and women and for the possibility of individual women constructing aspects of their subjectivity) and her refusal to formulate generalizations about the experience(s) of women make her definition useful to an inquiry into Arnim's construction of her textual Bettines.

As developed by Lauretis, Alcoff, and Adelson, the concept of positionality serves as a framework for exploring the relationship between Arnim and her textual figures, the many often contradictory roles she assigned to her protagonists, and the difficulty that scholarship has had in accounting for these differences. Because of the unique manner in which Arnim approached and appropriated writing (it is not necessarily the manner in which all writers, all women writers, or all letter writers have approached and appropriated discourse), she assigned to her textual personae various subject positions created out of an amalgam of memories, experiences with others, historical discourses, and future hopes. Writing bore traces of her past but also allowed her to invent new ways of conceiving her past, present, and future. More importantly, writing effected what Lauretis would term a "habit change" in Arnim—in the way she acted in public, and in turn, in the way she depicted her Bettine figures in subsequent texts. As a result, there is a dialectical continuity between the historical Arnim at various stages in her life and her Bettine personae, that is, between Arnim and the Bettine personae of her various texts in their roles as child, lover, friend, mother, and daemon. Her life experiences were the precondition for each work and each work contributed to the manner in which Arnim perceived and presented herself. The relationships between these various subject positions are often contradictory; it would be impossible to draw them into or construct out of them a single, unified subject. Yet they are related to one another through the experience of Bettina von Arnim as a unique historical site, and the experience of Arnim helps account for changes in the roles of her Bettine personae. As such, one can speak of a certain development (albeit, in the words of Mary Poovey, an uneven one) throughout Arnim's published texts. Most contemporary scholars share the opinion that Arnim's works constitute a developmental text. My project builds upon their work to delineate *how* her personae develop and to trace the transformations of Arnim's "Bettines" through all of her six major publications. In the following chapters, I will analyze Arnim's six novel-length texts in the order in which they were published. Focusing on specific roles played by Arnim's protagonists, I will show how Arnim used her texts to explore and develop various subject positions and how these positions changed over time.

CHAPTER ONE

The Child Speaks:
Goethe's Briefwechsel mit einem Kinde (1835)

Although the division of Arnim's life into neat and tidy compartments proves deceiving, the publication of her first epistolary text, *Goethe's Briefwechsel mit einem Kinde*, did serve as a turning point in her life. With this work Arnim began, albeit selectively, to re(en)vision and rewrite her past, and in so doing, to give shape to her present and future. In the process of creating her Bettine personae, the author Arnim did more than merely present her readers with fictional protagonists who possessed a significant degree of agency. She also employed writing to develop and express her own increasing sense of self-assurance.

The correspondence that served as the basis for Arnim's creative work is extant for only two of her six major texts: *Briefwechsel* and *Ambrosia*, and thus far only the original letters of *Briefwechsel* have received significant scholarly attention.[1] They document Bettina Brentano's relationships with Karoline von Günderrode, Goethe's mother, and especially Goethe, and they provide a partial record of the events that Arnim transformed into her first publication. The biographical version of this story is by now well known: Bettina Brentano developed an interest in Goethe after her brother Clemens presented her with a copy of *Wilhelm Meisters Lehrjahre* in 1801. Her discovery in 1806 of letters Goethe had written to her grandmother Sophie von La Roche expressing his love for Bettina's mother Maximiliane Brentano served to pique her interest. Following the death of her friend Karoline von Günderrode, the twenty-one-year-old Brentano befriended Goethe's mother Catharina Elisabeth in July 1806 and met Goethe for the first time in 1807. Their correspondence began in April

1807, and Goethe maintained a cordial but distanced tone for the first few years of their exchange. In 1810 Bettina Brentano met Beethoven and tried to interest Goethe in the composer's music. The two "geniuses" eventually met in 1811, and an account of one of their meetings made its way into *Ambrosia* in the form of a letter attributed to Beethoven. Later the same year, Brentano sent Goethe reports of conversations with his mother (who had died in 1808) for inclusion in *Dichtung und Wahrheit*—a point after which he became somewhat more attentive and his letters more intimate. In her Teplitz fragments, written while she was working on *Briefwechsel*, Arnim stylized their 1810 meeting at a spa in Bohemia into the erotic high point of their relationship.[2] In contrast, Goethe's diary entries make no mention of such a meeting.

After her marriage in 1811, Bettina von Arnim had a falling out with Christiane Goethe at an art exhibit in Weimar. In response to Arnim's criticism of one of Goethe's favorite artists, Christiane purportedly hit her, knocking off her glasses. In the aftermath, Arnim referred to Christiane as a mad blood sausage.[3] Not surprisingly, Goethe then cut off his end of the correspondence and most of their interaction despite Arnim's repeated attempts to rekindle the friendship. After Goethe's death in 1832, Arnim wrote to the administrator of his will, Friedrich von Müller, asking for the return of her letters "als Nahrung für mein Zusammensein mit ihm" (Quoted in Härtl, *Chronik* 30).

Beginning in the 1820s—and providing further proof of her activity during her years of marriage—Arnim began work on her Goethe Monument. Disappointed by the model she had seen of Christian Rauch's proposed Goethe sculpture, for which the city of Frankfurt had begun raising money in 1821, Arnim began sketching her own design. In 1825 she completed a plaster-of-paris model of her rendition depicting Goethe as Jupiter seated on a throne and a Psyche figure (herself) standing on one of his feet and plucking the strings of his lyre. Arnim endeavored the rest of her life to finance and complete this project.

In addition to the relationship with Goethe, other childhood and young adult influences on *Briefwechsel* included her relationships with Catharina Elisabeth Goethe and Karoline von Günderrode, her exposure to the ideas of early German romanticism, travels to Bavaria, Austria, and Bohemia, the French Revolution, the Napoleonic occupation of the German territories, the Tyrolean uprising of 1809, and exchanges with friends and acquaintances including her brother-in-law, the lawyer and later Prussian Minister of Justice, Friedrich Karl von Savigny (1779–1861) and the student Max Prokop von Freiburg (1789–1851), whom many thought Bettina Brentano might marry. Traces of all of these events and encounters can be found in *Briefwechsel* and provide evidence for those who would read the text according to the referential model of autobiographical representation.

Yet *Briefwechsel* was equally inspired by Arnim's adult life: by her friendships with the travel writer and garden-architect Prince Hermann von Pückler-Muskau (1785–1871)[4] and with the theologian Friedrich Schleiermacher (1786–1834);[5] by the heated debates over the question of Goethe's role in German cultural history following the author's death in 1832; by the July Revolution of 1830 and the Young German and Young Hegelian movements; and by Arnim's increasing political awareness and engagement. Much recent scholarship has been directed towards an investigation of the various sources of and inspirations for Arnim's work and these sources are well documented. The remainder of this chapter will inquire into the identity that Arnim created for the Bettine of *Briefwechsel*. Who did the girl-woman who had corresponded with Goethe, married and had seven children, and established contact with many of the leading thinkers of her day become in the pages of her first published text?

Upon a first reading of *Briefwechsel*, the familiar argument that the text lacks shape and direction, that Bettine merely "writes into the wind,"[6] might appear difficult to refute; the text initially seems to ramble for over three hundred pages and appears to be a bricolage of anecdote, emotional outpouring, and philosophical rumination. Such an impression remains unchallenged if one reads the text according to the rules established for traditional autobiography, for the insistence that the author is identical with her characters leads to a literal reading of Bettine's words rather than an understanding of the text as a poetically conceived whole. Arnim's texts demand recursive, interpretive reading, and such reading leads to a recognition both of the distinct structure of the text, and in the case of *Briefwechsel*, of the protagonist's development from a child without a voice of her own to an independent adult. Furthermore, Arnim's text does have a theme, namely that to which the protagonist points in the first lines of the final *Tagebuch* section when she writes: "In dieses Buch möcht ich gern schreiben, von dem geheimnisvollen Denken einsamer Stunden der Nacht, von dem Reifen des Geistes an der Liebe wie an der Mittagssonne" (427). *Briefwechsel* deals then with education, or *Bildung*, through love, and as writing in the lonely hours of the night would indicate, with the paradoxical combination of loneliness and self-sufficiency that Bettine encounters at the end of what I will demonstrate to be her years of apprenticeship. *Briefwechsel* can and should therefore be read as a text of female development.

Briefwechsel opens with a dedication to "Prince Pückler" that is signed "Bettina von Arnim" and dated August 1834. Arnim began her friendship with Pückler-Muskau just after her husband's death in 1831. He considered her "eine ächte Dichterin"[7] and encouraged her to write to him about her experiences with Goethe. Continuing a pattern that began with Karoline von Günderrode and would repeat itself many times in Arnim's life, however, he began to distance himself from her two years later; the married but separated Pückler was afraid that her increasingly passionate letters and advances would make him a laughing stock among his circle of friends. Arnim makes no mention of this tension in her dedication. Rather, she recalls the support and inspiration Pückler provided while the book was in process in order to suggest a role for the ideal reader of her finished product. She begins her dedication with a shortened and slightly altered version of "Haben sie von Deinen Fehlen" from the "Buch der Betrachtungen" of Goethe's *West-östlicher Divan*, a poem that denounces critics and asserts that only a few are equipped to recognize "das Allerbeste."[8] Following this citation, she offers an interpretation of the poem:

> Die Menge ist nicht dazu geeignet, die Wahrheit sondern nur den Schein zu prüfen; den geheimen Wegen einer tiefen Natur nachzuspüren, das Rätselhafte in ihr aufzulösen ist ihr versagt, sie spricht nur ihre Täuschungen aus, erzeugt hartnäckige Vorurteile gegen bessere Überzeugung, und beraubt den Geist der Freiheit das vom Gewöhnlichen Abweichende in seiner Eigentümlichkeit anzuerkennen. (11)

For the author, Pückler remains apart from the majority who cannot distinguish truth from appearance, and in praising him she invites her audience to read her text from a vantagepoint that recognizes the originality of its deviation from the norm.

The prologue, subtitled "Dies Buch ist für die Guten und nicht für die Bösen," offers further direction for the reader. Again Arnim uses the remarks of other readers to establish her authority. Perhaps in response to family members, including Clemens Brentano, who had advised against publication, she attempts to convince readers of her good intentions by quoting the supervisor of a book bindery who had assured her, "nur böse Menschen können [dieses Buch] übel ausdeuten" (14). In addition, she asserts the value of the letters themselves by claiming that both the administrator of Goethe's will, Friedrich von Müller, and Goethe himself had considered her letters something precious. Indeed, she declares that Goethe had told her he read her letters every day. By invoking the names of those who have found value in her letters, Arnim hopes to convince the reader to do the same.

Following these brief introductory sections, the voice of the author Arnim gives way to that of the protagonist Bettine who speaks throughout Parts One and Two. Part One can be divided into three sections: the correspondence between Bettine and Frau Rath Goethe, Bettine's final letter to Frau Rath recounting her friendship with Caroline von Günderode, and the first half of the correspondence between Bettine and Goethe. Each of these sections serves a specific function. In her letters to Frau Rath, Bettine writes her way into Goethe's genealogy, effectively becoming Frau Rath's daughter and Goethe's sister. The narrative of Bettine's friendship with Günderode recalls the disintegration of an intimate and intense relationship, thereby alluding to Bettine's hope that her relationship with Goethe will develop in a more positive direction, that she will not be abandoned by him as she believes she was by Günderode. Finally, in the first part of her correspondence with Goethe, Bettine emphasizes nature descriptions and her feelings of love for Goethe and assumes a subservient stance towards her *Meister*. At the same time, discussions of legal and educational measures taken to grant citizenship to the Jews of Frankfurt point towards her budding political awareness.

In Part Two Bettine assumes a more independent stance vis-à-vis Goethe. Whereas in Part One Bettine emphasizes her childlike qualities and her need for Goethe's approval, in the subsequent section she becomes far more critical, admonishing him for the apolitical stance of *Wilhelm*

Meister, criticizing his female characters in *Werther* and *Die Wahlverwandtschaften*, and arguing in support of the Tyroleans in their war against Bavaria.[9] Towards the end of this section, Bettine alludes to an increasing sense of distance between herself and Goethe, which stems not only from the distance he is placing between them but also from Bettine's newfound maturity and sense of individuation.

The final section of the text consists of a diary. Here the narrator, now clearly an adult, looks back on her past. She recalls not only her childhood experiences in a convent and her love for Goethe, but also Goethe's death, her conception of a monument to Goethe, and her plan to publish their correspondence. At times the narrator seems to be writing to herself, at other times to Goethe, and at still other times to someone she addresses as "mein Freund," a figure whom scholars have identified as a composite character influenced by Goethe, Schleiermacher, and Pückler-Muskau (*GB* 899). The subtitle of the diary, "Buch der Liebe," provides another reference to Goethe's *West-östlicher Divan*—this time to the third book—thereby linking this final section to Arnim's prologue; here the Bettine persona of Parts One and Two merges with the author Arnim, blurring the line between the two much more than in the previous sections.

At first glance, the diary appears to be a meditation on Bettine's/Arnim's love for Goethe. In elaborating her ideas and feelings, however, she makes the paradoxical assertion that while she needed the mirrors of others to develop her potential, her individuality, and her genius, in the end her love was self-love. This, in effect, relativizes the accounts of her love for Goethe and gives the reader a sense that both Bettine and Arnim have made it through their apprenticeship to find a place in the world both indebted to and independent of the relationship with Goethe.

Upon close examination, then, the various sections of *Briefwechsel* lend a structure to the text that enables the reader to chart Bettine's development. This, in turn, allows for the emphasis of different roles in the various sections and for changes in the manner in which these roles—including those of child, woman, lover, genius, and writer—are defined. I agree with Lorely French's contention that to focus on what are, in and of themselves, often narrowly-defined and stereotypical female gender roles in order to understand the character of Bettine becomes problematic insofar as "rigidly confining her character to prescribed functions ignores structural and thematic purposes which the character Bettine serves within these works" ("Bettina von Arnim" 188). I nevertheless argue that upon close examination of these roles one sees that, when assigning them to her Bettine personae, Arnim did not limit them to prescribed functions but rather worked to revise and reinscribe them with new meaning. Furthermore, she never felt compelled to limit these roles to one rigidly defined meaning. By viewing the text through the framework of these roles, I hope to illustrate how Arnim wove them together to create both the character Bettine and the subject positions for herself that made her subsequent texts possible.

The Child Bettine

One of the roles most frequently associated with Arnim's Bettine personae in general (and regrettably also with the author herself) is that of the child. Calling to mind both the child genius heralded by so many Romantic poets and the nineteenth-century tendency to infantilize women by equating them with children, the role is as troubling as it is appealing.[10] Stubborn, self-assured, insistent, *närrisch*, like the Bettina on the painted miniature this Bettine creates the impression of a much younger person. The title of the text points to the child as Bettine's central role, and in the first pages Bettine reminds her reader that Goethe not only corresponded with her but also suggested the role of child to her.[11] Writing to Frau Rath of her first encounter with Goethe, Bettine claims: "ich streckte die Hände nach ihm, glaub' ich,—bald wußt' ich nichts mehr, Goethe fing mich rasch auf an sein Herz. *Armes Kind, hab' ich Sie erschreckt*, das waren die ersten Worte, mit denen seine Stimme mir in's Herz drang" (25). In the first words he utters to Bettine, Goethe does not merely describe her as a child; he seems to name her, to baptize her into the role.

While many readers associate Bettine with the role of the child, they often fail to note the complexity and ambiguity of this role. Because Bettine's own narrative calls her account into question, it remains unclear in the above passage whether Goethe really bestows this appellative upon her. Phrases such as "Glaub' ich" and "wußt' ich nicht mehr" encourage the reader to pause and ask just who is doing the baptizing in this scene: Goethe or Bettine herself? In another letter she confides that, during conversations with others, she often finds herself distracted by thoughts of Goethe. Rather than offering resistance, she succumbs to her daydreams:

> Dann setze ich mich an die Erde und lege den Kopf auf Ihren Schoß, oder ich drücke Ihre Hand an meinen Mund, oder ich stehe an Ihrer Seite und umfasse Ihren Hals; und es währt lange, bis ich eine Stellung finde, in der ich beharre. Dann plaudre ich, wie es mir behagt; die Antwort aber, die ich mir in Ihrem Namen gebe, spreche ich mit Bedacht aus: *Mein Kind! mein artig gut Mädchen! liebes Herz!* Ja, so klingt's aus jener wunderbaren Stunde herüber, in der ich glaubte von Geistern in eine andre Welt getragen zu sein; und wenn ich dann bedenke, daß es von Ihren Lippen so wiederhallen könnte, wenn ich wirklich vor Ihnen stände,—dann schaudre ich vor Freude und Sehnsucht zusammen. (86–87)

Although the italics emphasize Goethe's appellation of Bettine as child, this anecdote stems from a fantasy in which Bettine plays the roles of both Goethe and herself as child. Because this scene is a daydream within the context of a work that emphasizes Bettine's relationship with Goethe, the reader comes away with a dual impression: that Goethe has valorized Bettine's role as child and that Bettine has consciously chosen to play this role.

Wolfgang Bunzel has argued that the strategy of calling into question what has been written characterizes the narrative style of *Briefwechsel*. Throughout this and all of her texts, Arnim's protagonists work to destabilize their own narratives as well as the reader's sense of the truth, not necessarily in order to deceive the reader, but rather to heighten "seine Aufmerksamkeit für den Akt des Erzählens" (Bunzel 13). By intentionally creating ambiguity and by opening space for multiple interpretations, Arnim's strategies force ever-closer reading. In the above passage, Bettine plays with the notion of naming, a process that, in regard to Goethe, involves exerting power over and sharing power with him, and in the case of Bettine, involves an assertion of her sense of identity and agency.

As *Briefwechsel* progresses, it becomes clear not only that Bettine has designated herself as child, but also that this child has many facets. On one level, Arnim employs narrative strategies that encourage the reader to interpret the role literally. At the same time, the child-Bettine stands in the tradition of early German romanticism, whose proponents saw childhood as representing both the refusal to conform to the norms of philistine society and openness to creative genius. Most importantly, Bettine's position as child represents her apprenticeship to her teachers Günderode, Frau Rath, and Goethe.

On the most literal level, the text deals with being a child. Describing herself as unintelligent, uninformed, and above all *unmündig*, Bettine emphasizes her childlikeness and, occasionally, her childishness throughout the text but especially in her earliest letters. She admits to Frau Rath: "daß ich nicht sehr klug bin, davon geb' ich häufige Beweise" (30). She reports that she told Goethe she never read the newspaper: "nichts interessiert mich als nur Sie, und da bin ich viel zu ungeduldig, in der Zeitung zu blättern" (25); and she describes her speech and writing to Goethe as "das unmündige Stammeln eines unbedeutenden Kindes" (87). To accentuate further her image as child, Bettine recounts to Goethe stories from her childhood. She tells him of her parents, offers anecdotes about the time she spent in a convent following the death of her father, and recalls the first time she saw herself in a mirror upon leaving the convent.

Bettine thus depicts herself as claiming to be and often acting like a child while at the same time recounting—as an adult—stories of her early years. As the text progresses, it becomes clear that Arnim intends this role to be understood metaphorically: openness to experience rather than age determines childlikeness. This means on the one hand that Bettine refuses to become like the overly rational and therefore unfeeling *Philister* whom she disdains. On the other hand, only as a child can she develop her creative capacities. She writes in the diary section: "So lang' wir Kinder sind im Gemüt, so lang' übt die Natur Mutterpflege an uns; sie flößt Nahrung ein von der der Geist wächst, dann entfaltet sie sich zum Genius; sie fordert auf zum Höchsten, zum Selbstgeständnis" (434). Bettine aims to develop her genius, and this can occur only through an openness to nature which, in turn, is facilitated by maintaining childlike openness and inquisitiveness.

As Bäumer has demonstrated, early romantic discourse informs Arnim's appropriation of the role of child.[12] Writers such as Friedrich Schlegel, Clemens Brentano, and Novalis describe a close connection between the child and the artist: the two share the originality associated with the romantic genius. Novalis states in an aphorism, for example: "Jede Stufe der Bildung fängt mit Kindheit an. Daher ist der am meisten gebildete, irdische Mensch dem Kinde so ähnlich" (333).[13] Because of this relationship between the child and the genius, not the well educated but the simple folk possess the capacity to recognize the originality of the child. Bettine expresses this belief in one of her many anecdotes: One day as she is walking in the country, she engages in conversation with a shepherd, and when they part he leaves her with the compliment: "ich sei gescheuter als alle Menschen, die er kenne; dies war mir was ganz Neues, denn bisher hab' ich von gescheuten Leuten gehört, ich sei gänzlich unklug; ich kann aber doch dem Schäfer nicht unrecht geben; ich bin auch gescheut und habe scharfe Sinne" (195). Recalling romantic novellas and fairy tales, and negating the claim of others that she is *unklug*, the intelligence of the child artist Bettine reveals itself not to the educated elite but to this shepherd.

Remaining a child in spirit therefore allows Bettine to learn both from her experiences, and most importantly, from those around her. In this role, Bettine can enter into an apprenticeship under the tutelages of Günderode, Frau Rath, and Goethe. Recounting to Frau Rath the story of her relationship with Günderode, Bettine relates that her friend taught her lessons not only on history and philosophy—disciplines that she claims made her physically ill—but also on friendship and the development of one's genius through another. Though not stated explicitly, Bettine also learns a more painful lesson from her friend, for her loss of Günderode teaches her the value of life. In contrast to Günderode's exclamation, following a discussion of *Werther*, "Recht viel lernen, recht viel fassen mit dem Geist und dann früh sterben; ich mag's nicht erleben, daß mich die Jugend verläßt" (65), Bettine's insistence on childlikeness and the emphasis on youth protect her from the ennui that eventually destroys her friend. This becomes a central theme in *Die Günderode*.

When Günderode distances herself as a prelude to her suicide, Bettine turns to Frau Rath Goethe for companionship. In this relationship, Bettine becomes daughter and pupil. Frau Rath writes to her: "Liebe, liebe Tochter, mein Sohn soll Dein Freund sein, Dein Bruder, der Dich gewiß liebt, und Du sollst mich Mutter heißen in Zukunft für alle Tag" (21). As Bernd Greiner has shown, this allows Bettine to place herself in Goethe's lineage, for Bettine makes no effort to hide the motivation behind her interest in Frau Rath: "Ich will nicht lügen: wenn Sie die Mutter nicht wär' die Sie ist, so würd' ich auch nicht bei Ihr schreiben lernen" (49). As daughter of the mother of the author, Bettine learns how to tell stories so that she can herself become a writer. Frau Rath encourages her to record Günderode's story and teaches her the value of memory by assertng: "Der Mensch wird begraben in geweihter Erde, so soll man auch große und seltne Begebenheiten begraben in einem schönen Sarg der Erinnerung, an den ein jeder hintreten kann und dessen Andenken feiern" (50). Engaging in her own form of remembering, Frau Rath provides Bettine with accounts of Goethe's childhood, which Bettine then recounts to Goethe for use in what he refers to as his *Bekenntnisse* (372). As mother and mentor, Frau Rath makes Bettine equal to her son as sister and writer, and as becomes more evident in *Dies Buch*, to herself as storyteller and mentor.

Although it is tempting to claim that the importance of Günderode and Frau Rath for Bettine's development equals that of Goethe, such an assertion overlooks the fact that, in this text, Bettine positions herself as child in order to approach and learn from the individual considered the greatest genius of his time: Goethe. It also fails to take into account that the author Arnim would not have gained the same public attention had her first publication been *Günderode*. Although it reflects sadly on women's lack of status and influence in the nineteenth century, the apprenticeship to Goethe was essential for the development of Arnim and her Bettine personae. Nevertheless, such positioning should not be understood exclusively to signify Bettine's submissive position in this relationship.

In Part One Bettine happily reports to Goethe that their relationship facilitates her development: "Ja Liebster, das macht mich glücklich, daß sich allmählig mein Leben durch Dich entwickelt" (184). While this fawning declaration may make the reader uncomfortable, one only has to recall Friedrich Schlegel's *Lucinde* to realize the radical nature of Arnim's appropriation of Goethe in this text. *Lucinde* also describes development through interaction with another, but as Becker-Cantarino has shown, the text strictly prescribes gender roles so that only the man's life (Julius's life) can unfold through interaction with a woman (Lucinde) as his mirror. In contrast, Bettine breaks out of the passive role assigned to women in Germany in the first half of the nineteenth century and actively seeks out Goethe. As Liebertz-Grün accurately observes, the life of Arnim's fictional Goethe—unlike that of Günderode—serves in this text as proof that one can remain an artist while still living in this imperfect world,[14] and Bettine desires to learn from him. For Bettina von Arnim, as for her protagonist Bettine, there were very few sisters of Shakespeare after whom she could model herself as an artist. Günderode committed suicide, neither Frau Rath nor Arnim's friend Rahel von Varnhagen ever published their own works, and writers such as Dorothea Schlegel and Caroline Schlegel-Schelling remained in the shadows of their husbands. Moreover, German-speaking women writers from earlier periods had virtually disappeared from the canon and those who were writing contemporaneous to Arnim did not have the reputation or influence that Goethe enjoyed.[15] With this in mind, Bettine's decision to turn to Goethe as her mentor must be viewed as a radical act of self-assertion.

Growing Up and Learning About Gender

Bettine plays the role of the child insofar as she narrates accounts of her childhood, and she employs this role metaphorically to express both her wish to remain creative and her position as one who develops through interaction with others. Yet, although she insists repeatedly to her readers (Frau Rath, Goethe, us) that she is a child, the person writing the letters in Parts One and Two is clearly a young woman, and the person writing the diary is a mature adult looking back on her relationship with Goethe following the latter's death. We thus witness Bettine maturing throughout the text, albeit not in a chronological sense. As she matures, Bettine openly confronts what it means to be a woman in her society, criticizing and rejecting some prescribed roles while accepting but redefining others.

In many of her letters to Goethe, Bettine rails against her family's expectations for her future: marriage and the acquisition of womanly virtues such as a calm temperament, passivity, and the ability to cook and sew.[16] Occasionally, she wishes to prove that she possesses these qualities. At one point she writes to Frau Rath:

> Erinnern Sie sich noch des Abends, den wir bei Frau von Schopenhauer zubrachten und man eine Wettung machte, ich könne keine Nähnadel führen?— Ein Beweis, daß ich damals nicht gelogen habe, ist beikommendes Röckelein; ich hab' es so schön gemacht, daß mein Talent für weibliche Handarbeit ohne Ungerechtigkeit doch nicht mehr in Zweifel gezogen werden kann. Betrachten Sie es indessen mit Nachsicht, denn im Stillen muß ich Ihnen bekennen, daß ich meinem Genie beinahe zuviel zugetraut habe. (144)

With her gift of the skirt, Bettine wishes to prove that she has mastered at least one of the feminine arts; with the same stroke of the pen—and recalling her tendency to relativize what she has just written—she calls her abilities into question, asking Frau Goethe for leniency when judging her handiwork. Within the context of the entire work, Bettine's inadequacy becomes one of her virtues, for it becomes clear that she does not wish to submit to and is often scornful of traditional female gender roles. Even when making a show of trying to adhere to gender norms, Bettine resists them.

Bettine is not always so flippant, however. In contrast to her remarks about sewing, she expresses sincere sorrow when she writes to Goethe of her sister's engagement: "Um wieder auf etwas Bitteres zu kommen, die Meline…heiratet einen Mann von dem die allgemeine Sage geht er sei ein ganz vortrefflicher Mensch. O wie ist das traurig, Sklave der Vortrefflichkeit sein, da bringt man es nicht weiter wie Charlotte es gebracht hat, man ketzert sich und andre mit der Tugend ab" (320). It appears that Meline has found a good match, but Bettine remains skeptical, drawing a parallel between Meline's supposedly excellent fiancé and Charlotte of *Die Wahlverwandtschaften*, implying that both entrap others in the snares of their virtue.

Bettine harbors no wish to marry or to sew or to keep house, and on occasion she seems to wish to be a man. She dresses in men's clothing the first time she travels to visit Goethe (18–19); when writing about the Tyrolean war, she expresses the desire to participate in battle: "Ach, hätt ich ein Wämslein, Hosen und Hut, ich lief über zu den gradnasigen, gradherzigen Tirolern und ließ ihre schöne, grüne Standarte im Winde klatschen" (249). The following expression of resentment towards the constraints placed upon her could also be read as frustration with being a woman: "Und da fühl ich, daß dies Leben ein Gefängnis ist, wo ein jeder nur eine kümmerliche Aussicht hat in die Freiheit: das ist die eigene Seele" (140).

The above passages have been cited as proof that Bettine engaged in cross-dressing or that, in creating her Bettine personae, Arnim was expressing an androgynous ideal.[17] The evidence notwithstanding, such an argument requires more nuance. Bettine's description of her first visit to Goethe is the only passage in any of Arnim's works in which one of her Bettine figures actively cross-dresses. In this instance one must consider that, like Bettina Brentano, Bettine travels to Weimar "durch die ganzen Armeen zwischen Feind und Freund durch" (19)—in the midst of the Napoleonic wars[18]—and, although it remains unspoken, she presumably wears men's clothing as protection against rape.[19] Neither Arnim nor any of her main characters ever cross-dresses as a conscious practice, something not unheard of in Arnim's day, as the examples of Madame de Gachet, whom we encounter in *Frühlingskranz*, George Sand in France, and Ulrike von Kleist, Emma Herwegh, and Louise Aston in Germany prove. Arnim's Bettines often express the wish to be a man and refer to themselves with male appellatives and pronouns, generally either in defiant response to a feeling of confinement or as expression of a feeling of strength. One must, however, make a distinction between this idealistic cross-dressing and those instances—literary and historical—in which women really were wearing the pants.

Arnim was a product of German Idealism and its belief in the power of education, and especially art, to influence human beings. Against this backdrop she depicts Bettine as a figure who recognizes the power of literature to influence and shape social mores, including gender norms. This may explain why Bettine directs her strongest criticisms of traditional female gender roles against female characters in Goethe's novels. Dissatisfied with the idealized image of a woman in a white dress with pink bows, she expresses to Frau Rath the wish to throw Werther's Lotte out the door: "Ihr Herr Sohn hat einen schlechten Geschmack an dem weißen Kleide mit Rosaschleifen. Ich will gewiß in meinem Leben kein weißes Gewand anziehen; grün, grün sind alle meine Kleider" (28). Furthermore, with the exception of Mignon, she expresses disdain for all of the female figures in *Wilhelm Meisters Lehrjahre*: "da sind mir alle Frauen zuwider, ich möchte sie alle zum Tempel hinaus jagen, und darauf hatte ich [bei der ersten Lektüre des Werkes] auch gebaut, Du würdest mich gleich lieb gewinnen, wenn du mich kennen lerntest, weil ich besser bin und liebenswürdiger wie die ganze weibliche Comitee deiner Romane" (297). Unimpressed by the female characters in novels she has read by Goethe, Bettine feels convinced that Goethe would find her version of femininity more appealing, indeed, that it is more appealing because of her refusal to conform to society's wishes for her.

Despite her criticism, Bettine finds herself drawn to two of Goethe's literary figures: Mignon of *Wilhelm Meisters Lehrjahre* and Ottilie of *Die Wahlverwandtschaften*. Bettine's identification with Mignon runs throughout this text and into *Günderode*, and despite her androgynous appearance, Mignon represents both the feminine lover and the "gewaltsam zurückgehaltener oder eingeschlossener Leistungsfähigkeit" (Bäumer, *Bettine, Psyche, Mingon* 139) suffered by so many nineteenth-century women, including Bettine's friend Günderode. In the course of the text, Bettine moves away from identification with the self-destructive aspects of Mignon to identification with other characteristics.

In Part One, following a dream in which she performs Mignon's *Eiertanz* for Goethe, Bettine expresses her fear, "daß auch mir das weiße Kleid ausgezogen werde, und daß ich in den gewöhnlichen des alltäglichen gemeinen Lebens einhergehen werde; und daß diese Welt, in der meine Sinne lebendig sind, versinken wird" (99). Whereas Bettine claims in her discussion of *Werther* that she wears only green clothing in order to contrast positively her free spirit to that of Lotte, here Mignon's white dress symbolizes the innocence of a child whose creativity and uniqueness are threatened by the drudgery of daily life. Of course, the white dress also becomes Mignon's shroud. Through her identification Bettine expresses the dual apprehension that she, like many of the women and literary heroines of her day, would be prohibited from living according to her credo, *es werde*,[20] and that there is no place on earth where she can develop her potential.

In Part Two, as a result of her experiences during the Tyrolean War and the confidence she has gained from her interaction with Goethe, Bettine no longer sees Mignon as a representation of her threatened existence. Rather, she comes to identify with Mignon as lover, and in addition, interprets her outside the context of *Wilhelm Meister* as an inspiration to personal as well as political and moral action.[21] Referring to Goethe as her master—and thus foregrounding her role as his apprentice—Bettine calls to him: "Siehst Du, Meister, wenn Du heute in der sternhellen kalten Nacht deine Mignon aus ihrem Bettchen holst…Du sagst ihr:…ich will allein mit Dir in die Fremde ziehen; O, sie wirds verstehen, es wird ihr nicht unglaublich vorkommen, Du tust was sie längst von Dir verlangte und was Du unbegreiflich unterlassen hast" (252). Loyalty and the desire for action become the virtues to which Bettine aspires, and her call to

Goethe serves as a plea not only to love her but also to become involved in the Tyrolean War rather than solely in the world of his literary characters: "Ach, ich muß klagen, Goethe...ich fühl mich jetzt so hülflos, so unverstanden wie damals die Mignon.—Da draußen ist heute ein Lärm und doch geschieht nichts, sie haben arme Tyroler gefangen eingebracht" (252–253). In criticizing Wilhelm Meister's indifference towards Mignon, Bettine reprimands Goethe for his indifference towards her and towards the efforts of the Tyroleans.

In addition to her identification with Mignon, Bettine provides a long commentary on Goethe's portrayal of Ottilie in *Die Wahlverwandtschaften*. Here one finds the clearest example of how she appropriates traditional female roles while at the same time redefining them. Again emphasizing the importance of action, she asks:

> und was hilft mich aller Geist und alles Gefühl in Ottiliens Tagebuch? nicht kindlich ist's, daß sie den Geliebten verläßt und nicht von Ihm die Entfaltung ihres Geschicks erwartet, nicht weiblich ist's, daß sie nicht bloß sein Geschick beratet; und nicht mütterlich, da sie ahnen muß die jungen Keime alle, deren Wurzeln mit den ihrigen verwebt sind, daß sie ihrer nicht achtet und alles mit sich zu Grunde richtet. (316)

For Bettine, to be childlike is to remain true to the lover in order to develop one's self through him (or her), to be a woman is to offer sober advice, and to be a mother is to accept responsibility for all of those with whom one comes into contact. In this passage, Bettine summarizes the gender roles that she accepts as her own and that Arnim explores further in her later works. As a result of this view of women's roles—and unlike many heroines of nineteenth-century female *Bildungsromane*—she is never consumed to the point of self-destruction by her love for Goethe and can therefore develop independently from her so-called master.

The Lover: As the Mirror, In the Mirror, Her Own Mirror

Briefwechsel often proves confusing and even disconcerting because Bettine simultaneously plays so many—often contradictory—roles and because she seems to be child and adult at the same time. One minute, she depicts herself babbling incoherently on Goethe's lap, and in the next she plays the self-aware lover. Despite their seeming contradictions, both the role of the child and that of lover allow Bettine to engage in *romantische Gesellgikeit*, a practice that Friedrich Schlegel describes in his "Gespräch über die Poesie" when he notes: "[Es] geht der Mensch, sicher sich selbst immer wieder zu finden, immer von neuem aus sich heraus, um die Ergänzung seines innersten Wesens in der Tiefe eines Fremden zu suchen und zu finden (286);" and that Günter Oesterle has summarized as "Eine Hermeneutik, die der Fremderfahrung zur Selbsterkenntnis bedarf" (62). While the child represents Bettine's creativity and her openness to experience, her role as lover indicates her willingness and ability to engage in intimate exchange. Recalling Altman's assertion that writing and reading, and intimacy and the need for an audience constitute epistolarity (186), one can see how the epistolary form serves as the ideal structural expression of romantic sociability.

Writing in a tradition that can be traced back to Plato's *Symposium*, and as is evident in the notion of romantic sociability that was taken up by early romantic writers, Arnim asserts through Bettine that love facilitates education. The more people with whom she comes into close contact, the broader her base of education, for each encounter allows her not only to share the experiences of others, but also to shape her own identity through them. Influenced by Friedrich Schlegel and Schleiermacher, Arnim's text implies that only through love can one find one's place in the universe, for love bridges the gap between the individual, constrained by death, and the continuity of all being.[22] This becomes evident early in the text when Bettine exclaims to Frau Rath: "Die Leidenschaft ist ja der einzige Schlüssel zur Welt, durch die lernt der Geist alles kennen und fühlen, wie soll er denn sonst in sie hineinkommen?—und da fühl' ich, daß ich durch die Liebe zu Ihm erst in den Geist geboren bin, daß durch Ihn die Welt sich mir erst aufschließt, da mir die Sonne scheint, und der Tag sich von der Nacht scheidet" (36–37). Bettine's love, not only for Goethe, but also for Frau Rath, for Günderode, and as becomes increasingly evident in Arnim's later texts, for her fellow human beings, unlocks the world for her.

In part, Arnim's appropriation of romantic sociability was inspired by her relationship with Schleiermacher. In summarizing the theologian's theories of individual development, Sabine Schormann notes his belief that in order to discover the world and herself the individual requires a medium, a *Mittler*. For Schleiermacher, finding a religion is the prerequisite for finding and becoming a medium: "Im Prinzip kann jeder, der die Religion für sich entdeckt hat, zum Mittler werden, allerdings gilt für Schleiermacher Christus als der erste und größte aller Mittler...Entsprechend ist auch das Christentum die heiligste aller Religionen" ("Was ich nur ahndete" 122). Schormann argues further that Arnim held a more secular understanding of the term: "[Arnim] sieht die Mittlergestalt dagegen im als Ideal gedachten Geliebten, einem Geliebten also, in dem sie den höheren Menschen, den Bezug zum Unendlichen sucht. Er soll ihr, sie soll ihm ermöglichen, die Vergänglichkeit zu transzendieren und im Ewigen aufzuheben." ("Was ich nur ahndete" 123). Arnim then projected this view onto her Bettine persona who uses not only Goethe but also Frau Rath and Günderode as *Mittler*, and to a lesser extent, serves them as *Mittler* as well.

While love serves as the basis for Bettine's interaction with others, it assumes many different forms: platonic love, erotic love, and *caritas*. Bettine's love is both intellectual and emotional. She learns to love through her personal experiences but the author's understanding of love is also shaped by her familiarity with the classical ideal of love as a means to education (*Bildung*) and with the romantic notion that love allows the individual to become one with others and with the universe. These components of love are present in varying degrees in Bettine's key relationships.

Bettine's earliest experiences with love occur during her childhood while she is living with her grandmother. In the *Tagebuch* she records the story of her first three kisses, the second of which is most important for her development. Herder bestows this kiss upon her in her grandmother's garden and then referrs to her as Psyche. As Bettine recalls: "so war mir dies unbegriffne Wort Psyche ein Talisman, der mich einer unsichtbaren Welt zuführte, in der ich mich unter diesem Namen begriffen dachte" (513). Referring to the heroine of Apuleius's tale of Psyche, who must win back her lover Cupid through a series of trials, this role assumes various functions for Bettine (as it did for Arnim). In her monument to Goethe, Bettine/Arnim depicts herself as a child Psyche stepping on Goethe's foot and plucking the strings of the lyre he holds, thus representing Bettine's openly assertive attempt to integrate herself into Goethe's life through love. Further, although by the end of this text Bettine has lost all of those most important to her (in contrast to Psyche who eventually wins back Cupid), her experiences have been a source of empowerment. Like Psyche, she has matured through love.[23]

Following the kisses of her youth, Bettines relationship to Günderode is her first love attachment. Günderode tutors Bettine in history and philosophy, but more importantly for Bettine, Günderode teaches her to become aware of her own thoughts and feelings: "Unser Zusammenleben war schön, es war die erste Epoche, in der ich mich gewahr ward" (64). Especially at the beginning of their friendship, creativity characterizes their mode of interaction, and playful exchange their correspondence. One sequence of letters, for example, involves a series of riddles: "Nun waren wir in's Rätsel *geben* und *lösen* geraten; alle Augenblick hatt' ich ein kleines Abenteuer auf meinen Spaziergang, was ich ihr verbrämt zu erraten gab; meistens löste sie es auf eine kindlichlustige Weise auf" (77). Their epistolary game thus involves fantasy and reciprocity.

Moments of happiness are, however, darkened by Günderode's despair and by Bettine's inability, despite her many efforts, to help her friend. The most intimate exchange between the two women occurs when Günderode announces to Bettine her plan to commit suicide. Bettine recalls:

> ich brach in lautes Schreien aus, ich fiel ihr um den Hals, und riß sie nieder auf den Sitz und setzte mich auf ihre Knie, und weinte viel Tränen und küßte sie zum *erstenmal* an ihren Mund, und riß ihr das Kleid auf und küßte sie an die Stelle, wo sie gelernt hatte das Herz treffen; und ich bat mit schmerzlichen Tränen, daß sie sich meiner erbarme, und fiel ihr wieder um den Hals; und küßte ihre Hände, die waren kalt und zitterten, und ihre Lippen zuckten, und sie war ganz kalt und starr und totenblaß und konnte die Stimme nicht erheben; sie sagte leise: Bettine, brich mir das Herz nicht. (73)

Through her kiss, Bettine expresses her wish for a union with Günderode, a symbiotic relationship of give and take, of mutual inspiration and education. Yet Günderode never reciprocates Bettine's physical overtures, and Bettine's outburst constitutes a powerful but fleeting moment in a relationship characterized by emotional intensity on the one hand and increasing distance on the other. The final break occurs when Bettine visits Günderode only to hear the words "komme nicht näher, kehre wieder um, wir müssen uns doch trennen" (81).[24] Bettine feels as if a lover has abandoned her: "Ach, erste Verzweiflung, erster grausamer Schlag, so empfindlich für ein junges Herz! ich, die nichts kannte, wie die Unterwerfung, die Hingebung in dieser Liebe, mußte so zurückgewiesen werden" (81). The relationship with Günderode leads Bettine to begin to formulate ideas about love and interpersonal interaction. The significance of this relationship for Arnim is attested to by her return to it in both *Günderode* and *Ambrosia*.

Looking back, Bettine realizes that her relationship with Günderode lacked the intimacy and reciprocity she desired: "Sie erzählte mir wenig von ihren sonstigen Angelegenheiten, ich wußte nicht, in welchen Verbindungen sie noch außer mir war" (72). Günderode's death proves to be the first of many instances that teach Bettine that it is one thing to love and quite another to have a truly reciprocal relationship or to expect love from others: "ich hab' geweint um mich, mit mir; hart muß ich werden wie Stahl, gegen mich, gegen das eigne Herz; ich darf es nicht beklagen, daß ich nicht geliebt werde, ich muß streng sein gegen dies leidenschaftliche Herz; es hat kein Recht zu fordern, nein es hat kein Recht" (71).

Remarkably, negative experiences harden Bettine only to the extent that she comes to rely on no one but herself for her sense of self. At the same time, they lead her to seek out further interaction with others. Following the break with Günderode, Bettine goes to the house of Frau Rath and announces, "ich will Ihre Bekanntschaft machen, mir ist eine Freundin in der Stiftsdame Günderode verlorengegangen und die sollen Sie mir ersetzen" (81). Bettine admits that she turns to Frau Rath in order to gain proximity to Goethe, but she then comes to value Frau Rath as friend and mother figure. This becomes particularly evident in Part Two when, in several of her letters, Bettine expresses to Goethe how much she misses his now-departed mother:

> Hätt ich die Mutter noch, so wüßt ich wo ich zu Haus wär, ich wurde ihren Umgang allem andern vorziehen, sie machte mich sicher im Denken und Handeln, manchmal verbot sie mir etwas, wenn ich aber doch als meinem Eigensinn gefolgt war, verteidigte sie mich gegen alle, und da holte sie aus in ihrem Enthusiasmus, wie der Schmidt, der das glühende Eisen auf dem Ambos hat, sie sagte: wer der Stimme in seiner Brust folgt, der wird seine Bestimmung nicht verfehlen. (358)

Helping Bettine to feel at home, Frau Rath serves her as mediator. Like

Günderode, Frau Rath teaches Bettine to listen to her own voice and to follow her vocation. We find in this passage an image of two individuals actively engaging with each other, and we encounter Frau Rath as an individual capable of both disagreeing with and supporting Bettine, characteristics that one does not find in the Goethe figure of *Briefwechsel*.

As significant as this relationship to Frau Rath may be, in this text (the story is different in *Dies Buch*) Bettine uses the mother to approach the son. She strives for her own education and the development of her genius; in order to achieve these goals she requires interaction with the best-known genius of her time. For this reason, I disagree with Liebertz-Grün's assertion that turning to Goethe serves merely to compensate Bettine for the loss of Günderode (*Ordnung im Chaos* 8). Neither the emphasis that the text places on the Bettine-Goethe constellation nor the significance of Goethe for Bettine's sense of self lends credence to this claim.

Recalling the gender attributes of Schlegel's Lucinde, Bettine depicts herself as the embodiment of love, writing to Goethe: "Ich zum wenigsten fühle, daß keiner mit mir wetteifern könnte in der Liebe, und darum siegt auch meine Großmut" (436). The notion of love that Arnim espouses in *Briefwechsel* becomes most complex in the representation of Bettine's love for Goethe. She adores him like a child, curling up in his lap as she might with an older brother or father, but then she describes their interaction with unmistakably erotic language. In one moment, she depicts herself wishing to assume a submissive, masochistic position: "Du! der es weiß, daß ich gern den *Nacken* unter deine Füße lege" (101). But then she gains the upper hand, confiding to Goethe's mother:

> Ich glaub' daß es eine Art und Weise gibt, Jemand zu besitzen, die Niemand streitig machen kann; diese üb' ich an Wolfgang, keiner hat es vor mir gekonnt, das weiß ich, trotz allen seinen Liebschaften, von denen sie mir erzählt.—Vor ihm tu' ich zwar sehr demütig, aber hinter seinem Rücken halte ich ihn fest, und da müßte er stark zappeln, wenn er los will. (32)

Here, Bettine expresses her sense of complete control over the relationship and depicts her submissiveness as no more than play.

Though these contradictory facets of Bettine's love exist simultaneously, as Bettine matures a self-assured, often erotic tone comes to dominate her expressions of love. This tone becomes particularly evident in the first half of Part Two and in the *Tagebuch*. That Bettine is no longer an *unmündiges Kind* is nowhere more apparent than in her description (based on her Teplitz fragments) in Part Two of a meeting with Goethe on a hot August night:

> so gedenke ich jetzt der Abenddämmerung im heißen Monat August wie Du am Fenster saßest und ich vor Dir stand, und wie wir Rede wechselten, ich hatte meinen Blick wie ein Pfeil scharf Dir in's Auge gedrückt, und so blieb ich drin haften und bohrte mich immer tiefer und tiefer ein und wir waren beide stille, und Du zogst meine aufgelösten Haare durch die Finger. (369–370)

Her gaze penetrating deep into Goethe, standing while he is sitting, Bettine pushes the moment to climax and release. Layering erotic and idealistic discourse, Bettine employs the metaphor of sexual intercourse to reflect her desire to become one with Goethe, as both artist and genius.

In her diary Bettine describes an occasion on which a similar erotic exchange with Goethe leads directly to creative birth on her part. Recalling a walk with him along the edge of a forest in Bohemia, she writes: "ich sah über mich und streckte die Arme nach Dir, Du beugtest Dich über mein Gesicht und legtest Deinen Mund auf meinen, und die Donner krachten, prallten aneinander, stürzten von Stufe zu Stufe den Olympos herab, und leise rollend flüchteten sie in die Ferne, kein zweiter Schlag folgte" (567). The topos of the storm represents sexual passion, climax and release. Ten years later, Bettine bears the fruit of this kiss: "Nach zehn Jahren war dies schöne Ereignis, was so deutlich in meinem Gedächtnis eingeprägt blieb, Veranlassung zur Erfindung von Goethes Monument" (567).[25] Bettine depicts this kiss as a moment of conception and her interaction with and love for Goethe as the inspiration for her development as an artist.

Despite, or more plausibly because of such intense moments, Goethe distances himself from Bettine in the second half of Part Two. In contrast to the situation with Günderode, in this text neither Bettine nor Goethe ever offers even a semblance of a reason for the growing distance between them. Based on the information Bettine provides, it appears Goethe fears Bettine and the authority she has gained through her growing self-assurance (ironically a product of her relationship with him) and through her knowledge about their relationship. The power of this knowledge becomes clear as Bettine recalls an evening when Goethe demanded that she love him forever:

> und ich sagte: "Ja."—Und eine ganze Weile drauf, da nahmst Du eine Spinnwebe von dem Gitter der Laube und hingst mir's auf's Gesicht, und sagtest: bleib verschleiert vor jedermann und zeige niemand was Du mir bist.—Ach! Goethe...ich erinnere mich gar nicht, daß ich mit Selbstbewußtsein Dir die Treue zugesagt hätte, es ist alles mächtiger in mir wie ich, ich kann nicht regieren, ich kann nicht wollen, ich muß alles geschehen lassen. (282)

Goethe asks Bettine to love him and, more importantly, to keep that love to herself. But Bettine cannot acquiesce, justifying her refusal to submit to his request by invoking a higher authority, that force more powerful than she herself, her genius. In Arnim's depiction, Goethe retreats in fear of Bettine's self-assurance and power.

Despite her confidence Bettine cannot reconcile herself to the loss of Goethe. She pleads to him: "Mit Dir hab' ich zu sprechen!—nicht mit dem, der mich von sich gestoßen,...Mit Dir Genius!" (414). But Goethe has fallen silent. Indeed, he falls silent twice in the text, for in the diary, Bettine writes of his death and her reaction to it. Bettine's reaction to the loss of Goethe serves as another indicator of how she has matured. Whereas, following her break with Günderode, she cried for and with herself and expressed the wish to become hard as steel, Goethe's parting reveals a very different truth to her: "ich habe keinen anderen Freund gehabt als mich selber" (471–472). Rather than finding her identity in her relationship to Goethe, Bettine's sense of self comes from within, a discovery indicated both by the development of the narrative and by the structural shift from epistolary to diary form. This calls into question the function that the beloved other serves for Bettine if, all along, she has been her only friend.

Throughout the text Bettine calls attention to her self-sufficiency. Her claim to Frau Rath in regard to Goethe: "ich will nur von ihm nehmen" (47) is echoed later by Goethe himself: "Eigentlich kann man dir nichts geben, weil Du Dir alles entweder schaffst oder nimmst" (335). Such passages portray Bettine as someone actively engaged in shaping her relationships and even her partners. It thus comes as no surprise that Bettine frequently employs the images of the mirror and the echo to describe the function of her counterpart, and that, as epistolary responses, the letters of Frau Rath and Goethe do more to provide additional insight into the character of Bettine than to give us a multi-dimensional sense of what her friends are like.

In the diary section, once she is left alone, Bettine repeatedly turns to her mirror for assurance:

> heut am Tag schreibe ich noch als psychologische Merkwürdigkeit her auf welche wunderbare Weise ich mich beschwichtigte, wie die geängstigte mit aller Willenskraft der Jugend ausgerüstete Seele sich half.—Auf dem Tisch vor dem Spiegel knieend, bei dem unsicheren Flackern der Nachtlampe, Hülfe suchend im eignen Auge. (555)

In turning to her mirror, Bettine turns inward for support, for help, and for love. In a series of aphorisms, she goes so far as to claim that love is, in essence, self-love:

> Willst Du den Geliebten erwerben, so suche Dich zu finden, zu erwerben in ihm. Du erwirbst, Du hast Dich selbst, wo Du liebst; wo Du nicht liebst, entbehrst Du Dich.
> Bist Du allein mit Dir, so bist du mit dem Genius.
> Du liebst in dem Geliebten nur den eignen Genius. (487–488)

Bettine's love evidences numerous paradoxes. In order to find herself, she requires another. But in loving that other, she loves no one other than herself and discovers nothing more than what she would call her own genius. Such a notion recalls and inverts the love relationship in Friedrich Schlegel's *Lucinde*, for here the woman Bettine uses others, including men, as her mirror, her vehicle towards achieving selfhood.

This dynamic results from a paradox inherent in the attempt to come to know others, summarized by Fichte in *Die Bestimmung des Menschen*:

> Alles Wissen [ist] lediglich ein Wissen von Dir selbst...dein Bewußtsein [geht] nie über dich selbst [hinaus, und]...dasjenige, was du für ein Bewußtseyn des Gegenstandes hälst, [ist] nichts...als ein Bewußtseyn, deines *Setzens eines Gegenstands*, welches du nach einem inneren Gesetze deines Denkens mit der Empfindung zugleich nothwendig vollziehst. (276)

All knowledge, and here one can also say all knowledge gained from love and loving, is only knowledge of the self. Echoing Fichte, Arnim illustrates here and in her later works the extent both to which love can only be self-love and to which one's knowledge of the other is no more than one's sense of one's self in the other.

Arnim's depiction of Bettine's love has left the author open to strikingly divergent interpretations: while some readers consider Bettine to be thoroughly narcissistic and self-absorbed, others have argued that, in her love relationships, Bettine abolishes all forms of hierarchy. I contend that the complexity of the ideas represented in *Briefwechsel* demands a more differentiated interpretation.

First, Bettine's love for Goethe (as well as for Günderode and Frau Rath) is indeed narcissistic. Her lovers do serve as her mirrors and they do help her to develop a sense of herself. Of course Bettine serves as a mirror for Frau Rath insofar as, by listening to the stories about Goethe, she allows Frau Rath to remember her role as Goethe's mother. She also serves as a mirror for Goethe insofar as she admires him and helps him to write his autobiography. Nevertheless, the text deals with Bettine's development, not theirs, and as such they become one-dimensional characters in contrast to the complex, chimerical Bettine. Second, although in an epistemological sense love may mean, "die Aufhebung der Herrschaftsbeziehung zwischen erkennendem Subjekt und Erkennungsgegenstand" (Bäumer, *Bettine, Psyche, Mignon* 150), this does not hold true for Bettine's love in this text. To the extent that Bettine uses her interlocutors as projection screens and to the extent that her individuality precludes complete reciprocity, the hierarchy does remain intact. Indeed, Bettine's knowledge of her relationship to Goethe and the manner in which she interprets and plans to write about this relationship—both forms of power—eventually drive Goethe away. Third, as a result of the narcissistic, hierarchical nature of her love, Bettine is left alone at the end of the text, with only herself to turn to as mirror.

Side by side with these negative aspects one also finds utopian qualities inherent in Bettine's notion of love. First of all, as a female literary figure in a century in which love led other literary and historical women to either death or loss of a sense of self, Bettine assumes what, in the nineteenth century, was form of agency generally available to men only: the ability to see herself in the mirror of others, to shape her sense of both herself and her relationship. Arnim contests the gender norms of the day, making Bettine into a female "Julius." In later works, this agency will develop into an awareness of the difference of others and it will help her to reflect on the manner in which she projects herself onto them. Second,

Bettine may be alone at the end of the text, but she has not been destroyed by her love. Finally and most importantly, and again paradoxically, we will see in later works that love is related to justice. What here is a personal statement will later on concern politics, for Bettine comes to assert that one must see oneself in others before one can judge them. Love thus becomes a plea for empathy: although one can never really know the other, one can strive to imagine oneself in that person's shoes.

Genie/Daemon

The title of *Briefwechsel* emphasizes Bettine's role as child, and the narrative itself recounts what is, in effect, a story of unrequited love. Nevertheless, the role most central to Bettine's sense of identity in this text is neither child nor lover but rather that of genius. Bettine's sense of her own genius would not be possible unless some part of her could play the child, for it develops out of her education and love relationships. At the same time, she asserts that her genius is an intrinsic part of who she is. To an extent, this sense of self allows her both to overcome gender dichotomies and to write. This proves significant not only for the Bettine of the text but also for Arnim, for publishing this text gives her a sense of self and public authority, both of which allow her to continue to write for publication.

Like the other roles I have described, that of genius has multiple valences. The term refers at times to an external source of inspiration, the godlike voice in and coming from another. Inspired by Socrates and the Platonic school, as well as by Goethe and Schleiermacher, Arnim also employs the closely related term *Dämon* to refer to the personal spirit assigned to each individual, "der ihn nicht blos schütze, sondern auch moralisch leite" (Stoll 157). Finally, Arnim employs the terms *Genius* and *Dämon* to refer to Bettine's inner voice in the sense of "eine innerste göttliche Stimme im Herzen, die uns geheimes offenbaren kann."[26] Goethe gives expression to this final notion in his poem "Urworte, Orphisch," which has as its subtitle "ΔΑΙΜΩΝ, Dämon." Here, Goethe depicts the human being as "Geprägte Form, die lebend sich entwickelt" and considers the *Dämon* the force that guides this development (*Werke*, vol. 1 359). As Bäumer observes, Goethe links "die Vorstellung vom 'Dämonischen' an den Gedanken der Entelechie und verlagert in Anlehnung an Sokrates die Ebene des Wirkungsbereiches des 'Dämons' von Außen zurück in das Innere des Menschen" (*Bettine, Psyche, Mignon* 210). Yet for Bettine, genius and daemon are both externalized and internalized. She considers others her source of genius while at the same time claiming to possess and to be a genius. She asserts that her daemon guides her actions and simultaneously comes to play the role of conscience and protector (daemon) in her relationships with others.

Although the Goethe of this text cannot be identified with his historical namesake, Arnim expected her readers to know who Goethe was and to bring their associations of Goethe as genius to their readings of her text. Bettine is not so much a passionate admirer of Goethe as author; she actually offers more criticism of than praise for his texts. Rather, Goethe becomes for her the embodiment of genius that she captures in her Goethe Monument and that she wishes to incorporate into her identity. In other words, she views him as her *Genius*.

Goethe does not stand alone in this role. Especially because of her love relationship with Goethe, Bettine views herself as his equal: "In der Liebe ist einer dem andern Genius und wird einer dem andern Element" (533). The text establishes links between Bettine's letters and two poems Goethe sends her to give the impression that Bettine has inspired his writing;[27] she shares with Goethe material for his autobiography; she also becomes an artist in her own right, designing the Goethe Monument and making plans to write *Briefwechsel*, activities she discusses in the diary. Paradoxically, then, due to the dynamics of romantic sociability and Arnim's/Bettine's complex understanding of the terms genius and daemon, Goethe as genius can be of no use to Bettine unless she has a sense of her own genius. Goethe does not bestow upon her any qualities she does not already possess, but she requires him to develop those qualities.

Arnim's notion of genius is related to her sense of self as an artist; it also derives from and influences her involvement in public affairs. Although she does not really thematize the role of the daemon as conscience until her later works, already in this text Bettine possesses a strong sense of the integrity of her actions and feels inspired to guide and protect others. In Part One, Bettine expresses this desire in regard to the proposed emancipation of the Jews in Frankfurt. Instead of sharing the skepticism of

Goethe and the Primate (*Fürst Primas*) of Frankfurt, Karl Theodor von Dalberg, Arnim positions Goethe as the foil to Bettine's conscience, allowing him to contend: "dem Fürsten Primas ist aber auch nicht zu verdenken, daß er dies Geschlecht behandelt wie es ist, und wie es noch eine Weile bleiben wird" (141). Such a claim allows for the depiction of Bettine as a supporter of the right of Jews to an education. She responds:

> Ich leugne auch nicht, die Juden sind ein heißhungriges, unbescheidenes Volk; wenn man ihnen den Finger reicht, so reißen sie einem bei der Hand an sich, daß man um und um purzeln möchte; das kommt eben daher, daß sie so lang in der Not gesteckt haben; ihre Gattung ist doch Menschenart, und diese soll doch einmal der Freiheit teilhaftig sein, zu Christen will man sie absolut machen, aber aus ihrem engen Fegfeuer der überfüllten Judengasse will man sie nicht heraus lassen;…es war…ein höchst genialer und glücklicher Gedanke von meinem Molitor, für's erste Christen- und Judenkinder in *eine* Schule zu bringen; die können's denn mit einander versuchen, und den Alten mit gutem Beispiel vorgehen. Die Juden sind wirklich voll Untugend, das läßt sich nicht leugnen; aber ich sehe gar nicht ein, was an den Christen zu verderben ist; und wenn denn doch alle Menschen Christen werden sollen, so lasse man sie in's himmlische Paradies,—da werden sie sich schon bekehren, wenn's ihnen gefällig ist. (147)

As I have argued elsewhere, this passage does not adequately support the assertion that Arnim was free of prejudice. She is unwilling to deny, for example, that the Jews are a ravenous, immodest people. Nevertheless, in comparison to Arnim's original correspondence with Goethe[28] and to the beliefs held by many throughout the nineteenth century, one cannot ignore the progressive nature of Bettine's support of Franz Joseph Molitor's educational project,[29] her argument for equal education for all, and her accompanying criticisms of church and state.

In Part Two, Bettine turns her attentions to the Tyrolean war, an issue barely touched on in the original correspondence. Here, Arnim begins to formulate her ideas about the role of the artist in society. In allowing Bettine to criticize Goethe's complete lack of interest in the war, Arnim chastises artists and art that remain removed from the world. Whereas Goethe writes Bettine that he turns to writing *Die Wahlverwandtschaften* "um weniger von allem Übel der Zeit ergriffen zu werden" (264), Bettine becomes educated through war:

> O, lieber Freund, während Du Dich abwendest vor dem Unheil trüber Zeit, in ein-

samer Höhe Geschicke bildest, und mit scharfen Sinnen sie lenkest, daß sie ihrem Glück nicht entgehen, denn sicher ist dies schönes Buch, welches Du Dir zum Trost über alles traurige erfindest, ein Schatz köstlicher Genüsse...während diesem hat es sich ganz anders in mir gestaltet.—Du erinnerst Dich wohl noch, daß die Gegend, das Klima meiner Gedanken und Empfindungen, heiter waren, ein freundlicher Spielplatz...Jetzt ist es anders in mir, düstere Hallen, die prophetische Monumente gewaltiger Todeshelden umschließen, sind der Mittelpunkt meiner schweren Ahnungen. (271–272)

Criticizing Goethe for retreating from the world, Bettine feels strongly moved by the events taking place around her. This exchange with Goethe foreshadows the attempts of Arnim and her Bettine personae to engage with the public sphere, to employ writing as a tool for social change rather than as a means to escape the troubles of the day.

As with the role of the lover, that of the daemon inverts the gender dynamics of *Lucinde*. Whereas Julius's development depends on Lucinde serving as his mirror, Bettine requires Goethe in order to develop her sense of genius. Moving through three phases in the text, Bettine begins by aligning herself with Goethe as genius in order to develop her own genius. In erotic encounters she then merges with Goethe not only as lover but also as artist. Finally, she comes to claim that Goethe is no more than a mirror of her own genius. Goethe leaves her twice in the text, first by ceasing to write and secondly in his death. Yet by the end of the text Bettine no longer has any need for him as interlocutor, for she has effectively usurped his authority as genius: "Und wenn dies alles wahr ist was ich hier sage, und wir werden einst uns wiedersehen in einem höheren Leben, dann denke, daß mein Genie Deinem Geist gewachsen sein werde" (543). Gone is the stammering of Part One, Bettine has made it through her apprenticeship and declares her genius as equal to that of Goethe.

Summary of a Development: Bettine as Writer

In depicting Bettine at various stages in her life, developing from young child to adult reflecting on her past, *Briefwechsel* recounts the story of a woman who not only becomes a writer but also defines how she wishes to write. Neither Bettine's correspondence nor Arnim's text provides a tightly-structured linear narrative. Arnim does not cover up the rough spots; the reader witnesses a text and a writer in the process of becoming.

Bettine possesses the qualities that German intellectuals of the early-nineteenth century attributed to the romantic writer: a childlike openness, natural genius, and the capacity to love and thus learn from others. She also has stories to tell. Nevertheless, the process of writing remains arduous. Describing her difficulty to Goethe, she writes:

> Wüßtest Du, was mich bei diesen einfachen Erzählungen oft für Unruhe und Schmerzen befallen!—es scheint Dir alles nur so hingeschrieben wie erlebt; ja!—aber so manches seh' ich, und denke es, und kann es doch nicht aussprechen; und ein Gedanke durchkreuzt den andern, und einer nimmt vor dem andern die Flucht, und dann ist es wieder so öde im Geist wie in der ganzen Welt. (196)

Bettine finds written language inadequate to express her myriad thoughts, feelings, and impressions. The attempt to record them in an orderly fashion leads to depression, and what she does produce seems only a shadow of her actual thoughts and feelings.

Bettine does not succumb to this emptiness of spirit, however, and she continues writing. She discovers through free association and through turning to and identifying her writing with music, especially that of Beethoven, that she can write, and those around her support her in this belief. Frau Rath encourages her to record Günderode's story; Goethe asks her to write down the stories she has heard from Frau Rath; and in reflecting on her life in her diary, she realizes that the story of her relationship with Goethe also needs telling. At this point, Bettine has also gained the authority (through association with Goethe) and self-assurance (through belief in her genius) to tell this story. Although *Briefwechsel* represents a crazy quilt of form and content, it recounts what it takes for a woman to become an artist and the result of this achievement: a strong sense of agency, albeit one coupled with loneliness.

Arnim's Bettine persona is not the only writer in or of this text; Arnim the author is present in the preface, and while one can distinguish between persona and author in Parts One and Two, it becomes more difficult to do so in the *Tagebuch*. Altman's analysis of the epistolary form elucidates the relationship between the author and her Bettine persona as well as that between the reader, the author, and that same persona. Altman has indicated that "the very fragmentation inherent in the letter form encourages the creation of a...coherence and continuity at new levels" (187). Out of the fragmentary form of her personal correspondence (with Goethe, Catharina Elisabeth Goethe, and Karoline von Günderrode) Bettina von Arnim the writer created her letter book *Briefwechsel* with Bettine as its semi-fictional heroine. At the same time, Arnim's personal engagement with the fragmentary form of her new text and with her literary persona led to what Lauretis would call a "habit change" in the writer, that is, a change in how she saw herself and in how she presented that self to her public. Furthermore, because Arnim blurred the lines between herself and her protagonist, and because the epistolary form invites active engagement on the part of the reader, she encouraged her readers to blur those lines as well.

Arnim was, of course, not free of her past or of the discourses of her time, something particularly evident in the manner in which she and her contemporary critics foregrounded Bettine in her role as child. As Adelson has noted, however, subject formation and positionality arise from both the construction of individuals *and* the possibility of the individual constructing herself. Against the dictates of her time, Arnim inverted the gender roles of *Lucinde* and allowed Bettine to assert her genius as equal to that of Goethe. In this way, she came to see herself as genius and encouraged others to do the same. The result of this process was not only the author of *Goethe's Briefwechsel mit einem Kinde* but also the woman who, five years later, completed *Die Günderode*.

CHAPTER TWO

Youth and Ideal Friendship: *Die Günderode* (1840)

The publication of *Goethe's Briefwechsel mit einem Kinde* transformed Bettina von Arnim into a public figure in Berlin. Her text received glowing reviews from such prominent critics as Willibald Alexis, Ludwig Börne, Karl Gutzkow, and Theodor Mundt. Others, such as the religious philosopher and poet Georg Friedrich Daumer, created poetic works inspired by the text. Throughout the 1830s and 1840s admirers sent Arnim numerous occasional poems that praised her by paraphrasing her texts.[1] In addition, the salon that Arnim had been hosting in her Berlin apartment at Unter den Linden 21 since 1834 attracted an increasing number of visitors wishing to bask in the light of someone who had been (as they believed after reading *Briefwechsel*) so closely associated with Goethe.[2]

This newfound popularity provided Arnim with the authority to become active in the interest of individual and political causes. Following the trial of the Göttingen Seven in 1837, she spent four years writing letters on behalf of her friends Jakob and Wilhelm Grimm; she eventually succeeded in persuading the new Prussian King Friedrich Wilhelm IV, just after his coronation in 1840, to grant them appointments at the Berlin University.[3] In 1838 she sponsored a lottery to raise money for the mentally ill Berlin painter, Carl Blechen. Moreover, through her salon she became involved in discussions about political reform. Her interest in the establishment in Prussia of a constitutional monarchy, which I will discuss in the next chapter, was an idea she shared with many liberals of the period. At the same time, Arnim also began work on an epistolary text that expanded upon the Günderode narrative of *Briefwechsel* to recall an almost forgotten woman poet who had committed suicide at the age of 26. Without the notoriety that Arnim had gained from her first publication, such an endeavor might not have been possible.

Arnim began working on *Die Günderode* in 1838 and published the text in 1840. The text was based on her friendship and correspondence with Karoline von Günderrode (1780–1806), a poet who, as the daughter of separated and impoverished parents, had been sent at the age of seventeen to live in the *Kronacher Damenstift für bedürftige Adlige*. She and Bettina Brentano met for the first time in 1799, and they developed a relationship that lasted until 1806 when Günderrode killed herself in the village of Winkel on the Rhine.

Like its predecessor, this work does not constitute a factual account, even though its sources include accounts of Bettina Brentano's friendship with Karoline von Günderrode and of the time the young Brentano spent living with Sophie von La Roche in Offenbach (1797–1802), with her older brother Franz in Frankfurt (1802–1805), and with her brother-in-law Savigny in Marbach and Trages (1805–1806). Rather, Arnim employs the events of this earlier period of her life as centerpieces around which she constructs a story of two personae, Bettine and Günderode, thus creating a montage of her past and her present, and of her real and imagined encounters with others, with the philosophical ideas of the first half of the nineteenth century, and with herself. As a result, inspirations for this text include not only episodes from Arnim's youth, but also experiences of the adult Arnim: her relationship with Schleiermacher, her salon conversations in the 1830s with a group of young doctors and medical students who referred to themselves as the *Doktorenklub*,[4] and the writing and publication of *Briefwechsel*. In addition the text clearly manifests the influence of the ideas of early romanticism (mediated through Clemens Brentano and Günderrode) and of the Young Hegelian and Young German movements.[5] Because Arnim was more concerned with the representational function of her characters than with the extent to which they were realistically depicted, figures also appear in the text who are most probably fictional (the mathematics teacher Ephraim), or whom Bettina Brentano never knew, or whom she met after Günderrode's death (Hölderlin, Primate Karl Theodor von Dalberg of Frankfurt, the educator Molitor).

This montage resulted in a text that achieved immense notoriety upon publication and that is considered by many today to be Arnim's strongest work.[6] The relationship between Bettine and Günderode is one of the most nuanced and complex of all relationships depicted in Arnim's texts, a factor that strengthens both the temptation to conflate the textual figures with their historical counterparts and the importance of resisting this temptation. As will become evident, the relationship between the two is intensely intimate and communicational on the one hand,[7] and it remains overshadowed by Günderode's wish to die and by the break between her and Bettine on the other. Even in this text, Bettine falls short of achieving romantic sociability's utopian goal of perfect, non-hierarchical communication. This tension notwithstanding, the epistolary exchange between Bettine and Günderode facilitates an exploration of youth and friendship, discussions of women's roles and possibilities, a redefinition of the functions of memory and history, and the advancement of the idea of art combined with activism. It also allows Bettine to gravitate more towards the teacher end of the pupil-teacher spectrum than was the case in *Briefwechsel*.

Whereas *Briefwechsel* depicts Bettine both as a child and as an adult looking back on her childhood, the time frame of *Günderode* is more unified, its primary action occurring between the years 1804–1806. Thus, while the author Arnim incorporates a lifetime of experience into this text, the reader sees the protagonist Bettine during one period of her life. As Altman asserts, epistolary narrative encourages the reader to read events as occurring in the present (187). This form and the unified time frame of *Günderode* do not so much emphasize the distant past as they draw the reader's attention to the continuity between the past and the present and to the lack of division between then and now, youth and old age. Further, while *Bildung* continues to be a central theme of this text, from the beginning Bettine is more sure of herself than in *Briefwechsel*, and rather than charting her own process of maturation, the text serves to illustrate the fine-tuning of her ideas.

Despite its narrow time frame, the story of Bettine and Günderode does not develop through a unified plot. Arnim works with themes and variations and develops her ideas through layering rather than through linear progression from one idea or event to the next. This stratified narrative technique notwithstanding, a series of guideposts helps the reader chart the development of the relationship between Caroline and Bettine.

Arnim divides this text into two parts. Part One is preceded by a dedication to *den Studenten* whom the author describes as "Euch *Irrenden Suchenden*" (297) and for whom she wishes that "das Göttliche erblühe und in der Zeiten Wechsel, ein milder Gestirn schützend über Euch hinleuchte" (298). Once the reader discovers in Part Two that, after moving to Marburg, Bettine spends her evenings scampering along the city wall, conversing with the stars in search of guidance, it becomes apparent that in this dedication Arnim is encouraging the students of Berlin (such as the members of the *Doktorenklub*) to view her as their guide and protector, or to use Schleiermacher's term, as their *Mittler*. As in *Briefwechsel*, then, she employs her dedication to suggest a standpoint for the ideal reader of her text. Following this opening, the voice of the author gives way to the correspondence between Bettine and Günderode, and at specific points within the text, to several poems by Karoline von Günderrode.

Far from serving as mere indicators of polite conversation, the first lines of the first two letters in the text establish a tone of intimacy between the two women. Bettine begins the correspondence by writing "Der Plaudergeist in meiner Brust hat immer fort geschwätzt mit Dir" (299); Günderode opens her first letter "Ich habe die Zeit über recht oft an Dich gedacht, liebe Bettine" (300). These letters mediate the impression of an exchange that continues in the interstices between letters and visits. Günderode's poem "Die Manen" follows these two letters. Its title referring to the good spirits/souls of the departed, the poem depicts a student and his teacher discussing the significance of memory and the past, recurring themes throughout the remainder of the correspondence. In the pages that directly follow this poem Bettine and Günderode both assume the dual roles of pupil and teacher in relation to each other. Whereas Günderode strives to instruct Bettine in philosophy and history, Bettine teaches Günderode the rules of her *Schwebereligion*. Despite this closeness, however, in the letters of Part One the women also express a sense of difference and distance from each other.

The fact that the reader is privy to different types of knowledge about each figure underscores the differences between them. Günderode communicates primarily thoughts and emotions in her letters and tells Bettine little about the activities and other relationships in her life. In addition, the reader gains access to Günderode's feelings through her poems, which are inserted between or integrated into the letters. In contrast, Bettine recounts far more than her ideas and sentiments. She complains to Günderode about difficulties with members of her family (who want her to conform to their gender-role expectations and live more like a proper lady) and especially with her brother Clemens (who wants her to conform to his idea of a writer). She describes people she meets in town, shepherds she encounters in the countryside, and visits with her grandmother. She writes of a ball she attends and of her flirtation with a neighbor's gardener. Throughout Part One, then, one gains a sense of a close friendship between two very different women, one whose life seems confined to a world of ideas and another who has access to and is equally comfortable in both the ideal and the social realms.

An epigraph summarizing both Arnim's belief in entelechy and her understanding of romantic sociability introduces Part Two. It concludes: "Wer das Ideal leugnet in sich, der könnte es auch nicht verstehen in Andern, selbst wenn es vollkommen ausgesprochen wär.—Wer das Ideal erkannte in Andern, dem blüht es auf, selbst wenn jener es nicht in sich ahnt" (563). Development of the individual requires recognition of one's own potential as well as of the potential in others. At the same time, the epigraph also recalls Bettine's criticism, expressed in *Briefwechsel*, of Günderode for abandoning her. The epigraph praises Bettine's stance vis-à-vis that of Günderode, for in the end, only Bettine is capable of at least trying to gain the understanding of self and other that she embraces.

This section begins with Günderode's poem "Mahomet's Traum in der Wüste," which not coincidentally deals with *Werden* and *Unsterblichkeit*, concepts that concern both Bettine and Günderode in this section. Again Günderode's letters, which deal primarily with her inner life, contrast sharply with those of Bettine, which provide detailed accounts of her travels. During a visit with her grandmother she learns of her grandfather who then becomes a role model for her. She moves with her sister Gunda and brother-in-law Savigny to Marburg where she meets the Jewish merchant and mathematician Ephraim as well as many of Savigny's students. She spends evenings walking along the city wall, meditating and conversing, as she claims in her letters, with the stars. Thus, while Günderode spends most of her time in her convent room, Bettine is able to move physically through the world. The differences between the two women become more palpable as their relationship develops, and their letters provide evidence of the resulting tension.

In the final letters of the text, Günderode assumes the role of teacher who wishes to send her pupil out into the world, and Bettine writes that Ephraim has counseled her to accept that Günderode must follow her own path. The final letter concludes with Bettine's description of Savigny's students walking past her window. The text itself ends with Karoline von Günderrode's poem, "Der Franke in Egypten," which deals with a pilgrim who, through love, finds his way home. Significantly, Günderode's death is not mentioned in this text. On the one hand, the theme of death pervades the correspondence, and because *Briefwechsel* as well as the history of Arnim's own life serve as intertexts for this work, the informed reader knows that Günderode commits suicide. On the other hand, Arnim's silence on this matter gives the text an open-endedness and a space for hope.[8] Like *Briefwechsel*, *Günderode* ends with both loss and gain, the loss (or within the space of the narrative, the silence) of a very dear friend and the gain of a strong sense of the need for friendship and of the role(s) of the artist, the individual, and the woman in the world.

Many of the roles ascribed to the Bettine persona in this text recall those discussed in the previous chapter. Again, Arnim deals with the roles of child, friend/lover, woman, the genius, and the writer. At the same time, the Bettine we encounter here differs from the figure who appeared in *Briefwechsel*. On a meta-level this difference stems from the myriad experiences that Arnim brought to *Günderode*, including the public acclaim she received following the publication of her first text. On the level of the literary figure, Bettine is dealing with a different interlocutor. Bettine herself best expresses this when she describes the difference between her relationships. Attempting to explain why her letters to Clemens vary so greatly from those to Günderode, she writes:

> Vom Clemens glaub doch nicht, daß ich ihn belüg, ich bin anders mit ihm in meinen Briefen, weil ich so sein muß. In Bürgel die kleine Orgel hat elf Register, groß und kleine Choralstimm, Harfenstimm, Trompetenstimm, Posaunen-Ton,

schnarrende Engelsstimm, was weiß ichs alles—und vox humana, der Hofmann hat mir gestern eine halbe Stund lang davon erzählt, und daß es Orgeln gibt die dreißig Register haben, er sagt meine Kehl wär wie so eine Orgel, ich zög allemal ein ander Register wenn ich sanft oder begeistert sing, oder schmetternd wenn ich tob, oder bewegt wenns zum Seufzen stimmt in meiner Brust, oder gewaltig wenn mirs ist als ob ichs allein alles zwingen müßt...Nun, ich mein, der Clemens zieht immer das Register der Kinderstimm aus meiner Brust.—In Frankfurt, in der Gesellschaft beim Primas, da prädominiert die quarrende Engelsstimm. Bei dir da muß ich immer das Gewalts-Posaunenregister mit Gewalt mit der sanften Vox humana unterdrücken. (419–420)

Encouraging her readers to identify her writing with music, Arnim introduces the metaphor of the organ to describe Bettine's writing. Not only does Bettine employ different registers with Clemens than with Günderode, these registers also differ from those that the Bettine of *Briefwechsel* used. Both the maturity of the author and the difference in interlocutor, then, modify the roles that Bettine plays. In *Günderode* the earlier emphasis on the child gives way to a foregrounding of youth, and Bettine comes to terms with the fact that she is a woman. The intensity of the friendship with Günderode throws into relief both the positive and negative aspects of romantic sociability more clearly than any other of Arnim's texts (except, perhaps, *Ambrosia*), and Bettine's sense of herself as genius and especially as daemon (in the form of guide or conscience) becomes more pronounced.

Youth

The title of Arnim's first text underscores the role of child as central to the development of the protagonist Bettine. She not only recalls her actual childhood, but also plays the child in order to emphasize both her opposition to bourgeois values and her openness to learning and development through unmediated contact with the world and others. The Bettine of Arnim's second text continues to play this role, but here the role of child becomes enmeshed with, and to an extent, gives way to an emphasis on youth, which the text presents as a more mature and informed but still open spiritual state.

At some points in the text, Bettine does seem very young. On occasion she plays the impudent child, affecting a childlike tone in several of her letters to Günderode. Furthermore, Günderode often writes to her as if to a younger sister, describing for example Bettine's disorderly room as a mirror of Bettine's "apparte Art zu sein" (312), and listening indulgently when Bettine rails against neighbors who have criticized her behavior (483). On such occasions, Bettine willingly dons the mask of the child in order to differentiate herself from the "rationalistischen Vernunfts- und Verstandesideologie, die sie im Prinzip des bornierten, unkindlichen Philisters attackiert und ironisiert" (Bäumer, *Bettine, Psyche, Mignon* 124), and her spontaneity stands in sharp and ironic contrast to the austerity of those she criticizes.

For Bettine, and at times even for Günderode, fantasy and childlike play serve as additional means of acting out against the confines others would place upon them.[9] Recalling one of their fantasy adventures, Bettine writes:

> Besinn Dich doch auf unsere Reise-Abenteuer die wir den Winter mit einander durchmachten, keiner von uns hatte eine trübe Minute den ganzen Winter nicht, Deine Sehnsucht ins Innere von Asien brachte uns immer unter die wilden Tiere...Was haben wir gelacht Günderode;—und haben unter Zimmetbäumen eine Tasse Chokolade getrunken die wir in Deinem Öfchen kochten mit wohlriechendem Sandelholz; und da kam ein Salamander ins Feuer und färbte sich da in allerlei Farben und warf die Chokoladenkanne um, und wir melkten die weiße Elephantin die ihr junges in unserer Nähe säugte und machten Elephantenbutter, ich wollt als immer Löwenbutter machen das littest Du nicht denn Du warst sehr vorsichtig. (504–505)

The realm of the imagination allows Bettine and Günderode to travel far beyond the boundaries generally demarcated for nineteenth-century women. Significantly, the capacity for childlike play that transports Bettine beyond the limitations of the real is greater than that of her friend. Günderode's insistence that Bettine make only *Elefantenbutter* as opposed to *Löwenbutter* emphasizes her own timidity and the latter's impetuousness.

Bettine has matured since her appearance in *Briefwechsel*, however, and the text includes fewer references to her actual childhood. Inspired by the students who frequented her salon, Arnim replaced the emphasis on childhood with an emphasis on youth. As Roswitha Burwick has noted, this becomes apparent in the dedication:

> [Arnim] widmete das Buch den jungen Studenten, den "Irrenden und suchenden," "Deutschlands Jüngerschaft." Die Alternde will damit keineswegs nostalgisch ihre Jugend durch die Erinnerung heraufbeschwören, sie will vielmehr ihre Definition von Jugend und Alter...offentlich mitteilen. Jugend ist die Begeisterung zum Leben, die Betonung des Selbst-Seins, die Warnung vor dem "Torengeschlecht der Philister," und der Glaube an der Zeiten Wechsel...Die Dedikation "Den Studenten" ist nicht allein für die revolutionären Studenten des Vormärz, die sich "Junges-Deutschland" nannten, sondern für den Leser schlechthin, der Bettinas Stimme nicht leicht überhören kann und sich unwillkürlich zum Dialog herausgefordert sieht. (67)

Youth implies not only a rejection of philistinism, but also a valorization of the self and of the infinite potential of the individual for action. As Burwick's analysis makes clear, it is the fifty-five-year-old author who first defines youth in the text. In so doing, she calls the reader's attention to youth as a central value of the text and as a central role of her protagonist. Arnim also invites the reader to see her (the author) as embodying youth; she facilitates this, as always, by blurring the line between herself and Bettine.

The emphasis on youth extends beyond the abstract, for in this text Arnim has created a Bettine who emphasizes and lives in the present (we recall the time frame) and who underscores her philosophy of youth to counter the death wish of her friend.[10] Bettine's repeated rejection of this wish (322, 462, 649, 699, 700) functions as a leitmotif. In contrast to the figure in the Günderode section of *Briefwechsel*, the Günderode of this text never expresses her wish directly. She does, however, voice in many of her letters the sense of malaise that one finds expressed not only by the Günderode of *Briefwechsel* but also in the texts of other early-nineteenth-century poets such as Hölderlin as well as in Arnim's own work.[11] For Günderode, the combination of gender, class, and marital status—in other words, aspects of her specific postitionality—compound this sense. In response, Bettine tries both to understand the reasons behind Günderode's death wish and to suggest an alternative in the form of a philosophical understanding of what it means to be young.

Echoing the sense of malaise expressed in Büchner's *Leonce und Lena* (written only four years before *Günderode* in 1836), and indirectly refuting those who would argue that either the historical Günderrode or her fictional counterpart killed herself solely in response to unrequited love,[12] Bettine believes her friend's death wish results from an existential boredom that, in turn, has grown out of restrictions placed on her ability to act in the world. Comparing Günderode's poem "Des Wanderers Nachtfahrt"—in which *Erdgeister* rescue a pilgrim from his attempts to escape to the underworld—to an untitled poem beginning with the lines: "Ist alles stumm und leer," Bettine proposes the following interpretation:

> Dein Gedicht was Du in der klanglosen Stunde geschrieben ist doch klangreich, es schöpft die Töne aus der Brust und stimmt sie zu Melodieen.—Doch weile ich lieber bei dem ersteren ["Des Wanderers Nachtfahrt"], denn das hast Du doch später gemacht nicht wahr? und fühlst auch wie ich daß die Schmerzen im Geist immer mit auf die Pein der Langeweile gegründet sind.—Denn nehms wie Du willst; bräche das Leben sich mit einmal eine neue Bahn und wär sie auch noch so uneben und holperig, die Verzweiflung hätt ein Ende. Denn alles Schmerzgefühl, alles Sehnsucht kommt doch nur daher weil die grade Bahn des Lebens gehemmt ist. (504)

Bettine cites a lack of opportunity for development as the cause of Günderode's emptiness and boredom—a lack that led to similar despair in fictional and historical middle class women in Europe and North America throughout the nineteenth century.

Günderode accepts this diagnosis but contends that existential boredom can be overcome—if at all—only by youth, a state that she defines according to age. She therefore wills to live as intensively as possible and then to die young. In response to Günderode's wish, Bettine offers her own solution: "Ach Günderode! atme aus um wieder aufzuatmen, Begeisterung zu trinken—denn: Ist Natur nicht bloß dieser Begeisterung Leben?—Und wär Jugend etwas, wenn's nicht ewig wär?" (649) Although she shares Günderode's abhorrence of restrictive middle-class values, Bettine does not consider philistinism an inevitable result of aging. She defines youth instead as an approach to life and presents herself as the embodiment of this youth. Here, one must again keep in mind that Arnim was actively engaged in creating herself through her Bettine personae. Through Bettine's efforts to educate Günderode in the ways of youth, the author was attempting to educate her readers.

This emphasis on youth brings about a change in Bettine's attitude towards Goethe's Mignon. She acknowledges her earlier idealization of Mignon's loyalty in love, but upon re-reading *Wilhelm Meister*, Bettine concludes that she has developed beyond her one-time role model:

> Ich lese jetzt zum zweitenmal den *Wilhelm Meister*, als ich ihn zum erstenmal las, hatte mein Leben Mignon's Tod noch nicht erreicht, ich liebte mit ihr, wie ihr, waren die andern in der Geschichte des Buchs mir gleichgültig, mich ergriff alles was die Treue ihrer Liebe anging, nur in den Tod konnt ich ihr nicht folgen.—Jetzt fühl ich daß ich weit über diesen Tod hinaus ins Leben gerückt bin, aber auch um vieles unbestimmter bin ich, schon so früh drückt mich mein Alter, wenn ich hier dran denke.—Ich hab mit ihr empfunden, ich bin mit ihr gestorben damals, und jetzt hab ichs überlebt, und sehe auf meinen Tod herab.—Gewiß stirbt der Mensch mehr wie einmal, mit dem Freund der ihn verläßt muß er sterben, und wenn ich mit jenem Kind leiden und sterben mußte, weil ich sein Geschick als das meine in ihm empfand und weil ich es zu sehr liebte und konnte es nicht allein in den Tod gehen lassen.—Wenn Du das alles überlegst, so wirst Du nachsichtig sein daß ich so furchtsam bin um Dich. (680)

Although she is now less certain of many things and has grown older since her first reading, Bettine realizes that her position relative to Mignon has changed. She no longer fears, as did the Bettine of *Briefwechsel*, that she will succumb to the routineness of a middle-class existence, "daß mir das weiße Kleid ausgezogen wird." Rather, she has gained a sense of agency that allows her to act in the present and offer help to Günderode, whose death is foreshadowed by that of Mignon.

Bettine's understanding of youth inverts many received ideas about this period of life. Not only does youth represent a spiritual state rather than physical age, it also carries with it responsibility. Insisting that she wishes to live the long and active life of her grandmother, Bettine writes:

> Ich will auch wie die Großmama einen Ewigkeitskreis mit meinem Leben schließen, nicht wie Du gesagt hast, jung sterben. Viel wissen, viel lernen, sagtest Du, und dann jung sterben, warum sagst Du das?—mit jedem Schritt im Leben begegnet Dir einer der was zu fordern hat an Dich, wie willst Du sie alle befriedigen?—Ja sage, willst Du einen ungespeist von Dir lassen der von Deinen Brosamen fordert?—nein das willst Du nicht!—Drum lebe mit mir, ich hab jeden Tag an Dich zu fordern. Ach!—wo sollt ich hin wenn Du nicht mehr wärst? (488)

Recalling the section of *Briefwechsel* in which Bettine criticizes Ottilie's choice of death over life, Bettine argues that the individual has too much responsibility for others to have the right to end her own life. On a more personal level, Bettine insists that Günderode has a responsibility to her as friend. Bettine thus strives to help Günderode, both by offering a counter-philosophy of life and by insisting that Günderode is responsible not only to her but to all whom she knows.

Sadly, Bettine lacks the empathy (more precisely expressed by the German word *Einfühlung*) to understand the depth of her friend's pain, choosing, for example, to optimistically read "Des Wanderers Nachtfahrt" as Günderode's own answer to "Ist alles stumm und leer" (Günderode never states which poem she wrote first) and employing an aggressive tone to accuse her friend of harming others with her wish for self-destruction. Bettine does not (and given the difficulty of coming to know another, perhaps cannot) recognize the differences in their respective situations. Although she herself emphasizes the importance of action and becoming, her faith in the power of ideas and idealism as themselves forms of action causes her to lose sight of the restrictions that material, experiential, and historical conditions have placed on Günderode; Bettine assumes that Günderode's positionality is constructed in the same manner as her own.

Yet the emphasis on youth represents more than a form of idealism or blindness, for it must also be read as Bettine's response to her own (and perhaps also to Arnim's own) sense and fear of nihilism and emptiness. She transforms the distance between youth and old age into one determined not by physical age but rather—in keeping with the dedication of the text—by the decision to remain a student of life rather than to sink into the ease of the *Philisterleben*.[13] Such an adamant stance elicits multiple, conflicting responses. On the one hand, Bettine's determination is admirable and the expression of her need for Günderode's friendship heartrending. On the other hand, she fails to recognize that different histories and life conditions make different degrees of agency (in Bettine's parlance, the possibility of "extending one's period of youth") possible.

Die Freundin: Between Reality and Ideal

Of all of Arnim's texts, *Günderode* is the most conversational, the text in which there is the most dialogue between the primary interlocutors and in which each of them engages to the greatest extent with what the other has written. Ironically, this dialogic form does not point solely to an ideal relationship; the intense and intimate exchange between Bettine and Günderode throws both the constructive and the isolating aspects of romantic sociability into greater relief than does *Briefwechsel*. Bettine turns to Günderode to educate and develop herself, and in turn, wishes to help Günderode develop her sense of self. This desire for friendship and mutual support runs parallel to a sense of increasing distance between the two, for Bettine's capacity for empathy is limited by her individuality, as is Günderode's. In the end, Bettine does not succeed at winning Günderode over to her belief in youth and passion for life.

Ruth-Ellen Boetcher Joeres writes that Bettine and Günderode choose to create a "loving and at times erotic epistolary relationship with one another [... and...] a group of likeness, a collective consciousness on however limited a plane" ("'We are adjacent'" 48). The two women are deeply attached to one another; Bettine avers that she loves and needs her friend, a sentiment she articulates when recalling a conversation in which she and Günderode discussed who would die first:

> Da hab ich aber gefühlt, und fühls eben wieder und immer: wenn Du nicht wärst, was wär mir die ganze Welt?—kein Urteil, kein Mensch vermag über mich, aber Du!—auch bin ich gestorben schon jetzt, wenn du mich nicht auferstehen heißest und willst mit mir leben immerfort; ich fühls recht, mein Leben ist bloß aufgewacht, weil Du mir riefst, und wird sterben müssen, wenn es nicht in Dir kann fortgedeihen.—Frei sein willst Du, hast Du gesagt?—ich will nicht frei sein, ich will Wurzel fassen in Dir. (300)

Calling to mind Bettine's expression of love for Goethe in *Briefwechsel*, this Bettine insists that she lives more intensely when with her friend, that every form of interaction leads to a rebirth in the form of new development. Bettine learns from and develops through Günderode, albeit (and as her readers by now have come to expect) not in any traditional sense.

Günderode communicates through less impassioned language, but (unlike many of Bettine's family members and neighbors) she also accepts Bettine for who she is and understands her desire for education:

> ich meine, Du könntest immer zufrieden sein damit, so empfunden zu sein durch Deine eigne frische Natur, daß Du meiner sicher bist. Wer im Ganzen etwas sein kann, der wird sich auch fühlbar zu machen wissen…Du bist ja auch heute nicht

was Du gestern gewesen, und doch bist Du eine ewige Folge Deiner selbst. (324)

This passage supports Waldstein's assertion that "cooperation, mutual respect, reciprocal enrichment and love are characteristic of the relationship between these two women and distinguish it from all other friendships portrayed in Bettine Arnim's novels. The two women reflect on themselves, on each other, and find themselves reflected in each other" (*Bettine von Arnim and the Politics of Romantic Conversation* 56). Recalling "Urworte, Orphisch," Günderode recognizes and accepts the inherent uniqueness of Bettine while at the same time encouraging her to continue to change and grow. In this sense, the relationship typifies the positive aspects of romantic sociability, for it provides a space in which the two women feel accepted and allows for growth through interaction with each other.

Yet this friendship is in no way perfect, and cannot be, for the two also remain trapped within their individuality, unable to understand each other completely. While Bettine lacks the empathy to comprehend the extent of Günderode's depression, Günderode remains distant from and independent of Bettine. She never claims to need Bettine the way that Bettine needs her; the reader often has the impression that Günderode is central to Bettine's development but hardly gets any sense of Günderode developing at all.

Scholars have frequently noted the use of the mirror motif in this text, and to a greater extent than Goethe in *Briefwechsel*, Günderode serves as echo or mirror for Bettine. On the level of the epistolary exchange, Bettine bounces her ideas off of Günderode, and Günderode's letters—far more resonant than those of Goethe—often serve to modify, magnify, and reflect Bettine's ideas back not only to her but also to the reader. Furthermore Bettine, who contends that she can speak to no one as to Günderode (377), refers to her friend as her echo: "Ewig Günderod —Du bist der Widerhall nur, durch den mein irdisch Leben den Geist vernimmt" (410). Bettine views Günderode as her mediator (*Mittler*) to a spirit that may be her own personal genius or a more universal, godlike spirit. As with Goethe in Arnim's previous text, Bettine's love of Günderode is as much self-love as love of another,[14] and their friendship leads in the end not towards increased intimacy, but for Bettine, to a stronger sense of self.

Bettine's approach to friendship appears selfish insofar as it is self-promoting. Yet as is the case with her emphasis on youth, and Bettine's self-centerdness notwithstanding, this self-promotion arises out of a need for self-protection. From the beginning of the text, and increasingly in Part Two, Bettine expresses a keen awareness of the difference and distance between herself and her friend:

> Ich hab Deinen letzten Brief noch oft gelesen, er kommt mir ganz besonders vor, wenn ich ihn mit andern vergleiche, die ich auch hier in derselben Zeit erhalten hab, so muß ich denken, daß es Schicksale gibt im Geist, die so entfernt sind von einander und so verschieden, wie im gewöhnlichen Tagesleben, der eine wird sichs nicht einbilden vom andern, was der denkt und träumt, und was er fühlt beim Träumen und Denken. (382)

She realizes that, despite her desire to understand and be understood by Günderode, the differences between them hinder understanding; echoing her new assessment of Mignon, she insists that she will continue to love but will not allow her love to consume her: "Es wird Dichtung meiner Natur sein daß ich so liebe;—aufnehmend, hingebend, aber nicht aufgenommen werdend" (670). More confident of her stance than the Bettine of *Briefwechsel*, this Bettine insists that love of another should not lead to loss of self.

The search in this text for a union in friendship faces narrative and theoretical limits, for it is hindered both by the two women's individual personalities and life circumstances and by the limits of romantic sociability, which not only asserts development through others but also leads to the sense of uniqueness and ultimate loneliness of the individual. Despite these limits, Bettine continues to strive for a utopia of understanding. Acknowledging their differences while at the same time expressing hope that these differences might be overcome, Bettine writes:

> Du redest von Dir als seist Du anders wie ich, ganz anders, ach und stehst mir doch allein unter allen Menschen gegenüber, und alles was wir mit einander besprachen, da waren wir nicht eins, Du warst anders gesinnt und ich anders, und doch hast Du mich immer vertreten, ja gewißlich ich bin anders wie Du, ich fühls auch heut aus jeder Zeile Deines Briefs, die mir doch so wahr sind und den tiefen Grund Deiner Seele beleuchten. Wie ist doch jeder Mensch ein groß Geheimnis, und bis alles ins Himmlische sich verwandelt, wie viel bleibt

da unverstanden. Aber ganz verstanden sein, das deucht mir die wahre alleinige Metamorphose, die einzige Himmelfahrt. (441–442)[15]

"Ganz verstanden sein," the goal of being understood without being absorbed into the other's *ich*, that is utopia.

The conclusion of the text—Günderode's unspoken death—implies that, on the narrative level, Bettine can no longer pursue this utopia through epistolary exchange. If we step away from the figures of the text to consider the relationship between the author and Karoline von Günderrode, however, we can opine that the process of rereading her letters and writing *Günderode* allowed Arnim to explore further her friendship. Admittedly, temporal distance enabled Arnim to present in her Bettine and Günderode figures a more idealized than historical relationship, but at the same time Arnim allows Bettine to express awareness that the friendship is not perfect, that the utopia of understanding has not been achieved. Furthermore, the idealization may indicate that and how Arnim tried, through the processes of memory and writing, to understand her friend and to develop their friendship further. Certainly neither Bettine nor Günderode is apotheosized as Goethe was in *Briefwechsel*. Both remain less than perfect human beings, individual women struggling to define themselves and each other through friendship, and as such they remain suspended between individual isolation and the utopia of understanding.

Gender Identity: The Wish to be a Man/Ordination as a Woman

Since the 1970s, discussions of gender in Arnim's texts have focused primarily on *Die Günderode*. Gisela Dischner has argued that Bettine rejects traditional gender norms and strives instead towards an androgynous ideal. Monika Shafi and Edith Waldstein have described in separate studies the relationship depicted in the text as an ideal female friendship. Shafi and Frederiksen, as well as Bäumer and Schultz, have cited the text as an example of "weibliches Schreiben" as defined by Hélène Cixous. These analyses are informed by feminist literary theory of the 1970s and 1980s, which pursued two important goals: the retrieval of forgotten women from the past to serve as models for the present and future, and the criticism of and search for alternatives to traditional gender norms. This approach has been immensely fruitful and has made my own work possible. As feminist scholars have become aware of the differences in and among feminisms, feminists, and women in general, however, it has become evident that the goals of earlier approaches often led to an essentializing view of women and women's writing and to the use of frameworks for understanding them that ignored historical, geographical, and individual differences.

The differences between Bettine and Günderode, and between the manners in which they experience the world, should give pause to those who would assert the existence of an essential feminine identity and/or form of writing. The positionalities of the two figures, and of the two authors, were constructed differently and for this reason, the friendship between Bettine and Günderode was, despite the utopia sought by Bettine, fraught with difficulty. In the remainder of this section I will show that, while Bettine does maintain an ambivalent stance towards feminine gender roles, and while she and Günderode often address each other with male pronouns, far from embracing an androgynous ideal, the Bettine of this text becomes reconciled with her womanhood (although not entirely with traditional gender roles) after reading Günderode's final letter to her.

Bettine undoubtedly feels constrained by the female roles assigned to her. Although she plays the coquette when, together with her sister Meline in Marbach, she flirts with the students who pass by her window on their way to Savigny's lectures, Bettine resists those who would restrict her to specific roles. She mocks Bostel, the family friend who wishes Bettine would act more like her well-behaved sister Lullu and who offers the unwelcome advice: "sprechen Sie ruhig mit Einem und bezeigen Sie doch nur ein klein wenig Teilnahme an" (305). She also resents family members who criticize her friendship with her Jewish mathematics teacher Ephraim. Whereas they wonder, "wo ich einen Mann hernehmen will wenn ich hebräisch lern?" and tell her, "So was ekelt einem Mann," she asserts:

> der ganz Jud [ist] nur in meine Tagsordnung einrangiert um mich vor dem Mottenfraß der Häuslichkeit zu bewahren, und ich [habe] gemerkt daß man in einer glücklichen Häuslichkeit Sonntags immer die Dachziegel gegenüber vom Nachbar [zählt]; was mir so fürchterliche Langeweile mache daß ich lieber nicht

heiraten will. (684)

The humor of Bettine's account notwithstanding, the ennui that she associates with housework is a form of the existential boredom that she considers the source of Günderode's depression and that she resists by fleeing the domestic sphere into nature.

In contrast to the burdens of housework, Bettine longs for the freedom that she believes a neighbor's gardener possesses:

> Heut Morgen kam ich dazu wie der Bernhards Gärtner mit einem Nelkenheber die dunkelroten Nelken in einen Kreis um einen Berg von weißen Lilien versetzte, in der Mitte stand ein Rosenbusch. Diese Früharbeit gefiel mir wohl und hab mit Andacht dabei geholfen, der Dienst der Natur, der ist wie Tempeldienst...Ach ich möcht ein Knab sein, Wasser holen in der Morgenfrische, wenn alles noch schläft, den Marmor polieren von den Säulen, meine Götterbilder still bedeutsam waschen, und alles reinigen vom Staub, daß es leuchte im Dämmerlicht; dann, nach der Arbeit die heiße Stirn auf die kühlen Stufen legen und ruhen, in heimlichem Genügen. (416–417)

Undeniably, Bettine communicates here an idealized perception of the gardener's life, especially since, despite the restrictions placed on her by gender, her class would presumably allow her more freedom of movement in many spheres than would be allotted to him. On a metaphorical level, however, his work in the garden stands in sharp contrast to housework as a more productive form of engagement: work that involves physical labor and creativity in an open space.

To resist feelings of boredom and limitation, Bettine also engages in fantasy play with Günderode. This includes not only planning imaginary trips, as described earlier, but also referring to one another with masculine pronouns and appellations (Er, Sokrates, Schüler, Lehrer, Platon). Intended to empower both of them with a sense of an ability to act, such role-play ultimately proves more productive for Bettine than for Günderode. Indeed, one wonders whether it does not serve to remind Günderode of the limits that have been placed on her. She writes in Part Two to Bettine:

> die Unmöglichkeiten dem nachzukommen was ich in Gedanken möchte, häufen sich, ich weiß sie nicht zu überwinden und muß mich dahin treiben lassen wie der Zufall es will, Widerstand wär nur Zeitaufwand und kein Resultat, Du hast eine viel energischere Natur wie ich, ja wie fast alle Menschen die ich zu beurteilen

fähig bin, mir sind nicht allein durch meine Verhältnisse, sondern auch durch meine Natur enge Grenzen in meiner Handlungsweise gezogen, es könnte also leicht kommen daß Dir etwas möglich wäre, was es darum mir noch nicht sein könnte. (724)

Günderode recognizes here that Bettine possesses the energy (in greater quantity than most women *or* men) and the will to offer unceasing resistance to the obstacles in her way. In contrast, she attempts to explain that both her "Natur"—her personality, the person who she is—and her station prevent her from benefiting from their playful exchange to the extent that Bettine does. She is more constrained by gender roles than Bettine. Coming from a family of little wealth, she must suffer the fate of the unmarriageable daughter: life in a convent. Wishing both to write and to love and be loved she encounters only men who seek subordinate partners and wives who can provide a dowry.

Although Günderode feels more constrained by her gender than does Bettine, in her final letter Günderode seeks to reconcile Bettine with the fact that she (Bettine) is a woman. Recalling a dream that Bettine once recounted in which she failed at rescuing a group of men about to be guillotined (the allusion to the French Revolution is clear), Günderode recognizes the prophetic significance of the dream's conclusion:

Du meintest, nicht im Traum sei Dirs gegönnt das auszuführen was in Deiner Seele spreche, vielmehr noch verzweifelst Du an der Wirklichkeit...ich stimme mit Dir ein, daß es ein Streich war den Dir Dein Dämon spielte, aber ein Weisheitsstreich;—wärst Du befriedigt worden im Traum, so wär Deine Sehnsucht das Große getan zu haben vielleicht auch befriedigt. (726)

Whereas Günderode views her own longing as both unfulfillable and destructive, she considers Bettine's desire a productive force. She therefore makes the wish that Bettine continue to feel challenged to action: "[so] daß nicht im Traum aber in der Wirklichkeit Dir das Rätsel auf eine glorreiche Art sich löse, warum es der Mühe lohnt gelebt zu haben" (726–727). At the same time she tells Bettine that, to put her talents to the greatest use, she must content herself with acting as a woman in the ideal sphere:

Sollt ich Deinen Charakter zusammenfassen so würd ich Dir prophezeihen wenn Du ein Knabe wärst Du werdest ein Held werden; da Du aber ein Mädchen bist so lege ich Dir alle diese Anlagen für eine künftige Lebensstufe aus, ich nehme es als

> Vorbereitung zu einem künftigen energischen Charakter an, der vielleicht in eine lebendige regsame Zeit geboren wird.—Auch wie das Meer Ebbe und Flut hat, so scheinen mir die Zeiten zu haben. Wir sind in der Zeit der Ebbe jetzt, wo es gleichgültig ist wer sich geltend mache...Ja, ich habe dir genug gesagt um Dir nah zu legen daß jene Anlagen des höheren Menschengeistes das einzige wirkliche Ziel Deiner inneren Anschauung sein müsse, daß es Dir ganz einerlei sein müsse ob, und wie fern Dein Vermögen zur Tätigkeit komme. (727–728)

As Bettine recognizes, here her friend and teacher Günderode is preparing her to enter into the world: "mir ist der ganze Brief...wie ein Ordnen vor dem Abschied, wo Du mich ins Leben schickst wie ein älterer Bruder den jüngeren" (729)—and Günderode's blessing is as troubling as it is moving. On the one hand she encourages Bettine to continue to develop her talents, to continue to pursue change. On the other, she advises Bettine that, in the times in which she is living, she must limit herself to the ideal sphere and not expect that her ideas become transformed into action. In so doing, she valorizes one of Bettine's most admirable strengths, the refusal to back down, while at the same time advising Bettine to restrict her action to a sphere that mid-nineteenth-century women such as Fanny Lewald, Luise Aston, and Malwida von Meysenbug were struggling more openly to escape. This passage may offer a clue as to why Arnim the writer never became actively involved in the political cause of women and why she focused so much energy on creating an idealized life and world in her texts; she transgressed gender boundaries in the realm of the imaginary but did not become involved in efforts to change women's material conditions. Within the context of German letters, such involvement would begin with the next generation of women writers.

Student and Teacher: Of History, Philosophy, Religion

As in *Briefwechsel*, the Bettine of *Günderode* learns about far more than gender roles and identity, for here, too, she interacts with those around her to further her own education. Bettine has matured since her last appearance, and in this text she plays the roles of student and teacher equally. She learns from those around her: Günderode, her grandmother, St. Clair (Arnim's spelling of Sinclair) who tells her of Hölderlin, and Ephraim. But she also assumes the functions of teacher and *Mittler*, instructing not only Günderode, but also—because her readers also assume the role of the "Du" in this epistolary exchange—both her intended audience (the students of the late 1830s and 1840s) and her readers today. To a greater extent than *Briefwechsel*—and thanks to the publication of this first work—*Günderode* allows Arnim not only to tell the story of a friendship from an earlier part of her life, but also to propagate the ideas she holds in the pre-revolutionary 1830s. As a result, the Bettine of this text becomes student and teacher of history, philosophy, and religion, three fields of knowledge that she defines over and against popular conceptions.

Bettine's position in various relationships often underscores her role as pupil. She is younger than Günderode and employs hierarchical models from classical antiquity to describe their relationship: "Weißt Du was, Du bist der Platon und Du bist dort auf die Burg verbannt, und ich bin Dein liebster Freund und Schüler Dion" (332), she writes early in the text. When she recounts her meetings with Sophie von La Roche, Bettine generally depicts herself as listening, her grandmother as speaking. This is also the case with Ephraim, who at the end of the text helps her come to terms with the loss of Günderode.

Ephraim—after Günderode the most important figure in the text with regard to Bettine's development—teaches Bettine to accept that Günderode must go her own way, that sociability cannot lead to an absolute union because the two individuals are so radically different:

> Heut war der Ephraim bei mir er wußte daß ich die andre Woche geh, wir sprachen von meinem Wiederkommen denn ich bleib nur drei Wochen mit der Lullu aus.—Wir sprachen von Dir, er sagte so viel Gutes von Dir, er las auch meine letzten Blätter an Dich, er sagte, man müsse nicht fürchten daß was man liebe, einem verloren gehn könne, weil er wohl erkannte etwas in Deinem Brief mache mir bang um Dich; er sagte Du seist einzig in Deiner Art, Du habest eine große Bahn, und wer nicht andre Wege gehe als die schon gebahnten und angewiesnen der sei nicht Dichter. Es sind nicht tausend Dichter, es ist nur Einer, die andern klingen ihm nur nach;—klingen mit.—Wenn eine Stimme erschallt, so weckt sie Stimmen. Dichter ist nur, der über allen steht. Der Dichtergeist geht durch viele und dann konzentriert er sich in Einem.—Oft wird er nicht erkannt und doch steht er höher als alle. (738)

In contrast to Bettine, who implores Günderode not to leave her alone, Ephraim believes that, as poet, Günderode must travel her own path.

Reading this passage, the informed reader has the sense that Günderode has already committed suicide and that only her voice, which lives on in her letters and poetry and in the memory of others, remains. Rather than consoling Bettine over the distant tone of Günderode's letters, Ephraim helps her to accept Günderode's death. The lines between protagonist and author, between past and present become blurred. It seems as if not only Bettine but also the author must be striving to learn from and find consolation in Ephraim's words.

The Bettine of the text is no passive pupil, however, and especially in her relationship with Günderode the boundaries demarcating the roles of teacher and student remain fluid. In response to Bettine's self-definition as pupil, Günderode writes:

> Es kömmt mir bald zu närrisch vor liebe Bettine, daß Du Dich so feierlich für meinen Schüler erklärst, eben so könnte ich mich für den Deinen halten wollen, doch macht es mir viele Freude, und es ist auch etwas Wahres daran, wenn ein Lehrer durch den Schüler angeregt wird, so kann ich mit Fug mich den Deinen nennen. (309)

In their reflections on history, philosophy, and religion, Günderode and Bettine do not always manage to alter each other's (often-differing) opinions; they do spur each other on to mutual reflection. Both historically and in this text, Günderrode/Günderode assumes the task of educating Bettina/Bettine in the areas of history and philosophy. Using her friend's teachings as a springboard, Bettine develops these disciplines to her own liking.

The theme of history and the attendant theme of memory run through the entire text, taking on both political and personal meaning. The student Bettine views history (in the form it is generally taught) as a series of facts and dates, to be remembered for their own sake, with no meaning for the individual in the present. Bettine's history teacher represents this "Selbstgenügsamkeit der Geschichtslehre" (Dischner 134), and Bettine has difficulty finding meaning in his lessons: "Tut der Lehrer den Mund auf, so sehe ich hinein wie in einen unabsehbaren Schlund, der die Mammutsknochen der Vergangenheit ausspeit, und allerlei versteinert Zeug, das nicht keimen, nicht blühen mehr will" (405–406). The history lessons consist of dry facts rather than living stories, and Bettine resists them despite

Günderode's well-intentioned advice that history could and should serve to ground her fantasy and philosophy: "Sei mir ein bißchen standhaft, trau mir, daß der Geschichtsboden für Deine Phantasien, Deine Begriffe ganz geeignet, ja notwendig ist.—Wo willst Du Dich selber fassen, wenn Du keinen Boden unter Dir hast?" (404).

Defying her tutor and Günderode, Bettine claims she prefers to live in the present rather than in the past: "Indes brennt mir der Boden unter den Füßen, um die Gegenwart, um die ich mich bewerben mocht" (406). This does not imply that she dismisses history; she does not ignore Günderode altogether. Rather, the past acquires meaning for her only when it is personalized and contextualized, given relevance with regard to the here and now. For Bettine, the past must be re-membered and *er-innert*, or reconstructed and internalized, transformed into a guide for action in the present. In this sense, Bettine reads histories in a manner described over a century later by Hayden White, not "as unambiguous signs of the events they report, but rather as symbolic structures, extended metaphors, that 'liken' the event reported in them to some [cultural] form" with which she has already become familiar (19). When Bettine looks to the past, she wishes to see details of private lives and find keys to understanding the present. This becomes apparent when she demands to know more than simply that the Egyptian King Sesotris took his life—"War er schön,—hat er geliebt?" (396)—and when she discusses the history of the twelve Roman emperors with Günderode.

In the epistolary exchange about Suetonius's *The Lives of the Twelve Caesars*, one sees how Arnim employs Günderode's questioning of Bettine's motives as a foil for her (Arnim's/Bettine's) ideas: she allows Günderode to express her fear that Bettine is idolizing Napoleon to serve as a warning about idolization of rulers in general, but then she allows Bettine to assert that she would never permit herself to be deceived by the pomp and circumstance surrounding Napoleon's rise to power. Günderode begins the exchange:

> Du hast bei Deiner Abreise, Ostertags schlechte Übersetzung des Suetonius in meine Behausung geschickt, vermutlich soll sie auf die Bibliothek zurück, noch in keinem Buch fand ich so Viel Spuren Deines fleißigen Studiums als in diesem; vier bis fünf Blätter mit Auszügen, wo Du alle Missetaten der zwölf Kaiser auf eine Rechnung gebracht hast. Was bewegt Dich zu solchen Dir sonst ganz

> fremden Forschungen? ich such mirs zu erläutern, denkst Du in Ansehung jener, die als große Männer nicht frei ausgingen von der Tyrannei Sünde, Deinen großen Mann zu absolvieren?—Ich scherze, aber ich möchte doch dabei in Dein Gesicht sehen ob Du ganz frei von jener Begeistrung bist die aus aufgeregtem Gefühl entsteht bei dem ewigen Gelingen aller Schicksalslösungen, und die ich lieber Schwindel nennen möchte, und den andre, Weltpatriotismus nennen und sich leicht verführen lassen eine Rolle zu spielen wenn sie ihnen geboten würde, weil es heißt Er hat einen Glücksstern, und da fühlt man sich gedrungen dem zu frönen, aus astralischem Emanationsgefühl, und da tritt man bald von der reinen Einfalt zum Götzendienst über. (622–623)

Günderode expresses both skeptical amazement at Bettine's thorough study of a history book and dismay that her friend's interest in the emperors may mean she has moved from admiring to idolizing Napoleon. Riled by these assumptions, Bettine responds:

> So viel prophetische Gabe kannst Du mir zutrauen daß es mir ahnend im Geist liegt, diese Strohflamen so gewaltig sie um sich griff, so schneller wird sie verflackern; bald wird alles in Asche versunken sein,—und du machst mirs zum Vorwurf daß ich mit des Ostertag schlechter Übersetzung mich so lang geplackt hab,—weil ich wolle die großen Kaiserrollen studieren? freilich hab ich diese zwölf Kaiser mit Interesse studiert, und hab gefunden was ich vorher hätte sagen können, daß alle Tyrannen arglistige kleinliche Naturen waren, sie gaben Befehle wo ihre Bitten genügt hätten, der Fortgang ihrer Macht entwickelt sich aus des Pöbels Eitelkeit…Das ists was ich in diesen zwölf Kaisern studierte, aber ich suchte nicht nach Ähnlichkeiten seiner Größe, sondern danach ob nicht alle Tyrannen niederträchtig sind wie er? (637)

Bettine has no intention of discovering whether any one of the past emperors was as great as Napoleon, but rather whether they were as malicious as he was. With the words of her protagonist, Arnim offers kindling for the fires of the student generation of the late 1830s and early 1840s as well as advice to all rulers to avoid hubris.

Günderode unabashedly mixes the personal and the political, and Bettine employs not only political history but also her personal history as guideposts for her thoughts and actions. Early in the text, the reader discovers that personal history bears the same weight as political history. As already mentioned, Günderode's poetic dialogue "Die Manen" follows the opening two letters of the text. It consists of a conversation between a pupil and a teacher and occurs following the pupil's visit to the tomb of the Swedish King Gustavus Adolphus. Although the student mourns the loss of a great leader, within the context of the entire work—and especially that of the discussions of death and suicide—the drama assumes a more personal meaning: the teacher conveys to the student that the past lives on in the present through creative remembrance. In response to the student's despair over the fleeting nature of life, the teacher replies: "Gegenwart ist ein flüchtiger Augenblick, sie vergeht indem Du sie erlebst, des Lebens Bewußtsein liegt in der Erinnerung, in diesem Sinn nur kannst Du Vergangnes betrachten, gleichviel ob es längst oder eben nur vorging" (302). Although this passage may initially strike the reader as contradictory to Bettine's claim that she wishes to live in and for the present, that impression dissolves as soon as one takes into consideration Bettine's revisionary approach to history: history has meaning only as personal memory employed to inform the present. In this regard Bettine writes towards the end of the text, at a point when the loss of her friend seems immanent, "Was ist Erinnerung?—Erinnerung ist viel tiefer als sich auf das besinnen was wir erlebten. Auch in ihren Verwandlungen berührt sie ewig den Geist—sie ist unendlich—sie wird Gefühl—dann wird sie Gedanke, der reizt den Geist zur Leidenschaft; als Leidenschaft erzeugt sie den Geist aufs Neue" (734). Memory—and with it both personal and political history—becomes a productive, inspirational force that, although it may become transformed through time (indeed, the passing of time itself proves productive), moves through a series of rational and emotional means of perception (feeling, thought, passion, spirit) to shape the individual spirit, and as a result, also the work of art inspired by that spirit. In this manner, Arnim points to the production of her own text, obfuscating, as is often the case, the distinction between art and life, past and present.

As with her conception of history, Bettine insists on defining philosophy against the manner in which it is taught to her. She rebels against "hoffartig[e]" and "unmögliche Kerle" (307) such as Fichte and Kant, insisting, "Die Weisheit muß natürlich sein" (307). This does not mean that either she or the text itself rejects philosophy altogether, and the reader cannot ignore the impact that leading philosophers of the first half of the nineteenth century had on Arnim. It is telling, however, that one of Arnim's closest adult friends was the theologian Schleiermacher, who strove in his writing and in his life to find a synthesis between the affective and the cognitive. As Sabine Schormann has noted, his influence is evident throughout *Die Günderode*:

> der Geist als heilende Instanz, als das intuitive, lebendige, gegen die philisterhaft-systematische Erstarrung gerichtete Bewegungselement, das dem Selbstdenken einen freien Spielraum eröffnet in Richtung Unendlichkeit. Dieses nach innen zentrierte, nicht bloß abstrakt-reflexiv, sondern ebenso sinnlich erfahrene Geistmoment vermittelt die Polarität von faktischer Lebenswirklichkeit und Sehnsucht und fängt damit das Wissen, daß die Synthese im Grunde nicht mehr funktioniert, auf in der Hinwendung zur in Bettines Werk so wesentlichen Trias von Musik, Liebe und Natur. ("Bettines Rezeption der frühromantischen Philosophie" 39)

Like history, philosophy must be experienced *am eigenen Leibe*, through the senses, and for Bettine it is communicated not through the rational written word but rather through music, love, and nature: non-human forces that also function as Bettine's educators.

Not surprisingly, philosophy for Bettine is closely related to religion, and she proposes to Günderode that they found a *Schwebereligion* in opposition to the dominant religious modes of the day (criticism of which will become more explicit in the *Dies Buch*). Whereas Bettine and Günderode argue back and forth about questions of history and philosophy, when it comes to religion, Bettine is clearly the teacher. Inspired by a voice that she also calls her *Genius* and her *Dämon*, Bettine proposes to Günderode:

> Ach ich hab eine Sehnsucht rein zu sein von diesen Fehlen. Ins Bad steigen, und mich abwaschen von allen Verkehrtheiten. Die ganze Welt kommt mir vor wie verrückt, und ich schußbartele immer so mit, und doch ist in mir eine Stimme, die mich besser belehrt.—Lasse uns doch eine Religion stiften, ich und Du, und lasse uns einstweilen Priester und Laie darin sein, ganz im stillen, und streng danach leben, und ihre Gesetze entwickeln, wie sich ein junger Königssohn entwickelt, der einst der größte Herrscher sollt werden der ganzen Welt.
> —So muß es sein, daß er ein Held sei, und durch seinen Willen alle Gebrechen abweise und die ganze Welt umfasse, und daß sie *müsse* sich bessern. (447–448)

Here again Arnim reveals the idealistic underpinnings of her writing. Like Schiller in his *Briefe über die ästhetische Erziehung des Menschen* and Goethe in his poem "Ilmenau," Bettine is convinced of the transformative power of ideas, albeit ideas that have their roots in feelings, emotions, and pantheistic nature worship. She maintains that her religion has the potential to transform and improve the world.

Throughout the text, Bettine outlines the basic tenets of her *Schweberurgion*:

> "Gott [ist] die Poesie…[und]…die Weisheit" (457).
> "Ein jeder muß ein inneres Heiligtum haben dem er schwört" (464).
> "Von mir soll niemand hören ich sei unglücklich" (465).
> "Es *werde*" (467).
> "Vor allem möcht ich Herr werden über mein Denken; daß ich nämlich die Zeit ausfülle mit lebendigem (lebengebendem) Denken" (519).
> "Alles was Dir geschieht soll Dein Geistesleben befördern" (691).

Bettine's religion emphasizes independent will and a belief in entelechy.[16] It centers on individual *Bildung*, which the individual can achieve only through a life of engagement with others and with what Bettine would call the individual spirit. At the same time, this religion does not emphasize rigid adherence to a strict codex of rules imposed from the outside. Rather, the rules stem from the individual's experience and conscience.

The basic tenet of Bettine's religion—based, as is the Judeo-Christian tradition, on conscience, free will, and human potential to distinguish between good and evil—centers on action: "Der Mensch soll immer die größte Handlung tun und nie eine andre, und da will ich Dir gleich zuvorkommen und sagen, daß jede Handlung eine größte sein kann und soll" (449). Within this sentence, the reader finds both the utopian thought for which Arnim has been praised and the naiveté for which she has been criticized. A product of a time that believed in the self, individuality, self-determination, and the inherent goodness of human beings, Arnim's text makes the claim that, if the individual listens to his or her own voice/daemon/genius, she will do good. Belief in her religion has a liberating effect on Bettine. She neglects, however, to take into account the material conditions and discourses that shape the individual.

Genius and Daemon: Consequences of the *Schweberurgion*

Bettine's sense of herself empowers her to believe that she can reject, or at least radically redefine, contemporary conceptions of history, philosophy, and religion. She herself would say that her inspiration stems from her genius or daemon, terms she uses interchangeably and to which she assigns multiple meanings. She considers herself a creative genius (German: *Genie*) but also describes her genius (German: *Genius*) as an external form of inspiration that assumes the form either of an individual or metaphorical figure or of nature itself. In this manner, Bettine makes the assertion that every individual is endowed with a form of genius (or: a *Dämon*), but that genius can develop and become only through continuous self-reflection and interaction with others and the world. Bettine depicts this dynamic as yet another form of mirroring when she writes Günderode, "es tut mir nichts leid als daß ich geh eh Du wieder kommst; daß ich geh und daß Du hier bleibst, aber ich tu es weil Du es sagst, weil ich Dich als meinen Genius anerkenne,—nein nicht Du—aber er nimmt Deine Stimme an" (605). Rejecting any gesture of possession, Bettine does not designate Günderode as her genius but claims that she recognizes her genius because of her interaction with Günderode. Others in whom she sees reflections of her genius include her deceased grandfather, Hölderlin, and Ephraim.

The sense of empowerment that Bettine gains from this unshakable faith in her genius expresses itself in an often repeated wish to rule the world: "Nun, obschon ich keine Weltgeschicht studieren mag, und bei dem Zeitunglesen vor Ungeduld mich kaum zusammennehmen kann, so ists doch die Welt die ich regieren möcht und mich reißts hin darüber nachzudenken" (513). Ironically, Bettine's gender serves to keep this wish in check and within the confines of utopian thinking. Unable to assume public office, Bettine does not have the opportunity to be tempted by the lure of power, as were the emperors she discusses with Günderode. Nor does she, as a woman, have the privilege of participating in the inherent messiness of politics and governing. Rather, she must content herself with defying public authority, refusing to defend herself when she is criticized: "laß die Leute bei ihrer herzlich schlechten Meinung von mir, es ist meine beste Freud, ich geh mit meinem Dämon um, der sagt: *Du sollst dich nicht verteidigen.*—Ich tu was er will, alles andere ist mir einerlei" (409). More importantly, she takes seriously her advice to Günderode—that the individual must assume responsibility for all with whom she comes into contact (a responsibility that in later works becomes overtly connected with motherhood)—and strives to come to the aid of others. Moreover, within the context of the work itself, she wishes to help Günderode, Ephraim, and Hölderlin directly. In other words, she wishes to serve as daemon to those who serve her as *Mittler*.

Bettine expresses her wish to help and inspire Günderode throughout their exchange. Her assertion, "da wollt ich Dir dienen und nichts Dich berühren lassen, was dir weh tun könne" (484), plays itself out in their debates as well as in Bettine's critical stance towards suicide. Although Bettine designates herself as Günderode's pupil, she strives to impart to her friend some of her enthusiasm for the present. In addition to learning from her friend, she wishes to serve Günderode as *Mittler* and to teach her that youth is not a matter of physical age.

Bettine and Günderode learn of Hölderlin through their mutual friend St. Clair, and recognizing the genius in his poetry, Bettine wishes to visit the sick poet and heal him through her love:

> gleich wollt ich das Gelübde tun diesen Wahnsinnigen zu umgeben, zu lenken, das wär noch keine Aufopferung, ich wollt schon Gespräche mit ihm führen, die mich tiefer orientieren in dem, was meine Seele begehrt, ja gewiß weiß ich daß die zerbrochnen unbesaiteten Tasten seiner Seele dann wieder anklingen würden. (429)

Illustrating here the give-and-take nature of the love in which she believes, Bettine insists that, by allowing Hölderlin to talk and by trying to understand what he has to say, she could not only nourish her own genius but also serve as a mirror in which he would see himself reflected.

Alone, the individual has no mirror and thus no means of securing his or her identity. As Bettine indicates in her meditation on Hölderlin, this is the reason behind both the externally imposed and the self-imposed marginalization of outsiders. Bettine insists that Hölderlin is mad because he has been defined as an outsider as a result of others' failure to understand him: "Wahnsinn, merk ich, nennt man das was keinen Widerhall hat im Geist der andern, aber in mir hat dies alles Widerhall" (548). Bettine believes she can heal Hölderlin by refusing to marginalize him because of what others perceive to be his insanity, his difference.[17]

Bettine's wish to protect, heal, and mirror outsiders extends from Günderode and Hölderlin to her mathematics teacher, Ephraim, for she ignores her family's warnings in order to spend time with him. In their conversations she allows him to give voice to the difficulties he encounters as a Jew in German society. Ephraim is the only one of Arnim's Jewish figures who speaks for himself. Furthermore, Bettine grants him a degree of acceptance and respect that he does not find among many outside his own faith.

Bettine's desire to help others does not mean she is always successful. Within the narration itself one could almost say that her efforts are in vain. It is not easy for her constantly to resist those around her. In a revised version of an original letter to Claudine Piautaz (cited in the introduction), Bettine writes: "Ich fang an zu glauben daß ich gar nicht fürs Gesellschaftliche geboren bin, konnt ich je meiner Phantasie nachgeben ohne mich zu erhitzen über den sinnlosen Widerspruch der Andern?" (613), and the reader senses that her repeated confrontations *do* drain her energy. Further, her desire to help others has only a limited affect on their real circumstances. She is never given the chance to visit Hölderlin, she cannot save her friend Günderode, and despite her respect for Ephraim, she is ultimately unable to express her love to him directly: "wahrlich ich hatte auf der Zunge ihm zu sagen, daß ich ihn unaussprechlich liebe und daß mir an seinem Segen mehr gelegen sei als an der ganzen Welt; aber ich schwieg still, was soll man so was sagen, er siehts ja, und fühlts auch gewiß innerlich als Wahrheit" (692). As Günderode has prophesied, Bettine's actions remain in the ideal world rather than in the public sphere. At the same time, in becoming a writer Bettine does become active.

Summary: Defining the Role of the Writer

As in Arnim's first text, the Bettine of *Günderode* experiences difficulty writing within the confines of a structured form. She considers her thoughts too evasive and too complex to capture on paper, and she finds it easier to write when she has already-written material to work with (that is, to serve as a source off of which to bounce and into which to integrate her own ideas). Bettine gives voice to this difficulty in pages upon pages of letters. At the same time, she comes, by means of the process of writing, to valorize her role as writer. In turn, this role allows her to act as *Mittler* and *Dämon*, not only for other characters in the text, but especially for her readers.[18]

Bettine's own remarks would indicate that she (and by association Arnim) is not much of a writer. She describes the tribulation of trying to give her ideas a written form as follows:

> daran denke ich jetzt immer wenn ich was neues in mir selber erfahr, daß andre dies alles wohl schon wissen und nichts Neues mehr für sie mehr sein mag, wie jene Violen und Gänseblümchen am Weg die ich mir sammeln wollte. So schreib ichs denn nicht auf, und auch weil die Gedanken sich an mich hängen wie Schmetterlinge an die Blumen, wer soll sie haschen?—sie merkens gleich und fliegen davon, und fasse ich einen so hab ich bald seine schöne Farbe abgewischt mit dem Schreibefinger, oder seine Flügel erlahmen. Und so ein Gedanke in der Luft flattert so lustig, aber auf dem Papier kann er sich nicht wiegen wie auf der Blume; und kann sich nicht auf die Rosen setzen von einer zur andern, er sitzt da wie angespießt. (522)

Writing ensnares words and ideas, depriving them of their freedom and of their ability to change shape and meaning in different environments.

When Günderode considers the letters Bettine has written, she seems to confirm that Bettine is not much of a writer: "Du kannst nicht dichten, weil Du das bist was die Dichter poetisch nennen, der Stoff bildet sich nicht selber, er wird gebildet, Du deuchst mir der Lehm zu sein den ein Gott bildend mit Füßen tritt, und was ich in Dir gewahr werde ist das gärende Feuer was seine übersinnliche Berührung stark in Dich einknetet" (436). Günderode sees Bettine not as a writer but rather as material waiting to be shaped by an external god, an attribute commonly assigned to women in the nineteenth century. Günderode's assessment certainly holds true if one considers those writers who used Arnim as the magic mirror for their own Bettine characters, but what does it mean within the context of this work?

We witness in *Günderode* a transformation of Arnim's Bettine persona. No longer a child, she emphasizes youth and strives to build an ideal friendship. Still a student of life, she also becomes a teacher of history, philosophy, and religion. She also tries to play for others the role of *Mittler* that Goethe played in *Briefwechsel*. If one recalls Bettine's dual roles as student and teacher, and her understanding of her genius as both an external and an internal source of inspiration, then it becomes clear that she views herself as both "clay for the gods" *and* as "god," or: as writer/shaper of that material (in other words, as shaper of herself). Bettine emphasizes her belief in her internal genius when she describes how she wishes to speak and write: "ich wollt immer so reden, wie es nicht statthaft ist, wenn es mir näher dadurch kommt in der Seel, ich glaub gewiß, Musik muß in der Seele walten, Stimmung ohne Melodie ist nicht fließend zu denken; es muß etwas der Seele so recht Angebornes geben, worin der Gedankenstrom fließt" (306). Bettine patterns her writing after music rather than after linear, univocal speech. She has a great deal to say, but her thoughts and feelings do not fit into traditional paradigms for written expression.

At the same time (and here she sheds light on Arnim's own process of literary production), Bettine asserts not only that she requires interaction with others to develop as an individual but also that she needs their inspiration (outside genius) in order to write. Bettine elaborates on this need when she wishes that her grandmother would bequeath to her the letters written by her grandfather:

> Das Wappen wollt sie mir aufheben und mir vor ihrem Tod noch schenken, ich hätte lieber den Briefwechsel gehabt.—Ich glaub zu so etwas hätt ich Verstand, es einzuleiten und zu bereichern für den Druck, da wollt ich wohl noch viel hinzufügen, mir kommt immer nur der Verstand wenn ich von andern angeregt werd, von selbst fällt mir nichts ein, aber wenn ich von andern großes Lebendiges wahrnehme, so fällt mir gleich alles dazu ein als sei ich aus dem Traum geweckt, vielleicht könnt ich hierdurch dem Clemens ein Genüge leisten der mich so zu manchem aufgefordert hat was mich ganz tot läßt. Erfinden kann ich gar nichts. Aber ich weiß gewiß wenn ich diese Briefe des Großpapa durchläse, es würde mir alles einleuchten was dazu gehört. (598)

Just as Bettine in her incarnations as youth, woman, teacher, and daemon learns to play these roles, in part, from others, so too does she receive nuturance for her writing from the written and spoken words of her interlocutors. Arnim used original correspondence as either the basis of or the inspiration for all of the six works I discuss here. For both Arnim and the Bettine persona of *Günderode*, then, writing is a recursive process. To begin, she must have a letter, an anecdote, a memory, or an encounter. Writing does not, however, mean merely recopying the letters or trying to remember the details and chronology of a specific invent. Rather, it involves transformation, using her experience to give the original document new meaning.

Bettine comes in *Die Günderode* to define her approach to writing, something that for her arises out of interaction, first with others and then with her own thoughts and writings. This process leads to personal development, and it is also a form of acting in the world. Indeed, within the constraints placed upon Bettine as a woman, it is the most effective means of action open to her. In her next text, Arnim will turn from an epistolary structure to written conversation in order to test the limits on her potential for action.

CHAPTER THREE

Behind the Mask of a Mentor:
Dies Buch gehört dem König (1843)

Die Günderode was enthusiastically received by the "feste Gemeinde" (Grimm 8) that had formed in 1835 with the publication of *Goethe's Briefwechsel mit einem Kinde*. With the appearance of her second letter book, and with the interest and support of her fans, Bettina von Arnim directed her attention with increasing frequency to issues of social and political justice. She took as guides for action both her interest in the notion of individual responsibility for others, as described in *Die Günderode*, and the liberal social, political, and religious views that had grown out of her engagement with the ideas of—and personal meetings with—such influential figures as Schleiermacher, the theologian David Friedrich Strauss, and the Young German and Young Hegelian thinkers who visited her salon. As Moriz Carriere recalls of a visit, as early as 1840 Arnim was pondering how she might influence Friedrich Wilhelm IV of Prussia and insisting, "Wir müssen den König retten" (90). Arnim's political beliefs led her in the summer of 1841 to step forward in defense of Gasparo Spontini, who had been General Music Director in Berlin since 1820 and who stood accused of treason following the interception by Prussian censors of one of his private letters. Not only did Arnim publish a defense of Spontini in the form of an open letter in the *Jahrbücher des deutschen National-Vereins für Musik und ihre Wissenschaft*, she also dedicated a collection of her musical compositions to him in order to help raise money for his legal fees. The authority that Arnim had gained from her publications and activity as a salon hostess insured that such engagement received significant attention: the king pardoned Spontini in 1842.

From this position of authority, and one year after the publication of *Günderode,* Arnim began to pen her third major work. As Ingeborg Drewitz has noted, in the two years it took Arnim to complete *Dies Buch gehört dem König,* she achieved "die vollkommen Identität mit der Rolle, die sie sich zudachte" (*Bettine von Arnim* 191). She had profited to such a great extent from self-reflection and interaction with her various mentors that she now considered herself in a position to inspire and mentor others, a sense enhanced by her newly discovered faith in the persuasive power of her writing. Within the personal context of Arnim's heightened sense of self-assurance and the political context of the pre-revolutionary 1840s, she directed the focus of *Dies Buch* away from the idea of individual development and towards a contemplation of the predominant social and political questions of mid-nineteenth-century Prussia.

Arnim's choice of personae in this text reflects her departure from an emphasis on the individual. Not Arnim's namesake, her Bettine persona, but Frau Rath Goethe holds center stage throughout a large part of the text. Arnim returns here to the relationship between Bettine and Frau Rath that she had begun to explore in *Briefwechsel.* In *Dies Buch,* however, their conversations no longer revolve around Goethe; in this text he represents only the object of a mother's love and is referred to more frequently as Frau Rath's son than by his own name. Rather, the moral bankruptcy of the church and the Prussian state becomes the object of their passionate discussions.

The action of this text consists primarily of speech: individuals speaking, conversing, or debating with each other, and telling stories. Furthermore, the action remains confined to a limited space. With the exception of the final depiction of scenes from nineteenth-century Berlin's notorious slum, the *Vogtland,* Frankfurt serves as the setting for the work. We occasionally see Frau Rath telling her stories at an open square in Frankfurt; most often she remains within the confines of her apartment where she engages in conversation with an unnamed friend (who recalls earlier Bettine personae), a minister, a mayor, and finally a *französischer Atzel* (a French magpie) that a French soldier gave her as he was leaving Frankfurt. The section headings tell us that these conversations take place in 1807, but references to events that occur into the 1840s such as the *Demagogenverfolgung* (the persecution of liberals and nationalists in the wake of the Carlsbad Decrees of 1819) make apparent that, in writing her "king's book" Arnim is more concerned with her own present than with the Frankfurt of the early part of the century. Although Arnim the writer did not choose Bettine as the central figure of this work, she continues to inhabit the main characters. In this text both the Frau Rath and the Bettine personae assume roles that, I will argue, develop out of roles played both by Arnim's earlier Bettines as well by as Arnim herself over the course of her life. In the figure of Frau Rath, one finds traces not only of the historical Catharina Elisabeth Goethe, but also of Arnim at various stages in her life and of Arnim's fictitious Bettines. Just as the Bettine of *Günderode* is a continuation of the character who appeared in *Briefwechsel*, the Frau Rath and Bettine personae of this text form a composite that can be viewed as a maturer and more self-confident version of these earlier Bettines.

Allusions to King Friedrich Wilhelm IV present the most conspicuous references to the political situation in mid-nineteenth-century Prussia. Arnim began to correspond with the ruler in 1840, when he was still crown prince, in the hope of gaining his support for the Grimm brothers following the trial of the Göttingen Seven.[1] Because one of his first acts as king was to grant the Grimms membership in the Berlin Academy of Sciences and the right to hold lectures at the Berlin University (originally called the Friedrich Wilhelm University after its first patron Friedrich Wilhelm III), Arnim had reason to hope that his regency would mark a departure from the more conservative, authoritarian reigns of his predecessors. Arnim was not alone in her hope. Upon his ascension to the throne in 1840, Friedrich Wilhelm IV was welcomed by a large number of German liberals who, because of the interest he had shown in liberal causes while crown prince, expected him to institute the constitutional government that had been promised by his father.

Friedrich Wilhelm III had twice pledged publicly to institute a constitution in Prussia, first in 1810 and again in 1815. Yet even following the ratification of Article 13 of the *Wiener Bundesakten* at the Congress of Vienna, with its decree that all states of the newly established German Federation were to introduce constitutions into their governmental systems, Prussia remained firmly within the tradition of enlightened absolutism. In 1840 German leftist intellectuals hoped Friedrich Wilhelm IV would establish a constitutional monarchy that, in turn, would lead to the easing of the Prussian censorship laws that had been tightened with the Carlsbad Decrees. Their hopes were soon dashed, however, for shortly after the coronation they came to see that the king followed the lead of his close circle of advisors and not that of the liberal movements of the day. Maintaining her faith in the king, when she sat down to write *Dies Buch*, Arnim hoped to draw his attention away from the voices of his advisors and towards her own suggestions for change.

In contrast to her first two publications, Arnim presents this work not as an epistolary exchange but rather as a series of conversations; working through *Dies Buch*, the first-time reader quickly becomes entangled among monologues and conversations that never seem to find their way to a quick resolution. This form, taken up again in *Gespräche mit Dämonen*, has led many scholars to classify these two texts as dialogue books in contrast to Arnim's letter books. In Schultz's estimation, the conversational tone and the way the work develops its themes through multi-directional dialogue reflect the salon-sociability at Arnim's address on Unter den Linden during the 1830s and 40s. He argues that Arnim's salon activity influenced the content and form of the work, especially its emphasis on the development of the individual and ideas through intellectual and emotional interaction, that is, through romantic sociability ("Euer Unglaube an die Naturstimme…").

In making his assertion, Schultz claims to disprove Liebertz-Grün's contention in *Ordnung im Chaos* that Arnim modeled her text at least in part on the Socratic dialogues and especially on Plato's *Politeia*. Yet the two models are not mutually exclusive but rather serve equally to elucidate this text. On the one hand, Schultz's contention is supported by the relationship between Frau Rath and the child Bettine, for here one finds an example of free and spontaneous interaction. On the other hand, Frau Rath assumes more control in her relationships with others in the text. Here the text tends towards a didacticism based on the Socratic model: while Frau Rath lets others take part in conversations with her, she directs and interprets what they say in such a way as to support her own arguments. In addition, the text indicates to the readers those figures with whom they should identify and those ideas they should favor. Although the text does not specify a solution to the problems it addresses, it does not meander aimlessly through a conversation with no beginning and no end but rather points in a specific and discernable direction. In this regard, many of Frau Rath's conversations do not maintain the free and open association attributed to salon sociability.

Furthermore, both the directedness of the text and its form are more indicative of written than of freely spoken language. The text has a discernible structure that does not replicate spoken language, nor can it accurately be described as spontaneous speech, even though within the individual sections one finds many sections in which such speech is imitated. Thus, *Dies Buch* remains an epistolary work in many respects. Arnim incorporated actual letters into her work (primarily from her correspondences with Friedrich Wilhelm IV, Prince Carl of Württemberg, and the Hungarian writer Kertbeny). The conversations in the text follow many of the principles of epistolarity as outlined by Altman: although spoken exchange is more immediate than an exchange of letters, conversations serve as both bridges and barriers to understanding. As opposed to writing and reading, here speaking and listening are granted equal importance, and successful exchange requires reciprocity. Each conversation is closed but then picked up later. We as readers are allowed to continue and expand on the often-fragmentary conversations to which we are privy. Moreover, like Socrates in his relationship with Plato, Bettine serves as the scribe for Frau Rath, and as the text presents it, Frau Rath's words can only achieve immortality through the written word. It is therefore no coincidence that, soon after its publication, Gutzkow posited that the text represented "ein[en] offen[en] Brief an den König" ("Bettines *Königsbuch*" 431).

Thus, while the distinction between letter book and dialogue book proves useful for distinguishing between the two different genres that Arnim used to frame her writing, Arnim never adhered strictly to one genre or another. Rather, she employed throughout her oeuvre what Friedrich Schlegel referred to as *Universalpoesie* and Christa Wolf has called a *Mischform* ("Nun ja!," *Ins Ungebundene gehet eine Sehnsucht* 346). Rather than addressing its readers in a genre with stark formal differences from *Briefwechsel* and *Günderode*, the text illustrates how Arnim destabilizes the categories of conversation and narration in her literary creations.

Critics have long noted a discernible structure in this work. In his review Gutzkow divided the text into two sections, the first of which criticized religion and the second of which promoted communism. More recently, Waldstein has shown that "the titles of the individual sections demonstrate a deliberate attempt at creating immediacy through a conversational atmosphere" (87). Expanding on Waldstein's argument, I contend that, although the sections relate closely to one another, each serves a specific and very different purpose.

As in her previous texts, Arnim establishes reader expectations in the title and introduction of the work. The title itself serves as a dedication, and more importantly, as a message to alert the king that the work's contents are intended for him.[2] This is underscored in the introduction. Functioning as a frontispiece of sorts, the introductory section of *Dies Buch* recounts a parable of a (genderless) child who presents his/her most precious possession, a perfectly rounded apple, to the king. That Arnim is working here within and against a tradition in which knowledge (and especially women's knowledge) is viewed with suspicion becomes evident with this positive appropriation of the apple as symbol of knowledge. The introduction thus presents one of the many instances in the text that inverts traditional interpretations of biblical stories. Knowledge acquires a positive value; it is something a child (and by inference the female author Arnim) possesses, and the child wishes to present this knowledge as a gift to the king. Although neither this child nor the child who appears periodically throughout the book to converse with Frau Rath is ever named, Arnim's strategies as writer and as public figure insured that at least her contemporary readers would associate this child with Arnim's other child Bettines and thus with the author herself. The reference to Alexander von Humboldt in the final lines provides further support for this association, for participants in Berlin social life were well aware that Humboldt served frequently as a mediator between Arnim and the king. With this reference to Humboldt, Arnim stepped outside the confines of her story to refer explicitly to the time in which she was writing. In so doing, she indicated to her contemporaries that the king of the dedication could be none other than Friedrich Wilhelm IV.

The introduction to *Dies Buch* does more than merely establish reader expectations and assert the value of the work itself; it introduces us to one of the narrative techniques employed throughout the remainder of the text: the use of allegory to illustrate a point. The story of the child with the apple offers a reinterpretation of the symbol of the apple of knowledge while at the same time serving as an allegorical representation of Arnim presenting her own work to the king. The fact that Humboldt must make this apple *genießbar* indicates the risk involved in such a gift and provides a hint as to why Arnim, in the words of Emily Dickinson, chooses to tell her truth at a slant.

Later in the text, Frau Rath offers an explanation for her use of allegorical stories as a means of describing, interpreting, and criticizing the broader world: "Da die Wahrheit vor lauter Anbetungszeremonien in ihrer göttlichen Nacktheit nicht vor diesen thronisolierten Menschenseelen auftreten kann, so tut es not daß sie im Gewand der Fabel wie den unschuldigen Kindern sich zeigt" (101). Frau Rath considers the king, who remains isolated by the trappings of the throne and palace, incapable of facing, or at least certainly removed from, the naked truth; storytelling provides a means of communicating this truth to him.

Stories offer accessibility, which is in keeping with Frau Rath's desire to educate others. Moreover, stories allow simultaneously for concealment and revelation, thus offering a clever means of conveying radical ideas and skirting censorship. In an atmosphere in which prescribed gender roles limited women's public participation in political debate, Arnim created the seemingly innocuous personae of Frau Rath and the child Bettine, and she employed the strategy of storytelling to slip her ideas into public consciousness surreptitiously. At a time when the public expression of ideas by liberal men was increasingly restricted, the fact that Arnim and her protagonists were women, and that in the nineteenth century, the stories of women and women writers were not taken seriously, proved to be a distinct advantage. As Heinrich Houben notes, the work's contents placed "Bettinens Königsbuch in die vorderste Reihe der als revolutionär betrachteten vormärzlichen Literatur" and would have landed any male writer in jail (36). Yet her evasion strategy was only partially successful. Whereas Arnim's text did get past the Prussian censor, the ensuing public stir led to the banning of this text in Bavaria and Austria and, somewhat later, to the temporary censorship of *Clemens Brentano's Frühlingskranz*.

Following the introduction, the text turns from the allegory of the child with the apple to Frau Rath. Part One of the text bears the title "Der Erinnerung abgelauschte Gespräche und Erzählungen von 1807" and portrays Frau Rath telling stories to her Frankfurt audience. This section begins with a series of aphorisms entitled "Aussprüche der Frau Rath." Here again the line between Frau Rath and her Bettine personae becomes fluid. Not only do the aphorisms recall passages from the diary section of *Briefwechsel*, they also espouse ideas central to Arnim's earlier works: freedom, individuality, and development of genius or spirit (*Geist*). Yet this half-page of adages does not merely reiterate what Arnim has written before. To the above list of values one finds added, with no small amount of humor and provocation, a new virtue: inconsiderateness. As one of the aphorisms states, "Rücksicht ist das Unkraut auf dem Feld der Freundschaft und der Liebe, oft überwuchert es den ganzen Boden so daß kein gesundes Pflänzchen drauf gedeiht" (16). Although she must convey the truth of her stories obliquely, Frau Rath speaks her mind. In contrast to the Bettina Brentano who wrote to Goethe, and even to an extent, in contrast to the Bettine figure of *Briefwechsel*, Arnim's literary Frau Rath has no need to please and no concerns about hurting anyone's feelings. She minces no words. Honesty and directness become the only acceptable means for interacting with her listeners, but that directness is softened by a laugh and a wink. If *Günderode* is Arnim's most poignant work, *Dies Buch* is without a doubt her most humorous.

From these "Aussprüche," the narrative moves to the first of Frau Rath's stories. In the section "Die Frau Rath erzählt" she begins to recount a tale that evolves into a collage of stories within frame stories. In the most external frame, Frau Rath recalls an invitation she receives to have tea with Queen Louise of Prussia and her subsequent visit to the queen's court in Darmstadt.[3] Frau Rath narrates her adventure from the beginning, when she receives the invitation, to the end, when she returns home to Frankfurt and to friends and neighbors who ask incessantly to hear the story again and again. Each time she relates her story, however, she tells a slightly different version, inserting not only new details about the trip but also insights she acquired along the way. A story of a visit to a royal court thus becomes a series of digressions on such diverse topics as: why Frau Rath refuses to believe in the seven days of creation, the advantages of old age, praise of motherhood, criticism of the church, praise of the political system of the *Freie Reichsstadt* Frankfurt, and her refusal to be impressed by the accouterments of court society. For Frau Rath, these digressions *constitute* the story. At the beginning of a new day of story telling, she asks if any of her listeners can tell her where she left off the day before:

> Kann mir Einer sagen wo wir geblieben sind?—"Im Garten im Mondschein."— Ja, ja, ganz recht, aber was haben wir da verhandelt?—Denn sonst wär meine Geschicht gleich aus, wenn ich wie die große Herrn mit Relaispferd durchsause wollt, ohne die geringste Erfahrung zu machen unterwegs, ohne die geringste Entdeckung oder Bemerkung als bloß daß es wie der Wind über Stock und Steiner hinausgeht!—Nein, wir fahren mit einem Zauderer—der alle Viertelstund ein Schnäpschen nimmt, und alle Anrand Futterung hält.—So bin ich einmal nach Heidelberg gefahren mit siebenzehn Futterungen und einundzwanzig Schnäpse und hab doch Geduld gehabt; so muß man mit der Frau Rath auch Geduld haben und heut hab ich grad Lust nach einem kleinen Räuschchen; denn von den Wirklichkeiten ist so nicht mehr viel zu erzählen—nur noch von denen Einbildungen. (43)

For Frau Rath, a linear account of her journey would mean neglecting much of what had actually happened. Her visit to Queen Louise did not progress from her arrival to her visit and then to her departure; it included the thoughts and feelings she had along the way. Including them in her story and digressing from the main point means refusing to accept a traditional hierarchy of meaning. In *Ordnung im Chaos*, Liebertz-Grün has described digression as one of the central narrative strategies of *Dies Buch*, and this section exemplifies the manner in which Frau Rath exploits the strategy to explore all of the possible valences of her story. Digression, then, serves to illustrate the complexity of everyday life, to challenge the authority of linear stories and histories, and to foreground subjective experience.

In the next two sections of Part One, "Ein vertraut Gespräch 1807" and "Zweites Gespräch," Frau Rath turns from telling her stories before an audience to conversation. "Ein vertraut Gespräch" begins with Bettine arriving at the home of Frau Rath. Notably, when Frau Rath offers to discuss "Wolfgang" Bettine declines. In contrast to the Bettine of *Briefwechsel*, this Bettine persona is far more interested in her own experiences and her friendship with Frau Rath. When the minister arrives, Bettine retreats into the background, but her occasional comments to Frau Rath let us know that she is always present, listening. With the minister, Frau Rath soon begins to criticize the church. In "Zweites Gespräch," still conversing with the minister, she turns her attention to the penal system. When the minister leaves, Frau Rath is again alone with Bettine.

In all of the sections of Part One, the reader witnesses Frau Rath engaged in various forms of communication. She becomes meditative and self-reflexive in her aphorisms. She engages a wide audience with her storytelling. Her exchanges with Bettine are playful but also fruitful. She assumes an almost pedantic tone when conversing with the minister. These modes of expression allow her to explore various self-expressive and communicative possibilities. Together with her strategy of digression, this allows her to tell the more rounded story for which she is striving.

Part Two of *Dies Buch*, the section that Karl Gutzkow described as *kommunistisch*, is also divided into three sections. The first bears the heading "Sokratie der Frau Rath (Bruchstück: Die Verbrecher)." Over the course of a series of visits from Bettine, the minister, and a new figure, the mayor, Frau Rath addresses Prussia's treatment of and the church's attitude towards criminals and the poor. Using state-produced evidence against the state, Frau Rath appropriates crime reports written by Prussian bureaucrats to illustrate the injustices of the Prussian legal system. With this evidence she substantiates her contention, still valid today, that a direct correlation exists between poverty and crime, and she illustrates how government and church policies have been responsible for both. The conversational form allows the characters to jump from one topic to the next, and Arnim employs digression throughout this section as a means of allowing Frau Rath to expand and embellish her arguments. Despite her digressions, Frau Rath returns again and again to very specific themes: the causes of crime and poverty, the role of the state and the church, the need for education for all citizens, the role of the mother, and friendship. Frau Rath may digress from her topic, but like any good orator she returns to the main idea both to insure that the audience is following her and to give her point added emphasis.

The next brief section bears the title "Das Gespräch der Frau Rath mit einer Französischen Atzel" and constitutes, philosophically and politically, the most radical section of the text. Frau Rath relinquishes her position of authority here, shifting from teacher to pupil of a French magpie that she received from a French soldier during the occupation of Frankfurt. The magpie symbolizes Lucifer, the bringer of light. Arnim thus writes here in a tradition, in existence since the Enlightenment, that appropriates this figure as a bestower of knowledge.

The magpie asserts it has come to educate the world by sowing chaos in the form of a revolution of ideas. The aim of this revolution is to free humankind from the bonds imposed by church and state. In contrast to Frau Rath, who vehemently opposes the ideas espoused by the *Atzel*, Bettine defends its ideas. Notably, she is not only sitting in the room listening but has the magpie perched on her head while it is speaking and is thus positioned in a manner that associates her with the bird's ideas. Indeed, there are similarities between the magpie and earlier Bettine personae: the bird associates with the stars, takes walks late at night in order to commune with nature, and emphasizes knowledge and development. Although the Bettine of this text generally plays, or at least appears to play, the more receptive roles of friend, listener, and scribe, at this point she takes the reins from Frau Rath, pushing the ideas developed by her mentor to their limits. At the end of the section, a storm arises and lightening strikes a church tower in Frankfurt. Within a Western narrative tradition that she certainly knew from the works of Goethe and Klopstock, Arnim employs nature to represent feelings and events, here: both the personal desire for change and the revolution that is brewing in Germany as she is writing her work.

Should there, at the end of Parts One and Two, be any question as to why the revolution called for by the magpie might be imminent, Arnim provides a final piece of evidence. In the "Erfahrungen eines jungen Schweizers im Vogtland (Als Beilage zur Sokratie der Frau Rat)," Arnim incorporates the reports that Swiss educator, Heinrich Grunholzer, had written for her describing the destitute area of Berlin known as the *Vogtland*. This section limns a picture of the social ills whose cause Arnim so clearly pinpoints in the earlier sections, and according to Geist and Kürvers, it provided the mid-nineteenth-century reading public with its first shocking glance into the lives of the poor in Berlin (192). Although a large portion of *Dies Buch* consists of demanding, philosophical language, Arnim closes the work with concrete discussions of readily visible problems, thus emphasizing that she intends her philosophical and religious ruminations as a call for social and political action.

Into the text's complex structure Arnim weaves a number of central themes and ideas: she criticizes policies of the church and state towards their subjects, especially towards the poor and criminals; she suggests a constitutional monarchy combined with local government based on the pre-Napoleonic model of the *Freie Reichsstadt* Frankfurt; and she suggests the king withdraw from politics per se to serve as a public, moral figurehead. In addition, the figures of Frau Rath and Bettine allow for further exploration of the concept of friendship, which Arnim wishes to transpose onto the political realm. In discussing and debating these ideas, the two women assume numerous roles, many of which have their roots in earlier Bettine figures as well as in Arnim's life. Arnim writes the personae of Bettine and Frau Rath against the backdrop of her (Arnim's) own experience and thus stands behind the masks of both the child Bettine and the elderly Frau Rath. These figures share the roles of friend and teacher, yet they are by no means identical. Whereas Frau Rath assumes the roles of mother, wise woman, and orator, Bettine plays the child, the scribe, and in her identification with the magpie, the revolutionary.

In *Dies Buch* Arnim splits Bettine into not only two but four distinct personae: Frau Rath, an unnamed child who is clearly Bettine, a French magpie, and a young Swiss educator. If we recall how her texts encourage readers to identify the author with her literary personae it becomes apparent that, with this division, she stakes out multiple subject positions for herself. One can only speculate on the reasons for this split. Why didn't Arnim simply call Frau Rath *Bettine*, for example? Perhaps she wished to pay homage to the influence of the historical Catharina Elisabeth Goethe in her life; perhaps she wished to indicate that she now saw herself in a role that resembled that played by her mentor: Arnim was an authority within a circle of friends and admirers but had little influence outside that realm. On a more somber note, like Frau Rath, who never saw her son during the last eleven years of her life,[4] Arnim had, despite her popularity, experienced her share of isolation, to an extent from her immediate family, but also from the individuals she cared about and had hoped to influence (Goethe, Pückler, Günderrode, Friedrich Wilhelm IV, Clemens, Nathusius). She therefore may have identified with Frau Rath's isolation. At the same time, by including the child Bettine and her elderly friend Frau Rath in her work, Arnim allowed herself to hide, to seek refuge behind the masks of women in positions often considered harmless. She could also hide behind figures not at all associated with the Bettines of previous texts. Indeed, the most radical moments in this text are carried by a bird that appears to speak madness and defecates all over Frau Rath's apartment and by the "junger Schweizer" who records the *Vogtland* report. In dividing Bettine not only into separate roles but also into four distinct personae, Arnim can pay homage to her mentor Catharina Elisabeth Goethe and smuggle her ideas into the Berlin public sphere. The remainder of this chapter examines the roles played by these personae.

Frau Rath—The Old Woman

Far more than in *Briefwechsel*, the Frau Rath of *Dies Buch* becomes stylized as a woman whose age and experiences have left her undaunted by the authority of others and without any longing for younger days or a return to better times. She possesses self-respect and faith in her ideas but resists any temptation to take herself too seriously. These qualities extend to all of the roles she plays: youthful and elderly woman, mother, friend, teacher, and daemon.

In contrast to the female figures in *Briefwechsel* and *Günderode*, who occasionally express the wish to be men, Frau Rath valorizes what she considers to be feminine attributes (including the empathy that she believes develops out of being a mother) while at the same time challenging those who would assign to women the characteristics of meekness and frailty. In addition, she resists the purely rational thinking that, in the nineteenth century, was associated with masculinity:

> Mut hab ich, womit ich den Leuten, wenn sie den Kopf verlieren ihn oft wieder zurecht gesetzt hab. Ja bei Gelegenheiten, von denen eine Frau keinen Verstand zu haben behaupt wird, da steht als dem Mann derselbig ihm allein zugemessne Verstand still, daß er wehklagt: Ach was fangen wir an?—Da antwort die Frau und schlägt dem Nagel auf den Kopf. (24)

Frau Rath does not reject reason altogether; she insists that because it has been confined to and defined by the masculine domain, it has become a counterproductive force. For this reason she offers resistance when, in an attempt to praise her, the minister tells her she has "einen männlichen Geist." She protests: "Ich mag Ihr Prädikat nicht. Staun an den Mut eines

Weibes und ihre Heldenkraft, wie sie mit furchtlosem Blick den Kampf besteht! Hoch über Gefahr hinweg trägt ihr Herz die Streiterin; unermeßlicher Stärke genießt sie, von keiner Furcht die Seele bestürmt" (181–182). Behind the effusive tone of this passage, one finds Frau Rath making a case for courage, heroic strength, and reason tempered by empathy as the feminine gender attributes with which she identifies.

Important, too, for Frau Rath is her age. In contrast to the child Bettines of Arnim's previous novels—and to the childlike person sitting at her feet—Frau Rath emphasizes her maturity:

> so schön und luftig die Blütezeit ist, so muß man doch die Zeit wo das Obst reift am meisten respektieren! Denke doch einmal sie steigt herauf, die Natur, in alle Baumzweigelcher und so schön ihr die Blütezeit läßt, und so verliebt sie auch in ihre eigne Jugendschönheit ist, sie schüttelt sie sich ab, und nun arbeit sie eifrig in der heißen Sommerzeit, alles sammelt sie, den Regen, den Sonnenbrand, bis sie ihre Kirsche zu Stand gebracht hat, nun gibt sie's dem Menschen hin; ist das nicht eine große Lehr die sie gibt? (30)

Within the context of Arnim's work up to and including *Dies Buch*, this passage performs the dual task of alerting the reader to the accomplishments of the fictional and the historical Frau Rath as an older woman, and indirectly, to Arnim's own accomplishments and to the position that she has achieved at the time of writing this text. Taking recourse to the by now familiar language of nature, Arnim valorizes age and maturity by analogy with the process of ripening. And in a gesture of self-referentiality that recalls the ripened apple in the introduction, she uses this passage to assert that the now-ripened fruit of her labor—her text—can now be shared with others. Arnim thus positions herself next to Frau Rath as a woman who has benefited from her age.[5]

In addition to Frau Rath and the implied adult Arnim standing in the shadows of the text, one other older woman appears here whose significance resonates with that of the other two: an elderly beggar woman whom the mayor describes with abhorrence after she catches his eye at the end of a popular uprising. He recalls:

> Mir ist viel schon in meiner Staatspraxis vorgekommen, aber nichts so schauerlich als dies verdammte alte Weib mit dem Sattel auf dem Kopf der sie vor dem Regen schützte, es goß fürchterlich sonst hätte die Revolution auch noch länger gedauert, aber einem langweiligen Landregen widersteht keine Revolution. (205)

Although a summer storm frightens away most of the would-be revolutionaries, one beggar woman remains, insolently grinning at the mayor from underneath a saddle she uses to keep the rain off her head. Responding half with mocking irony and half in anger, Frau Rath exclaims:

> Es lautet schrecklich!—So ein Staat von alten Weibern die im bösen Mut aufbrausen.—Ich möcht ihn nicht regieren, noch weniger von ihm regiert werden! Ja leider—Was ist des deutschen Vaterland? Nicht Pommerland nicht Schwabenland; es ist das Altweiberland![6]...Es gibt so alte Kater die ihre Jungen würgen, und die schauderhafte Alte die unterm Sattel hervor die würdigen Beamten so verhöhnte, ist ein Wahrhaft prophetischer Anblick. (205–206)

Only this old woman can look the mayor, as a representative of the state that devours its young, in the eye and elicit from him a sense of terror that Frau Rath considers prophetic of times to come should the state refuse to concern itself with the old woman and those like her: "Warum wißt Ihr nicht woher sie kommen? Woher sie verschwinden? Warum will der Staat sie nicht finden und ihrem Verderben vorkommen?" (206) This elderly woman joins forces with Frau Rath and Arnim[7] in an effort to place before the mayor (and, consequently, the king) a mirror: not a mirror in the sense that Bettine used Goethe as a mirror in which she could reflect (on) her own development as a writer, or in the sense that Günderode and Bettine mirrored each other in friendship, but rather a mirror as a tool of critique. These women have seen and experienced the world and now *re-present* that world to the male representatives of the state with a healthy dose of criticism.

Like a spider web, the lines of thought in this text tend to be barely visible, barely tangible, but at the same time artfully woven together. Arnim spins a strand that connects Frau Rath, the elderly woman under the saddle, and herself the writer: old women, seers, sages, they reveal to male representatives of the state and the church not only the present consequences of their actions but also what those actions might lead to in the future. Consciously or unconsciously, then, Arnim appears to be working within the tradition of the *Fürstenspiegel*, holding up her text to the king as a reflection of his actions (and lack thereof) and as evidence for the need for reforms in Prussia.

For Frau Rath, wisdom is a product of age and maturity. In her account, it also stems from motherhood. Whereas mid-nineteenth-century mothers traditionally had responsibility for the education of younger children, the mother figure of this text serves as an educator not only of the young person sitting at her feet, but also of the mayor and minister, and indirectly, of the king to whom the text is dedicated. There are, in fact, four figures who share this mother-role: Frau Rath as the mother of the genius Goethe and as spiritual mother to her listeners and especially Bettine; Queen Louise, for whom Frau Rath makes the wish that she will bear a son who can pull the German states out of the political turmoil of the Napoleonic wars, and who historically gave birth to the future Friedrich Wilhelm IV; the state, which Frau Rath insists should assume a mothering role towards its subjects by encouraging them to develop through independent thinking; and finally Arnim the author who, in writing this work, positions herself as second mother to the king insofar as she wishes to educate him both through her publication and through the earlier letters written to him.

Regarding her philosophy of mothering, Frau Rath claims that she encouraged her son to become independent, in effect taking credit for his achievements. She tells, for example, of her refusal to listen to an outsider's advice on how to raise her child:

> Nun also auf eignen Füßen stehen soll der Geist. Das ist bei mir eine unumstößliche Wahrheit, an der manches zerschellen muß, was dagegen anstößt. Woher hab ich sie mir als junge Mutter von einem großen Sohn denn so fest einbilden können, daß ich dem Herrn Haberlein nicht gefolgt hab, wenn er sagte: *Man muß das Kind führen und es stützen* und was weiß ich als!—Ich aber dachte man muß das Kind locken und nicht führen, und muß ihm alles wegnehmen, woran er sichs lernt nicht auf den eignen Beinen zu stehn. (48)

Frau Rath claims to have encouraged her son to learn, to develop, to become. She provided an environment in which education was possible, but she did not tell him how or what he should learn—an approach to education that the Bettines of *Briefwechsel* and *Günderode* endorse but rarely experience in their elders.

Of course when Frau Rath visits Queen Louise, her little Johann has left the fold long ago whereas the Queen has apparently not yet conceived her son. Yet motherhood, or rather potential motherhood, draws the two women together. As Frau Rath exclaims, "Muttergefühl ist eine Wünschelrut die schlägt in allen weiblichen Herzen an" (67). With this statement, and with her emphasis on women as childbearers and educators, Frau Rath essentializes but also valorizes motherhood as an integral aspect of femininity.

At the same time, she proceeds to carve out a space for motherhood within the sphere of public decision making. Speaking in 1807, the hopes that Frau Rath once tied to Napoleon have diminished, but she recalls that, when she returned home from the court in 1804,[8] she made a wish: "Gewiß ist, daß ich in selbiger Nacht von Herzen gewünscht hab, die Frau Königin möchte der Welt einen tapfern Sohn gebären, der den freien Geist, die Unsterblichkeit nämlich, nicht fürchtet" (81). Frau Rath wishes for the birth of a king whom Arnim the author, in the early 1840s, wishes to educate to his full potential, a wish that continues to be expressed in *Dämonen*. Furthermore, she wishes for a transformation of the state into an entity that would play a nurturing role vis-à-vis its citizens. Indeed, in her estimation the state is already the mother of its citizens, but the representatives of the state must determine how they will define that role:

> Der Staat ist Mensch, die Menschheit zur Freiheit heraufbilden ist seine physische Geschichte. Er trägt die Krankheitsstoffe in sich, und soll sich aus ihnen erlösen. Ist die Menschheit Kind, dann liegt Anlage und Gesundheit im Keim!—Der Staat muß diesen Freiheitskeim in ihr entwickeln sonst ist er Rabenmutter, und sorgt auch für *Rabenfutter*. (234)

In a sly and politically astute move, Arnim manipulates the view, long defined for masculinist intentions, that relegates motherhood and femininity to the private sphere. Equating mothers with the state, Frau Rath both valorizes the strength of mothers and feminizes the state. The private becomes the model for the public; motherhood becomes a model for the relationship between the state and its citizens, one that discourages dependence and strict adherence to a specific set of norms in favor of the development of individual potential.

Frau Rath thus transforms motherhood, a role traditionally associated with the private sphere, into a model for the public sphere. A similar transformation takes place with the role of friend. Whereas being a mother implies directing another's development without necessarily being directed, friendship implies reciprocity. Within the context of Arnim's body of work, these two roles are closely related, and *Dies Buch* sharpens an idea that Arnim began to formulate in *Briefwechsel* and *Günderode*, namely that the prerequisite to a friendship of equals is a mother-child relationship constituted in the manner described above. The goal of the mother/state is to raise children/subjects to the status of equals, to the point where a hierarchy no longer exists. Only then is friendship possible.

The most balanced relationship and the only friendship in the text is that between Frau Rath and Bettine. As in *Briefwechsel*, Frau Rath encourages Bettine's development while at the same time acknowledging that Bettine has a thing or two to teach her as well, an awareness that becomes particularly evident in the segment with the French magpie. In the friendship between Bettine and Frau Rath we find a relationship marked by a reciprocity matched in Arnim's texts only by that between Bettine and Günderode, but without the impending sense of separation that pervades *Günderode*. Furthermore, within *Dies Buch* this friendship is the least hierarchical of Frau Rath's relationships, for both figures oscillate freely between the roles of teacher and pupil, and while Frau Rath does most of the speaking, Bettine does all of the writing (and editing) of the text.

As with motherhood, Frau Rath extends the concept of friendship beyond the personal realm to the public sphere. Not only must the king rear his subjects, he must also recognize that, once this project of education begins, it will transform the king's relationship to the people into a friendship in which his so-called subjects will begin to shape *his* character:

> Was ist Freundschaft?—leider das unverstandenste, gemißbrauchteste, versäumte Geistesfeld, falsch einwirkender Richtungen, fremder Weltinteresse und nicht Interesse der Liebe. Poesielose Selbstigkeit, statt Poesie der Selbstheit, und Phantasie, die edelste Trägerin aller erhabenen Wirkungen auf einander ist ohne Macht. Dies alles ist verborgne Zukunftsanlage. Der Freund dem du dich hingibst, ihm zu lieb dich heiligst und bildest, dem du deine erhabnen Gedanken zuhauchst, der wird die kräftigste Weihe deines Charakters;—aber auch der ganze Charakter dessen den du so als Genius in dir trägst steigt aus dir empor. Einer kann göttlich vollendet werden durch die beziehende Empfindung zum Andern, so erzeugt sich der Fürstencharakter aus dem Volk, so erzeugt sich der Genius aus dem Freund. (268–269)

Like the Bettine of *Günderode*—and despite her friendship with the Bettine figure of this text—Frau Rath realizes that the friendship she envisions is a utopian wish that will be realized, if at all, in the future; the concept as it is presently used and realized is, in her mind, misused.⁹ Yet her prescription for the relationship between a ruler and his subjects is ultimately friendship, a relationship that, if pushed to its limits, would make the roles of ruler and subject superfluous. The idea of friendship as a model for this relationship is, then, a step beyond and more radical than the model of motherhood, for it implies not one-sided but mutual *Erziehung*.

The model for the relationship between a king and his subjects serves a strategic function for Frau Rath, for it licenses her to criticize those representatives of the church and state with whom she comes into contact. Significantly, once she enters into conversation with them, she no longer plays the role of friend that she plays with Bettine. Rather, she shifts into the role of the teacher (*Mutter*). We see her discussing her ideas with Bettine, various citizens of Frankfurt, and a mayor and a minister, but her messages are also intended for Friedrich Wilhelm IV and the readers of the text. With the exceptions of Bettine and the magpie, Frau Rath engages with her interlocutors not in order to learn from or develop herself through them, but rather for the purpose of instruction. She compares herself to Socrates, and while she encourages her counterparts to speak their minds, she remains in control of the direction of the conversation, guiding them in their thinking. Using these tactics, she succeeds in voicing her criticisms of the present relationship between the church and state and the people.

Frau Rath's criticisms of the church extend from the present back to the Inquisition, and although she converses with a protestant minister, she draws parallels between the Catholic church's repression of individual expression and the manner in which the nineteenth-century Lutheran church in Prussia tries to force its adherents into a mold of behavior that disregards their individual needs. She asks the minister incredulously: "Wie können und wollen Sie die Grausamkeit der Inquisition rechtfertigen. Jedes Antasten der Geistesfreiheit ist Inquisition, Ersticken des freien Bewußtseins aus einem verborgnen falschen Grund, den man sich selbst nicht wagt zu bekennen?" (115) Rather than forcing church members to conform to a moral ideal, Frau Rath asserts that those who lead them must address their needs. Resorting to a metaphor common in Arnim's work, she criticizes the minister for delivering sermons that find no resonance among his listeners: "Ihre Predigten! Ja ich bin überzeugt, daß Sie das

Wort Gottes, die Bibel, in voller Kraft erschallen lassen, aber keine Ohren, keine Herzen dieses Vernehmen. Was wollen Sie Herr Prediger?...Es ist kein Widerhall im Menschengeist" (125).

For Frau Rath, then, spiritual and moral development does not result from passive acceptance of or adherence to a fixed doctrine, but rather from active engagement with religious teachings and stories. With this in mind, she recounts the story of a missionary excursion to Africa: "die Missionsdamen machten aus, daß ein getaufter Kaffer unmöglich könne mit unbekleideten Beinen mehr vor Gott der alles sieht herum laufen" (287). The women therefore sewed pants for the potential converts in the dark of the night, "denn da es ein Werk der Schamhaftigkeit war so wollten sie's nicht beim hellen Tag, sondern bei Mondenschimmer und bei Talglichtern betreiben!" (288) As Frau Rath gleefully reports, after all of this hard work the converts did not use the articles of clothing in the manner intended:

> die Hosen sind auch glücklich ohne Sturmwetter am Kap der guten Hoffnung angelangt, sichtbar hat die göttliche Vorsehung grad in der glühenden Sommerzeit gewaltet, wo die Passatwinde sich oft karambulieren und meist viel Schiffsladungen dem Krieg der Elemente zum Opfer fallen, da ist diese Ladung ungefährdet angekommen, denen Täuflingen ausgeteilt worden, sie sind zu Haufen zur Tauf herbeigestürzt, und haben mit Tanzen und großen Luftsprüngen sich taufen lassen, auf den Kopf gesetzt die bunten Blumenhosen, auf beiden Seiten hingen die blumigen Beine herab, und der christliche Glaube und Alles geht herrlich und in floribus in dem Afrika her! (288)

The actions of these *Täuflingen* represent the manner in which one should appropriate Christian teaching: with inventiveness and according to one's own needs. The present-day reader cannot overlook the paternalism inherent in Frau Rath's remarks about the converts. Nevertheless, she limns a vivid picture of the foolishness of colonial policies. Frau Rath considers the church an institution whose primary aim appears to be self-preservation and propagation, and she chastises its remove from those it is supposed to serve.

Drawing a parallel between the church and the state, Frau Rath turns in Part Two to the treatment of the poor and criminals. Ilse Staff has insightfully located *Dies Buch* within the context of Prussian law at the turn of the nineteenth century. Illustrating how crime prevention assumed two different forms—general prevention (instilling fear of the consequences of committing a crime) and special prevention (the attempt to reform prisoners)—Staff notes:

> Das Allgemeine Landrecht für die Preußischen Staaten vom 5. Februar 1794, dessen Entstehungsgeschichte noch in die Zeit Friedrichs des Großen fällt, nimmt durch die eindeutig fixierten gesetzlichen Strafdrohungen den Gedanken der Generalprävention, der Abschreckung, auf; andererseits geht es spezialpräventiv davon aus, daß der Wille des Täters durch die Strafe in die "vernünftige" Richtung gelenkt werden könne und müsse. Das wird insbesondere darin deutlich, daß das ALR neben die eigentliche Strafe die Sicherungshaft stellt, durch die die Resozialisierung des Täters erreicht werden soll (sog. dualistisches System der Verbrechensbekämpfung). So wird z.B. im Paragraph 5, II. Teil, 20. Titel ALR für Diebe und "andere Verbrecher" bestimmt, daß neben der Strafe so lange eine "Verwahrung" erfolgen soll, bis der Nachweis ehrlicher Erwerbsmöglichkeiten erbracht wird. (46)

Frau Rath responds directly to this legal situation—still in place at the time Arnim was writing—when she poses the question:

> Voll welcher Frevel steckten alle Gefängnisse?...Sie habens gewagt frevelhafte Hand anzulegen, an *Den* zu legen für dessen Erlösung der Gott-Sohn sich hingegeben hat, und zwar unter dem Vorwand diesen Gott-Sohn an ihm zu rechtfertigen. Den armen menschlichen Leib haben sie mit großer Grausamkeit geplagt, damit der Geist solle verzagen. Mitten in den kräftigsten Lebensjahren die Männer aus ihrem Familienschoß gerissen, die unschuldigen Kinder, die Mütter der Verzweiflung preisgegeben. Kein Stern hat denen je mehr geleuchtet. *Eine* Krankheit, *ein* Geschwür vom Kopf bis zur Sohle ließen sie diese Gefangnen im Unflat dahinschmachten.—Dabei regierten sie die Welt nach Belieben, genossen alle sinnliche Freuden und es regt sich nicht ein Funke des Gewissens in denen! (162–163)

As the final section of *Dies Buch* so poignantly and prophetically illustrates, neither the moral approach nor the attempt to inspire fear prevents crime. Rather, they lead to its perpetuation, for as soon as one member of the family is thrown into jail, be it for begging, for falling behind in the rent, for theft, or for prostitution, the family has lost a source of income, and with limited legal means of earning more, must turn to crime or begging, the latter also against the law in Berlin at the time. As the *Vogtland* section makes explicit, the need to have food in one's stomach inevitably precedes moral behavior as dictated by laws.

Frau Rath holds the church and the Prussian state responsible for failing to serve their subjects and citizens. Implicit in this criticism is her view that the state and its citizens are intimately bound together. She insists, as Gutzkow noted in his review, "Sünder und Richter stehen im engen Verband. Beide müssen einander auf die höhere Stufen heben. Wahre Menschenliebe ist die innigste Selbstliebe" (198). Frau Rath declares not only that judges must reform sinners and criminals, but that the reverse is also true. Her approach to penal reform is therefore a politics of empathy: one combats social ills by trying to understand them rather than by judging and immediately punishing the perpetrators. She suggests therefore that the church and the state direct their actions towards serving their servants.

In her criticisms of the inquisition, the minister's sermons, and the treatment of criminals and the poor it often seems that Frau Rath is more prepared to criticize than to offer positive advice. The minister registers this feeling in his accusation: "Sie bleiben immer bei den Negativen bei dem was man nicht soll, aber kommen Sie doch auf das Positive auf das was man soll, damit man die Wege der Weisheit offen vor sich sieht!" (226). Frau Rath's response may appear evasive, but it conforms to her ideas about the roles of the mother and the friend, roles that she encourages the king and the state to assume: "Es wär mir lieber Sie möchten's erraten, so weiß ich Sie wären einverstanden mit mir" (226). Rather than neatly packaging solutions in a system, Frau Rath prefers that her listeners (and readers) discover their own answers. This does not imply, however, that Frau Rath advocates a relativity of ideas. Again employing the Socratic method, Frau Rath guides without dictating.

In her relationships with the representatives of church and state, Frau Rath plays the role of mother and teacher rather than that of friend. As a guide, she does not suppress her own ideas entirely, and in her discussions she suggests some specific changes. On the most basic level, she insists on more education for both the king and the people of the state: "Entstehen, sich bilden ist nichts anders als frei werden. Jed sinnlich Wesen ist zugleich ein Geist der aufsteigt aus sich in die Freiheit. Gesehen gefühlt werden vom höheren Wahrnehmungsvermögen, ist die Freiheitswelt des aus der Sinnenwelt aufsteigenden Geistes" (136). Education implies a process in which a self develops through interaction with others and with the environment and vice versa. In response to this need, and in contrast to

Bettine's rejection of formal education in *Günderode*, Frau Rath proposes a *Verbrecheruniversität* as an alternative to the so-called education that criminals and the poor receive in church. She claims they would benefit far more in the "Anstalten von Lehrstühlen, Musensitze, Zenosgänge und sonstige klassische Böden" than from the tautologies offered them in sermons, adding with humor, "Ein geschwätzig Weib erzählt alles dreimal aber die geschwätzige Theologie schwätzt ohne Aufhören dasselbe...was kann davon ein gesunder Verbrecher inspiriert werden" (251).

Frau Rath also comments on the distance between the king and his followers. The text alludes to the attention that Friedrich Wilhelm IV paid to his close circle of advisors when Frau Rath visits the court of Queen Louise and Friedrich Wilhelm III. She describes the *Hofchargen* she meets there as a *heraldischer Tierkreis*: "Löwen Büffel Pfauen Paviane Greife, aber auf ein Gesicht das menschlich schön zu nennen wär besinn ich mich nicht. Das mag davon herkommen, weil diese Menschengattung mehr eine Art politischer Schrauben oder Radwerk an der Staatsmaschinerie und keine rechte Menschen sind" (25). Frau Rath insinuates that this nonhuman *Tiervolk* functions only as a cog in the state machinery and suggests that it should be placed on a separate island to keep it from doing harm: "wie im Traum dacht ich wenn ich König wär ich hielt mir eine apparte Insel vor das heraldische Tiervolk, da könnten sie so fortleben bis sie sterben wollten, aber mir jederzeit unter den Füßen herum zu grabln, daß man alle Augenblicke über sie stolpern müßt, das litt ich nicht" (26). In 1840 Friedrich Wilhelm IV was in the process of handing over his father's collection of exotic animals, kept up until then on the *Pfaueninsel* between Berlin and Potsdam, to the newly founded Berlin Zoological Gardens. It may not be too far-fetched to infer that Arnim was using her sharp sense of irony to suggest that he now had room on the *Pfaueninsel* for his coterie of advisors.

Rather than surrounding himself with advisors, Frau Rath suggests the king assume a less mediated relationship with his subjects: "je näher das Volk seinem Fürsten, je grösser ist dessen Kraft, er schlägt wie ein elektrischer Schlag durch alle Herzen" (87). His ministers would not keep her ideal king isolated from his subjects. He would concern himself with the elevation of humankind in general, provide housing for the poor rather than build monuments to himself, and have no "Gelüste nach Pantheon,

Kirchen, Museen, Naturalien-Kabinetten, Wintergärten und dergleichen" (217). Echoing her concept of friendship, here she envisions the king as a servant rather than one who is served.

The notion of a symbiosis between *Volk und Staat* is, of course, not new in 1840. Härtl has demonstrated the influence upon Arnim of Clemens Brentano and Achim von Arnim's ideal of an "engere[n] Bindung zwischen Dichtung und Leben, [idealem] Volk und Nation" (Arnim, *Werke*, ed. Härtl. vol. 2 909). Further, Wyss has convincingly illuminated the parallels between Arnim's thinking and Novalis's conception of the relationship between people and their ruler in *Glauben und Liebe*. Inspired by these earlier thinkers, Arnim projects the model of romantic sociability onto the structure of the state.

Because Arnim employs the model of romantic sociability, I disagree with Hahn's contention: "Bettina's Zeitgenossen ist die Tendenz dieses Buches völlig klar gewesen. An eine Absicht, sie wolle dem König einen Spiegel vorhalten, um ihn so zu seinem hohen Beruf zu erziehen, hat ernsthaft niemand geglaubt" (38). Hahn argues that Arnim intended her work solely as criticism rather than as an attempt to educate the king. Although this reading may make Arnim's thinking more attractive to the liberal-minded reader, such an interpretation does not make sense within the context of her entire body of work. While the author unquestionably became increasingly disillusioned with the king and with the power of the written word to influence the king or shape the public sphere, she maintained a belief in communication and its potential for bringing about change in the political sphere.

In addition to Arnim's exposure to German romanticism, she was in her adult life also involved in the liberal intellectual movement of the 1830s and 1840s. Leonard Krieger's discussion of the liberal thinking of the *Vormärz* generation proves helpful for understanding the influence of its ideas on Arnim's work. Like many liberals, Arnim desired "the application of ideals to practical activity" (Krieger 279), and she expressed in her texts deep concern about what came to be known as *die Soziale Frage*, that is, the living and working conditions of the poor. At the same time she, like the Young Hegelians, maintained into the 1840s a belief in "the enduring vitality of [the] association between monarchical authority and popular liberties" (275). Like many of her day, she was and remained a monarchist, albeit one who provocatively insisted that the monarch should share sovereignty with the people. Krieger situates the liberals of the 1840s in a spectrum ranging from moderate to radical. At the moderate end one has such thinkers as Friedrich Dahlmann, one of the Göttingen Seven, who attributed "great value to existing institutions" (304) and absolute sovereignty to the monarch. At the opposite end Krieger places the radicals such as Edgar Bauer and Arnold Ruge (both whom Arnim knew), describing them as figures who "look to the people as the agents of a philosophically, morally, and religiously conceived reform" (326). Although one must take seriously Drewitz's warning against "jede radikale Deutung ihrer [Arnim's] Entwicklung" (*Bettine von Arnim* 210), Arnim's thinking and the ideas she expressed in *Dies Buch* tend towards the radical end of the liberal spectrum. For example, although Frau Rath promotes the idea of the monarchy, she does not conceive of the king as directly involved in the day-to-day operations of the state. Rather, the king is to serve as a figurehead, a source of identification, a moral leader whose actions should be governed not by his sense of divine authority or by the advisors of his *heraldischer Tierkreis* but rather by representatives from the general population:

> Wär ich Kaiser ich würde auf dem Römer als der edelsten Schul großer Staatsmänner meine treuen Räte wählen meine Reichsstützen. Was im Kleinen sich erprobt kann im Großen als helles Licht scheinen. Die helle Ansicht moralischer und politischer Fragen traue ich ihnen zu. Wer im Kleinen das Allgemeine im Aug hat umfaßt immer das Ganze, nicht durch Bücher und diplomatisches Studium sondern durch Erfahrung und geübte Bürgertugend, durch Aufmerksamkeit auf Gewinn und Verlust.—Nun Herr Bürgermeister, man rufe mich einst zum Kaiser aus!—was doch meiner Seel auch einstens bei einer Wiederkehrung geschehen kann, denn es ist nicht gesagt daß sie dann grade wieder in einem Weiberrock stecken wird. (301)

The day-to-day business of running the state should fall to a representative government. As a model for this form of government Frau Rath suggests Frankfurt and the manner in which the city was governed before the Napoleonic occupation, when the city was still a *Freie Reichsstadt*. During this time, the Frankfurt Magistrate was responsible for what Frau Rath describes as *das äußerliche Leben*. Without specifying a preference for a parliamentary form of government, Frau Rath insists that rulers (*die Fürsten*) be responsible only for *innere Politik* (85). According to Frau Rath, "sie sollen in allem sich selbst fühlen und für sie heißt es also: Alles was Du andern tust das tust Du Dir selbst!—Wie Nun!—Wär es schwer zu regieren?" (85) Adopting this model, Frau Rath reduces the responsibilities of the king to adhering to the golden rule, to treating his subjects as if there were no difference between himself and them, in other words: to treating them as friends.

Admittedly, with her promotion of both a king and a representative form of government, Frau Rath's message is mixed. She argues that Frankfurt offers "ein Exempel vom schönsten Verhältnis zwischen Fürst und Untertan, Republik und Monarchie zugleich," and she sees two advantages to such a system:

> Daß wir nicht vergebens seufzen nach was wir schon besitzen, die Republik ist unser Himmelbett, die Monarchie ist unser guter Stern am Himmel.—Das zweite Gute, was daraus entspringt. Daß ein großer Monarch wirklich als von göttlicher Abkunft gehalten wird, daß er nämlich nicht in allen Stank sich zu mischen hat…, sondern bloß dann eingreift wenn seine Großmut den Anschlag geben kann. (83)

Here Frau Rath argues that, while she advocates a monarchy, the monarch should serve only as a figurehead and not intervene in the day-to-day operations of the state. Yet one must question the extent to which Frau Rath's solutions are truly radical. She wishes for a representative form of government, but she maintains the belief that it is possible for a king to act in a manner directed by his conscience in the interests of those he serves.

It is also worth noting that Frau Rath never calls for a constitutional monarchy per se. Indeed, when the idea of a constitutional monarchy is raised, she claims that an emotional, spiritual bond between a king and his people has the potential to be much stronger than any legally defined relationship, an idea shared by many of Arnim's Young German contemporaries. In response to the mayor's fear that her ideas "auf eine Konstitution hinaus[laufen]," Frau Rath responds, "Ei was!—Macht das Blut Rechte geltend gegen das Herz?—Kann der Geist eine Grenze ziehen zwischen sich und der Seele?—Bin ich König, so ist das Volk mein Blut." (274) For Frau Rath, then, what ties a king to his people is not the governmental framework of a constitution, but rather a sense of social and familial responsibility to them. The conservative aspects of this text have less to do with the plea for a constitutional monarchy and more to do with Arnim's faith in the power of conversations and social interaction and with the ability of the king to intuit the needs and wishes of his people and then to act on them. Frau Rath's criticisms are thus far more radical than the solutions she hints at. While Frau Rath does make a plea for a change in the actual relationship between the king and his subjects as well as in the manner in which people are governed, and whereas she does, through conversation, poke significant holes in the explanations for state and church actions offered by the minister and the mayor, the most radical voices in the text do not belong to Frau Rath, but to three other personae: Bettine, the magpie, and the "junger Schweizer."

(Bettine): Child and Friend, Scribe and Teacher

Sitting in Frau Rath's shadow throughout most of the text, playful and impudent, we find a nameless figure with whom, of all of her interlocutors, Frau Rath has the closest relationship. As Adolph Stahr recognized in his incendiary review of the text: "Die Stumme Person ist Bettina, auf der Schawell hinter der Frau Rath kauernd,—freilich eine Hauptperson, denn sie ist's, die alle die Reden…in den darauf folgenden Tagen und Nächten zu Papier bringt" (6). Although I would not equate this figure with Arnim herself—especially since traces of the author are to be found in both the child and Frau Rath figures—I would argue that this figure is a continuation of several aspects of Arnim's earlier Bettine personae: she is an impudent child and she is a friend to Frau Rath. The two female characters speak directly with one another with no need for the *Rücksicht* that Frau Rath finds so disagreeable, and this directness leads not to antagonism but to a heightened sense of intimacy and respect.

This Bettine persona plays a small but significant part in the text, for she represents the youthfulness that Arnim valorized in *Günderode*. This reveals itself in the figure's spontaneity: the first time we see her, she has just stolen pears from a garden near the Bockenheimer Gate. It is also evident in the pupil role she often assumes: she sits on a *Schawell*, or stool, next to Frau Rath and listens intently to what the older woman has to say. By presenting her readers with both the Bettine and the Frau Rath personae, Arnim provides representatives of inquisitive, spontaneous youth and mature wisdom, pupil and teacher, child and mother. Furthermore, by valorizing the friendship between these two figures, she emphasizes that these roles are not bipolar opposites but rather part of a fluid continuum.

In her role as child, Bettine not only learns from but also serves as an inspiration for Frau Rath. Significantly, the two are no longer bound by their ardor for Goethe but by their desire to engage with the present. In one conversation with Bettine, Frau Rath's exasperation turns quickly into an expression of warmth:

> Ei ich möcht doch wissen wer mehr vertragen muß, ich oder Du?...Aber ich will nicht undankbar sein, denn daß ich Dich hab das kann ich nicht leugnen, das ist meine Freud! Andre Leut sind mir nichts, Du bist mir alles. Seit Du Dich alle Tag bei mir einfindst gefällt mir mein alt geblümt Tapet wieder, und die Schawell grünt wieder auf! Siehst Du das ist die Verwandtschaft zwischen Deinem Herzen und meinem. Du belebst die Abgestorbenheit des Lebens aufs neu! (307–308)

Whereas Bettine poses as the student, her presence also inspires Frau Rath. She mirrors Frau Rath and serves as her muse, albeit without losing her sense of self in the process. The two are thus autonomous and united, unique individuals with identities that change through interaction with one another.

Although Bettine mirrors Frau Rath, she does not remain passive. Her activity reveals itself first in the fact that she also serves Frau Rath as a teacher, something Frau Rath acknowledges throughout the text. Frau Rath recalls, for example, a conversation with Primate Dalberg:

> Letzt macht mir der Primas sein Kompliment über Deinen Geist wie der Blitz;— ich fragt ob er mich wollt verantwortlich machen für all Deine tolle Einfälle, er meint Dein aufgeweckt Temperament müßte mir Plaisir machen; ich dacht wenn der wüßt wie sie der Frau Rath mitspielt! Alle Augenblick fällst Du mit Deiner unberufnen Verkehrtheit mir über den Hals. Die Judenschulen, die Dorfschulen, die Universitäten, die politische Lage, das deutsche Reich samt den Kurfürsten, das vergangene Jahrhundert, das kommende Jahrhundert, die Sternguckerei. (307)

It is as if this Bettine has shared all of the letters and conversations of the Bettines in *Briefwechsel* and *Günderode* with Frau Rath, and the latter insinuates that many of her own ideas are, in fact, Bettine's. In this manner, the text implies that neither Frau Rath nor Bettine views herself as the original source of the idea she espouses. Recalling Bettine's musings about writing in *Briefwechsel* and *Günderode*, the text presents thought as a collective process.

More obscure than the source of the text's ideas is answer to the question, Who is speaking? *Dies Buch* begins with the section entitled "Frau Rath erzählt" One cannot forget, however, the almost invisible frame of the text: Bettine writing down what she has heard. Although hidden, we have here one of Bettine's most important roles: writer. Whereas Frau Rath communicates entirely through conversation, Bettine sits in the background, recording what Frau Rath says, embellishing and shaping the older woman's words to suit her own purposes. At one point, she asks, "Will sie [Frau Rath] wissen was sie gestern und vorgestern geredet hat?—Da ist alles aufgeschrieben!" to which Frau Rath replies, "Acht und zwanzig Seiten!—Nun du wirst mir manchen Placken da hineingefleckt haben, der nicht von meinem Zeug ist.—Der Sokrates hat sich das auch müssen vom Plato gefallen lassen" (184). As the disciple of Frau Rath, this figure serves as the creator, the shaper of Frau Rath. Apparently the listener, she becomes the ultimate recorder of the story. In a move that underscores the genealogy that she began to create with *Briefwechsel*, Arnim positions Bettine as *Mittler* between Frau Rath and us, the readers of the text, thus encouraging us to see in Bettine a daughter of and heir to Frau Rath.

Die französische Atzel: Devil, Daemon, Mother, Revolutionary

In the penultimate section of *Dies Buch*, "Das Gespräch der Frau Rath mit einer Französischen Atzel," we find Frau Rath and Bettine alone with a French magpie, a gift to Frau Rath from a French soldier with whom, according to Bettine, Frau Rath had fallen in love. Frau Rath appears annoyed with the bird because "[er] den ganzen Stubenboden voll macht" (305), but she is reluctant to take Bettine's advice to set it free. As Bettine tells her, "Nun ja da kanns die andern Ätzeln klug machen und kann eine Apostel in die Wüste senden unter die Menschheit" (307). From the beginning of this section, Bettine aligns herself with the magpie and understands its function as a messenger. This is further emphasized when she invites the bird: "Komm Satan, setz dich auf mein Kopf und parlier mit der Frau Rath" (309). Teamed together in this manner, the magpie and Bettine assume a radical position against which Frau Rath plays the foil. Indeed, at times Frau Rath's responses to her counterparts seem so exaggerated that one has to wonder whether she is not winking as she responds to the magpie: "Ei Teufel Du machst mich Toll Du hasts drauf abgesehen mich zu ärgern mit Deinen dummen Behauptungen" (309). Throughout Arnim's writing, one finds protagonists who require opposing opinions in order to develop their own ideas. In the absence of the minister and the mayor, Frau Rath assumes the position of the skeptic.

As is evident from the passages cited in the preceding paragraph, the text associates the magpie first and foremost with the devil. As Bunzel et al. point out, "Die Teufelsgestalt im *Königsbuch* vereint zwei Traditionsstränge: die des aufklärerischen Lucifer, der für das Prinzip der Erkenntnis steht, und die der romantischen Satansfigur, die als unerbittlicher Kritiker an den gesellschaftlichen Verhältnissen und damit in der Rolle des Sozialrevolutionärs auftritt" (*DB* 1031).[10] The magpie as devil becomes both a figure of enlightenment and a revolutionary, and both roles come together for Arnim under the rubric of daemon. It is thus no coincidence that Bettine describes the bird to Frau Rath as "ein Dämon der schon eine Stunde da sitzt und ihr die Geheimnisse einer neuen Erlösung demonstriert" (325).

In keeping with Arnim's understanding of the term, this daemon is both teacher and inspiration. Its ideas stem from those of earlier Bettines, and they presage the musings of the title figure of *Dämonen*. As teacher, the magpie humorously suggests an inversion of heaven and hell. Hell proves to be a holding pen for nobility and philistines similar to the island that Frau Rath suggests for the king's *heraldischer Tierkreis*. Here they are fed illusions in the form of "Preisausteilungen and Orden" (310) to keep them out of trouble. While the magpie must help the other devils to keep the inhabitants of hell pacified, it claims a far more important function as creator and inspiration. As the magpie reminds Frau Rath, it was the devil who encouraged human beings to eat the "Frucht der Erkenntnis...das war das erste Prinzip der Selbsterzeugung" (318). Furthermore, the devil is a proponent of revolution, and like earlier Bettine figures, maintains as a motto the phrase *es werde*. As daemon, the magpie bears a message of individual development free of interference from church or any other external dogma. Such development is not a product of order and moral dictates but rather of chaos and freedom. Frau Rath recalls after the magpie disappears: "Rätsel hat sie vorgebracht die kein Mensch erraten mag, die die moralische Welt in ihrem Mittelpunkt erschüttern, und die gefährlichsten Kräfte der Einbildung wild untereinander stürzen und alles zertrümmern was Gewohnheit, Sitte und Glaube geheiligt haben!" (325)

The last page of the section underscores the magpie's message of upheaval and change; a bolt of lightening causes a fire at the *Kathrinenturm*, a symbol of church authority. As in the scene with the old woman and the saddle, optimism and idealism collide here with a keen awareness of the difficulty inherent in achieving lasting change:

> Da seh nur unserm Kathrinenturm sein Zopf brennt!—guck nur wie er seine Stirn kraus zieht. Ja guter Kerl deine Nachtmütz brennt ab.—Wann werden sie dir dein Wetterdach flicken? da werden Jahrszeiten drüber hingehen, und das Wasser wird dir in die Ank laufen! nehm dich in acht! daß du den Schnupfen nicht kriegst.— Guck jetzt steigen sie aufs Dach.—
> "Ja und da kommt die Feuerspritz und spritzt alles daneben!" (328)

The pigtail ascribed to the church recalls the hair style introduced by Friedrich Wilhelm I and rejected by the liberals in the French Revolution; moreover the night cap was commonly associated with the *Philister* and especially *der deutsche Michel*. As such, the church tower comes to stand for the outdated church and state that, for a moment, seem about to be consumed by the fire of revolution. The fire has been extinguished, but as Frau Rath points out with no small hint of sarcasm, the structure leaks, and water will continue to cause damage over decades. The reader is left to wonder whether this slow leak will ultimately cause more damage than a raging fire that attracts attention and is quickly extinguished. The fact that Arnim ends this section with her official dedication of the text to the king suggests that she hopes her work will effect gradual but permanent change.

Der junge Schweizer, another face of the Daemon

One final figure in the text bears mention: the narrator of the final section, the unnamed *junger Schweizer* who records his impressions of the infamous *Armenviertel*, the Berliner Vogtland. Aspects of the Bettine personae in Arnim's first two novels—fragmented but held together under the rubric of the name "Bettine"—become divided in this text among three personae: Frau Rath, Bettine, and the French magpie. They have distinct identities and personalities but also have their origins in earlier Bettines and in the ideas and experiences of the author herself. The intertextual links in Arnim's works encourage the reader to make these associations, and Arnim reception has shown that Arnim was especially effective at creating a link between herself and the Frau Rath and Bettine personae of her texts. One can also read the magpie as an extension of Bettine incarnated as representative of an anti-religion of the individual. *Der junge Schweizer* is yet another extension and fragmentation of Bettine.

The author of the Vogtland report was indisputably no fictional character. In February of 1843, Arnim met the young Swiss pedagogue Heinrich Grunholzer at the apartment of Jakob and Wilhelm Grimm where he was staying while attending lectures at the Berlin University. Upon learning that the head of an organization to help the poor had promised to acquaint Grunholzer with charity projects in Berlin, she asked him to collect material for her. She included this material, for which she paid him 50 talers, in slightly altered form in *Dies Buch*.

Just as in the case of Catharina Elisabeth Goethe, *der junge Schweizer* to whom Arnim attributes the final section of *Dies Buch* loses a degree of historical identity to become a part of the net of meanings and associations that Arnim has woven around "Bettine." Arnim's works encourage this identification, for this section continues the social engagement that one finds in the depiction of Ephraim in *Günderode* and in that of the Tyrolean uprising in *Briefwechsel*. Like the Bettine persona of *Dies Buch*, the young Swiss man assumes the role of listener and scribe, giving voice to but also commenting on stories told by the poor inhabitants of the *Vogtland*. Finally, this figure's presence in the *Vogtland* resonates with Arnim's activities in the service of the poor and oppressed: her engagement during the cholera epidemic of 1831 and her letter writing campaigns on behalf of the Grimms and Spontini, for example.

The reception of *Dies Buch* would indicate that readers have associated Arnim with the person visiting the *Vogtland* even though there is no evidence that Arnim, her social engagement notwithstanding, ever set foot in the area (Geist and Kürvers 215). On September 19, 1843, the Berlin newspaper *Die Stafette* published an article entitled "Bettina in den

Berliner Familien-Häusern" that attributed the final account to Arnim. The article begins:

> Man denke sich! Bettina, die einst als Kind nur in den überschwenglichen Idealen schwärmte und keine größere Seligkeit kannte, als vor Göthe, ihrem Liebes-Abgott, wie ein unsterbliches Kind genienhaft zu tanzen, ist jetzt als Greisin herabgestiegen in das tiefste Elend Berlins, in die schmutzigste Wirklichkeit, in welche jede Spur von Idealen unter Lumpen, Hunger, Schmutz und Thränen verkümmert ist. (Quoted in Geist and Kürvers 211)

Novels and scholarly works have followed this lead. In his 1850 novel, *Reaktionäre und Demokraten*, Karl Ludwig Häberlin describes Arnim as the "Erzähler" of these accounts (111); in the 1977 study of the *Sozialroman*, Erich Edler's discussion of *Dies Buch* emphasizes Grunholzer's appendix but generally attributes the ideas expressed in it to Arnim. Like Frau Rath, then, the young Swiss man can be viewed as yet another Bettine persona.

Whereas the magpie makes a case for the emancipation of the individual, the young Swiss educator takes up the cause of those whom church and state refuse to treat as individuals. One of the most unique and moving aspects of this section is that it allows the poor to speak for themselves. In this report we hear from women who must prostitute themselves to stave off hunger, a family that falls ever deeper into debt after the husband is arrested for begging, 2,500 individuals living in tenement buildings with only four hundred rooms. Together with the narrator's commentary, the stories told by the interviewees reveal the false logic behind the policies governing treatment of the poor. As the figure G. remarks, "Man gibt uns keine Arbeit, verbietet das Stehlen und wirft uns ins Loch, wenn wir betteln" (337). Rather than locking the poor in a vicious circle of imprisonment and further poverty, the narrator (echoing Frau Rath) suggests: "Wo die Not so groß ist, muß man tätig unterstützen, nicht moralisieren, bis die Leute vor Hunger sterben. Auch ist zu bedenken daß die Hoffnung wieder aufzukommen, Kraft gibt zur Bekämpfung des Leichtsinnes" (335). Rather than warding off criminality, this report suggests that the laws of the *Allgemeine Landrecht* actually promote it. With this account, the young Swiss man reveals the mistreatment of the poor by the state while reminding the reader that the poor are individuals deserving of a chance to educate and develop themselves. In so doing, he provides evidence for the need for the changes proposed in the earlier sections of the text.

Summary: Conforming? Transgressing?

In *Dies Buch gehört dem König* Arnim no longer presents us with one central figure who assumes multiple roles. Rather, four different personae possess attributes that can be found in and have developed out of earlier Bettines. In Frau Rath we find a valorization of old age, wisdom, and female attributes. As the most visible figure in the text, she serves as teacher, philosopher, critic, and daemon. The figure who sits on a stool next to Frau Rath plays a childlike role, describes herself as the Plato to Frau Rath's Socrates, and records everything Frau Rath says; this figure resembles most closely the Bettines of earlier texts. The French magpie represents the philosophy of "becoming" and of revolution. Finally, the young Swiss educator is a figure who has had direct contact with the poor of Berlin. His report offers concrete evidence of the need for changes proposed by Frau Rath and the magpie.

One might be tempted to argue that, in a time of censorship and of spying associated with the *Demagogenverfolgung*, Arnim fragmented her "Bettine" as a means of distancing herself as author from the more critical aspects of her text in order to avoid censorship. If this was the case, it certainly was not effective, as the story of Arnim's dealings with Prussian censorship laws reveals.

Before it appeared in July of 1843, the text was not subject to censorship. First, Alexander von Humboldt had secured permission from the king for Arnim to dedicate the text to him. Second, because of the book's length, Arnim was not required to present her book to the censors before publication: the most recent censorship law of October 4, 1842, based on the Carlsbad Decrees of 1819, released all books longer than 20 signatures[11] from this obligation.[12] Nonetheless, as Houben notes in *Verbotene Literatur von der klassischen Zeit bis zur Gegenwart*, this loophole did not mean that the book was forever safe from confiscation, nor did it indicate growing tolerance of free speech on the part of the state:

> Man maß damals die geistige Nahrung nach dem Scheffel; den Leser eines Buches von 21 Bogen hielt man für weniger gefährlich als den einer Broschüre

von vielleicht nur wenigen Seiten; deren Verbreitungsmöglichkeit war schon durch den Preis größer, deshalb behandelte man das kleinere Buch strenger als das größere. (35–36)

Once Prussian officials actually read Arnim's book (the king most certainly did not do so initially), its challenge to state authority became clear. In a report to the king dated August 17, 1843 the Prussian Minister of the Interior, Count Adolf Heinrich von Arnim-Boitzenburg, enumerated the treasonous aspects of *Dies Buch*. He claimed that Arnim derived her worldview "aus einem excentrischen an Fanatismus grenzenden Eifer für die abstracte Idee des Rechts" and insisted that her work was an affront to all "Prinzipien des bestehenden Staats, des Christenthums und der socialen Einrichtung jeder Art" (quoted in Houben 34). Finally, he asserted that only the ecstatic style of the text hid its radical message from the majority of readers:

> Wäre das Buch, statt in dem nur für einen kleinen Leserkreis geeigneten Tone prophetischer Exstase, in der dem größern Publikum zugänglichen Form einfacher Logik und verständiger Reflexion geschrieben, und trüge nicht der abentheuerliche Charakter der wenn auch nicht genannten, doch bekannten Verfasserin dazu bei, die praktische Richtigkeit und Anwendung der darin enthaltenen Doktrinen in Zweifel zu stellen, so würde dasselbe, den gesetzlichen Bestimmungen nach, vermöge der darin dargelegten und vertheidigten Irreligiösität und vermöge des darin gepredigten heillosen Radicalismus für eine der gemeingefährlichsten Schriften erklärt werden müssen. (35)

The danger of *Dies Buch* lay in the possibility that someone would translate its contents into plain German. Because it was dedicated to the king, this would create the dual impression that the king approved of its contents and that the state was easing up on its interpretation of censorship laws.

As Karl August von Varnhagen wrote, once Friedrich Wilhelm IV actually read the text that initially had his blessing, his mood became "wahrer Unwille."[13] Furthermore, Arnim-Boitzenburg's report proved prophetic, for Stahr's positive review of the text (1843, dated 1844) distilled the ideas of Arnim's text to an abbreviated and more accessible form. Because no newspaper was willing to print the review, Stahr published it as a pamphlet, which was immediately banned in Prussia. In response, Bavaria and Austria banned the pamphlet and confiscated all available copies of Arnim's text. Of course, the banning of the book only increased its popularity. As Konrad notes in his edition of Arnim's works, *Dies Buch* was second only to *Briefwechsel* in the number of tributes, and in the number of criticisms, that it received (vol. 3 461).

As this summary of Arnim's fencing with the Prussian censor would indicate, there was never any question about the author of the text, and Arnim's readership automatically associated her with at least two of the figures in the text: Frau Rath and the child. Rather than interpreting the division of Bettine into four personae as a means of evasion, then, I suggest that it allowed Arnim to depict communication in what she considered to be its ideal form. Whereas the mayor and the minister serve as little more than foils for Frau Rath, the conversations between Frau Rath, Bettine, and even the magpie are characterized by a combination of intimacy and *Rücksichtslosigkeit*. These figures challenge and question one another, and their ideas develop dialectically through conversation. Arnim offers this portrait of communication to Friedrich Wilhelm IV as a model for the relationship that she envisions between a king and his people. Reverting to the metaphor of the apple, the wisdom of the text can be found not only in the ideas it champions but also—one could even argue especially—in the manner in which those ideas are developed.

In addition to contributing to the message of the open letter to the king, these four figures may have served a more personal function as well. As Ursula Püschel has observed, Arnim's possibilities for action were fairly limited. She could act in the interest of individuals such as Spontini, or later, Hoffmann von Fallersleben, who lost his professorship in Breslau following the publication of his *Unpolitischen Lieder* in 1840 and 1841. The only possibility she had to effect change in a larger public arena was to whisper into the ear of the king.[14] In contrast to her day-to-day life in Berlin, she created in *Dies Buch* an ideal space in which she could try on a wider variety of roles. In Frau Rath she could see herself reflected as salon hostess and valorize her aging, something that, as her correspondences with Pückler-Muskau, Döring, and Nathusius indicate, did not come easily to her. In the Bettine figure, she could portray herself as writer while holding on to the role of the youthful sprite. The magpie allowed her to present herself as a radical with the means of communicating her message to a broad group of listeners/readers. The mask of the young Swiss educator allowed her to become a man who could move freely from one country to another and who had publicly recognized authority. Thus, although the text itself does not focus on issues of individual development, it can be argued that it allowed the author Arnim to develop in ways not open to her in the public sphere.

Arnim's text was very much a response to contemporary politics, and reception of *Dies Buch* has addressed this text as a political novel. Yet while some (Stahr, Fromm, Hahn, Püschel) have focused on the progressive elements of the text in order to emphasize what they consider to be its socialist or even communist tendencies, others have argued that Arnim's support of a constitutional monarchy was illusionary or even reactionary (Staff, Waldstein), especially since the radicals of her day, disillusioned by the broken promises of constitutions after the Wars of Liberation, were already calling for a republic.

The text certainly makes a case for a more even distribution of wealth, and it convincingly illustrates how the church and the state alienate those whom, according to the text, they are supposed to serve. The text also hints that the continued inaction of church and state will lead to revolution. Indeed, the book presages not only the coming revolutions of 1848 but also the relative ease with which those revolutions were ultimately squelched. As Waldstein has indicated, it does not, however, offer any "alternative political framework or ideology, within which many of her specific suggestions concerning social welfare could come to fruition" (100). One finds in *Dies Buch*, for example, no systematic model for how wealth should be redistributed or for how labor should be valued. It would thus be inaccurate to claim that Arnim's texts advocated any form of a democratic or pre-socialist state as an alternative to the monarchy, even though one must recognize that Austrian and Bavarian authorities considered these texts threatening enough to ban them and that, after the publication of this text, Prussian authorities were so leery of Arnim that *Frühlingskranz* was immediately confiscated upon publication.

Although Arnim worked within the framework of a constitutional monarchy, she was not a naive monarchist who was "unable to overcome her desire for a hierarchical structure" (Waldstein 100). Arnim was, and here I would agree with Püschel, a pragmatist who knew that, in order to have any influence on public affairs, she had to work within the structure in which she was confined. She knew how to level quite damaging criticism, but she also knew she could not afford to alienate the king entirely, something that happened in spite of her intentions. Furthermore, while Arnim may be criticized for her inability to join the most radical voices of her day by calling for an abolition of the monarchy, one must recognize that, as she does with so many other concepts she employs, she uses her text to redefine the monarchy and the power ascribed to the king. By suggesting, for example, that not the king but a body similar to the pre-Napoleonic *Frankfurter Magistrate* would be in charge of day-to-day government operations, she would deprive the king of his ruling powers and introduce a republican form of government. The king's function is to be a moral authority and educator of the people in a manner parallel to that in which Bettine and Frau Rath educate each other. By employing romantic sociability as a model for the relationship between a king and his people, the text makes a plea for breaking down political hierarchies and for empowering citizens to play a role in governance. Admittedly, Arnim was idealistic insofar as she falsely believed that a ruler could be persuaded to voluntarily give up his power and to consider the people as "das Höhepunkt nach dem der Lauf der Sterne berechnet wird" (297). But insofar as her model for the relationship between the king and the people, like her model for conversation, appears to have been intended to break down rather than sustain hierarchies, she wrote her text in the spirit of the revolutions that were to come later in the decade.

CHAPTER FOUR

Child Turns Woman:
Clemens Brentano's Frühlingskranz (1844)

Bettina von Arnim published the majority of her works during the turbulent 1840s, and her writing bears the mark of the political upheavals of the decade preceding the revolution of 1848. In addition to the activities of the moderate and radical liberals, the Young Germans, and the Young Hegelians, one other group deserves mention within the context of this period: the diverse and not always unified women who made up the women's movement. With their literary and journalistic endeavors and social and political activism they began the unified public struggle, still continuing today, to achieve equal rights and opportunities for women.

In research on women's social and literary history published since the mid-seventies, feminist scholars have generally agreed not to include Arnim among this group. As in so many aspects of her life and writing, here again she defies categorization. She does not belong to the group of women writers born before her, including Wilhelmine Eberhard (1757–1817), Sophie Brentano-Mereau (1761–1806), Karoline von Wolzogen (1763–1847), Johanna Schopenhauer (1770–1838), and Fanny Tarnow (1783–1862) who, according to Renate Möhrmann, did not question traditional gender roles in their writing (*Die andere Frau* 30). The women generally considered to be Bettina's romantic sisters—Caroline Schlegel Schelling (1763–1809), Dorothea Schlegel (1764–1839), Rahel Varnhagen (1771–1833), and Karoline von Günderrode (1780–1806)—did actually question prescribed gender roles in their letters and other texts, but unlike Arnim, experienced significant difficulty crossing as writers from the private into the public sphere. Neither Schlegel

Schelling nor Varnhagen published her own work, and both Dorothea Schlegel and Günderrode published under pseudonyms. Moreover, Arnim did not share the group identity of those women, born in the first two decades of the nineteenth century, who founded the women's movement in Germany, and who, again in the words of Möhrmann, "selbstständig und selbstbewußt ihre eigenen Interessen [verkündeten]" (3). Members of this group included Mathilde Franziska Anneke (1817–1884), Louise Aston (1814–1871), Ida Hahn-Hahn (1805–1880), Fanny Lewald (1811–1889), Malvida von Meysenbug (1816–1903), Clara Mundt (1814–1873) writing under the pseudonym of Luise Mühlbach, and Louise Otto-Peters (1819–1895). In their novels, journalistic writing, and public activity these women attended to four main concerns: the improvement of educational opportunities for girls, women's development of an autonomous sense of self, the opening the workforce to women, and the eradication of marriages of convenience (Möhrmann, "Die Teilnahme..." 378).

Of course, Bettina von Arnim's texts deal extensively with the issues of education and development of the individual. She became a working woman following Achim von Arnim's death in 1831. She expressed her criticisms of the institution of marriage in her public and private writings. She also shared with women such as Louise Otto-Peters a deep concern for the poverty that she saw growing out of the arrival of the industrial revolution in the German territories. Nevertheless, Arnim never addressed the issue of the emancipation of women *qua* women, nor did she ever indicate any sense of identification with women as a group. In contrast to Otto-Peters, who chose as the motto for her *Frauen-Zeitung*, "Dem Reich der Freiheit werb' ich Bürgerinnen"[1] (Frevert 74), Arnim was more interested in the broader (and more abstract) concept of freedom for all human beings.

With regard to the documentation of the German women's movement, then, Möhrmann was justified in her decision not to include Arnim in her anthology *Frauenemanzipation im deutschen Vormärz*. Equally insightful, however, was her presentation in *Die andere Frau* of Arnim as an important transitional figure. Indeed, many of those writers whom Möhrmann includes among the first generation of the German women's movement— Louise Aston, Fanny Lewald, Malvida von Meysenbug, and Clara

Mundt—recognized this by paying homage to Arnim in their memoirs and fictional texts.

According to Möhrmann, Arnim created a bridge between eras not in her early epistolary texts but rather in *Dies Buch gehört dem König* with its assertion: "die Domäne der Politik [ist] nicht nur das Reservat der Männer" (36). Frau Rath actively promotes her ideas as those of a woman and strives to feminize the public sphere. One cannot forget here that change—in this case a change in gender roles and the position of women in society—is a long and difficult process requiring both personal and political, private and public effort: laws must change, the workplace must change, men must change, women themselves must change. Furthermore, as Adelson and Lauretis remind us, change occurs in different ways for different individuals depending on their individual positionalities. Although Arnim does not write in the service of the women's movement, the development of her Bettine personae documents a remarkable change in her perception of women and women's roles. In contrast to Möhrmann, I would argue that in no text is Arnim's consideration of gender roles more foregrounded than in *Clemens Brentano's Frühlingskranz*.

Following the publication of *Dies Buch*, Arnim turned again in her writing to material from her past, namely to her relationship and the letters she exchanged with Clemens Brentano between the years 1800–1803. The beginning of this time frame is marked by Bettina Brentano's re-acquaintance with her brother in October of 1797 when she was twelve and he nineteen. Clemens and his sister Sophie had been sent to live with relatives, initially to relieve the child-rearing duties of their mother Maximilane Brentano, who had born twelve of Peter Anton Brentano's twenty-one children and who died 1793. At the end of the text's time frame, in 1803, Clemens marries Sophie Mereau. Although Clemens and Bettine, as well as later critics, would agree that their temperaments were the most closely matched among the Brentano siblings, what began as an emotionally intense relationship soon showed signs of tension. Despite the fact that both Bettina and Clemens prized individuality and therefore refused to conform to the mores of middle-class German society, both the paths they chose and the fates that befell them insured that they would defy social norms in starkly differing manners. Arnim's development included a marriage and seven children, widowhood, a professional life as writer of her own works and publisher of the works of Achim von Arnim, and an impressive record of social engagement. She remained politically active throughout her life, and she held on to early romantic ideals of the autonomy of the individual (ideals that were to an extent imparted to her by her brother). In contrast, Clemens Brentano's first marriage ended in sorrow with Sophie Mereau's death in childbirth in 1806. He married the sixteen-year-old, emotionally unstable Auguste Bussmann in 1807 only to divorce her in 1812.[2] In 1817 he returned to the Catholic faith from which he had strayed in his youth, and he moved to Dülmen in Westfalia in 1819 in order to record the visions of the stigmatized nun Anna Katharina Emmerich.[3] Despite their divergent paths, Bettina and Clemens maintained contact with one another until the latter's death in 1842. The tension in their relationship reached its peak with Clemens's objection to the publication of *Goethe's Briefwechsel mit einem Kinde*, but correspondence continued, and Arnim often wrote letters of introduction for those among her admirers who hoped to meet Clemens during their travels.

In writing *Frühlingskranz*, Arnim erased almost forty years in order to focus on the first six years of a relationship with an individual with whom she had become acquainted before she met either Günderrode or Goethe. Indeed, when she published her collected works beginning in 1853, *Frühlingskranz* appeared as the first volume in the series, apparently indicating that she considered the Bettine of this text to be the predecessor of the main figures of her subsequent texts. Lorely French posits two reasons for Arnim's decision to publish her fourth text as the first volume in this series: "Historically, *Der Frühlingskranz* is the first correspondence. Aesthetically, the correspondence with her brother is an effective introduction to her epistolary theories and their application in praxis" (*Bettine von Arnim* 426). The argument for reading *Frühlingskranz* as the first work of Arnim's sextology also finds support in the three extant original letters of those Arnim incorporated into her text. Here one sees that "Bettine bei der Überarbeitung zwar konzentrierte und modifizierte und auch die Chronologie durchbrach, um die Briefe zu einem 'Kranz,' einem lesbaren Briefroman, zusammenzufügen, aber dabei doch in der Regel behutsam vorging" (Schultz, "Nachwort" 357).[4] Although this claim cannot be proven because most of the original letters of the correspondence have disappeared, the argument that Arnim's spring wreath was woven solely out of original correspondence would appear to support a reading of this text as the beginning of the story of Bettina/Bettine.

As such, one could also read Arnim's depiction of the relationship between her fictional Bettine and fictional Clemens as her answer to Brentano's depiction of his sister in *Godwi* (1801), the second part of which he also dedicated to her. Here one finds the young Bettina Brentano thinly veiled in the figure Annonciata, a "Wunderkind" (318) and a "stilles und oft heftiges Wesen" (310). In her own artistic rendering of herself, Arnim presents us with a persona who has no wish for her brother to admire her, who wants to be accepted for who she is and for the person she determines herself to be.

Yet despite the time frame of the text, the reader who approaches Arnim's works in the order in which they were written cannot help but be struck by the self-assurance of this figure in comparison to that of the main figures in *Briefwechsel* and *Günderode*, by the manner in which this Bettine's refusal to be a "Weib wie es sein sollte" echoes not only debates about gender roles taking place during early romanticism but also those current in the 1840s. As opposed to Arnim's earlier works, this figure distances herself from the role of child and consciously looks to adult women as her models. At the same time, the return to a focus on individual development does not neglect issues of politics and questions of the good life for society as a whole; Bettine's defense of heroes of the French Revolution reminds her readers that personal struggles for autonomy are the basis for the political visions foregrounded in this text's immediate predecessor, *Dies Buch*, and in Arnim's later *Gespräche mit Dämonen*.[5]

As with her earlier works, then, *Frühlingskranz* must be read with double vision: as a product of Arnim's youth and of her adult life, as inspired by early romantic discussions of gender and by the frustrations of a woman striving to be publicly active in the mid-nineteenth century. Varnhagen's diary entry from 28 April 1844, in which he describes discussions with Arnim about the progress of the work, confirms that she made changes to the original letters: "Sie sagte mir selbst, daß sie jetzt beim Abschreiben manches hinzufüge, ausbilde, näher bestimme" (*Tagebücher*, vol. 2 291). Because the text stems from two developmental periods in the life of the author Arnim, one can read it not only as the first work of her autobiography but also as a continuation of the story of her

Bettine personae, figures who are sometimes older (as when they hide behind the mask of Frau Rath) and sometimes younger (as when they play the child), but who continuously adhere to their collective motto, *es werde*.

Arnim returns in *Frühlingskranz* not only to what, on the surface at least, seems to be the setting of her youth, but also to epistolary writing as a vehicle for exploring the development of the ideas and the characters in the text. Here, to a greater extent than in *Briefwechsel* and *Günderode*, the epistolary form reveals the increasing distance between the correspondents. Letters cross in the mail, both Clemens and Bettine write second letters without having received and read responses to first letters. Recalling Altman's description of the literary letter as both bridge and marker of distance (186), the correspondence in this text serves the latter function. As the text evolves, the letters communicate less and less with each other, creating the impression of an increasing sense of isolation felt by both correspondents, but especially by Clemens.[6]

Arnim begins this work as she does her previous ones with a brief introduction and dedication. The text is prefaced by two quotations, attributed to Clemens, in which he admonishes Bettine to keep his letters. The second offers the purported source of the title of the text: "Verliere keinen meiner Briefe, halte sie heilig, sie sollen mich einst an mein besseres Selbst erinnern, wenn mich Gespenster verfolgen, und wenn ich tot bin so flechte sie mir in einen Kranz—Holland 1808" (9).[7] With these epigraphs, Arnim reintroduces herself as sister, writer, and literary historian, for she is taking on the task of reacquainting the public with her deceased brother's poems and letters. Furthermore, as Hartwig Schultz has argued, Arnim uses these introductory passages to justify the publication of *Frühlingskranz* to her family ("Nachwort" 346). Around the time of the publication of her ode to Clemens, her brother Christian Brentano was working on the publication of his brother's collected works, editing out evidence of the younger, wilder Clemens Brentano to whom Arnim pays homage in her text. The epigraphs thus serve as proof (offered, perhaps, with a wink) that she was doing no more than carrying out the express wishes of her brother.

Whereas the introductory pages pay homage to Clemens Brentano, Arnim dedicates the text to His Royal Highness, Prince Waldemar of Prussia (1817–1848), son of Wilhelm of Prussia (the future Emperor

Wilhelm I). A close friend of Arnim's children and enamored for a time of her daughter Maximiliane, Prince Waldemar frequently visited Arnim's Berlin salon in the 1840s. According to Drewitz, by dedicating her text to this prince (who was more open to Arnim's pedagogical efforts than was Friedrich Wilhelm IV) Arnim gives voice to her "tiefe Sympathie" (202) with this sensitive, politically liberal son of a much harsher father.

In the wake of the scandal caused by *Dies Buch*, Berlin censors brought publication of *Frühlingskranz* to a halt on May 24, 1844, and it was not released again until June 10. The reasons cited for the censorship included her choice of the left-leaning Edgar Bauer as publisher, the "respektwidrige[n] Inhalt der Zueignung" (*CBF* 999), and the fact that—as with *Dies Buch*—the author's name was missing from the first page. Whereas any informed reader would have quickly ascertained who the author of the text was, thus making the problems with the title page a mere matter of formality, Arnim's dedication was indisputably provocative. Although she begins by addressing the prince, "Lieber Prinz Waldemar," she then says that she cannot decide how she should behave towards him: "Da man aber einem Prinzen gegenüber durchaus schicklich sein muß, Aufrichtigkeit aber Unschicklichkeit ist, so machen sich *Euer Hoheit* gefaßt, entweder was Unschickliches zu hören oder was Unaufrichtiges" (11). With irony, Arnim discloses the complications one encounters when trying to address a member of the royal family with candor. To avoid this difficulty, she decides instead to address herself to the people in the marketplace, in other words to a public:

> In welchem ich mich heimisch fühle, das mich angeregt durch seinen Beifall und durch sein Einverständnis mich inspiriert, zu dem kann ich doch wohl reden ohne Einwendung; da Aufrichtigkeit bei diesem auch Schicklichkeit ist. Nun also: Ihr Leute auf dem Markt!—Ich hab dies Frühlingsduftende Buch nur dem darbieten können, gegen den ich keinen Zweifel hege, der Feldblumenkranz könne ihm zu gering sein. (11)

Anticipating the text's allusions to the French Revolution, Arnim praises the people for valuing honesty and frankness. She tells them further that she can dedicate her text only to those who appreciate its honesty. Such a claim calls into question whether Arnim actually intended the text for Prinz Waldemar or for a broader reading public that she terms *das Volk*.

With one exception, the remainder of the text consists of a letter exchange between Clemens and Bettine, interspersed with poems by Clemens. Initially these letters flow out of one another, but by the end of the text they contradict and bypass each other. The first two letters of the text provide a sense of the nature of the relationship between the two siblings. They dearly love each other but also talk past each other when attempting to express this love. In his first letter to Bettine, Clemens, standing in the long tradition of men who wished the women in their lives to mirror them, endeavors to claim her as his muse:

> Ich habe jetzt außer Dir für keinen Menschen ein ganz lebendiges Interesse das mir selbst Mut geben kann mich in die Höhe zu arbeiten. Du gibst mir Kraft und Mut und Aussicht, wenn Du in allem Guten gedeihest, denn Du gedeihest meinem wärmeren Anteil an Dir. Suche Dich über das was man Dir als Pflicht zumutet zu erheben, mache daß Alles um Dich zufrieden ist. Was Du mehr in Dir fühlst als das gewöhnliche *Bravsein* dafür hat die arme Welt ja doch keine Ordnung, das mußt du still in Dir bilden und Gott selbst dafür Rechnung stehen und mit der ganzen Harmonie der Gefühle dafür dankbar sein…Lebe wohl! sei recht fleißig am Ofenschirm damit er bald fertig wird, ich freue mich darauf, daß die Flamme durch sein Gewebe schimmert und ich klimpere dann auf der Guitarre dazu Lieder und Melodien die Dein sind. (13)

The first line of this letter recalls the correspondence in *Günderode*: Clemens tells Bettine that she gives him the strength to develop and form himself, just as Bettine told Günderode that there was no one else with whom she could speak, in whom she could see herself reflected. Then, Clemens proceeds to describe the Bettine in whom he wishes to see himself. She must be "good," she must do more than is expected of her in order to please others, and she must engage in the women's work of adorning with needlework a screen for a tile oven.

In her response, Bettine wishes she could meet her brother halfway, that she could reciprocate his love for her, but she seeks a type of friendship and love markedly different from what he can offer her:

> Ja Du willst daß ich Dich immer so liebe wie Du mich liebst. Und warest Du doch ganz nah bei mir und könnt Dich ans Herz drücken dafür daß ich in Dir finde was ich vergebens in Anderen suchte, ein Gespräch wo die Seele in der Pforte steht in ruhender Stellung zwar, aber so hingebeugt zum Nachbar, so sanft lockend daß der aus sich ausspreche. (14)

In contrast to Clemens, Bettine seeks reciprocity in their relationship, a conversation or a correspondence in which the individual can maintain her autonomy while still leaning towards (not on) the other, and in which the very presence of the other inspires thoughts and language.

In their exchange Bettine and Clemens return again and again to specific themes: education in general and in particular Clemens's attempts to educate his sister, female gender roles, notions of authorship and Bettine's struggles to pen the story of her (daily) life, and intersections of Bettine's local activism and the French Revolution. Liebertz-Grün has argued that the main theme of the text is the "Ideal der harmonischen Bildung" (*Ordnung im Chaos* 94). While I believe that the text discusses education in depth, I would modify Liebertz-Grün's assertion to maintain that the central theme of the text is women's education, namely, Clemens's understanding of women's education and Bettine's arguments against his assertions and for her vision of herself as a woman. Indeed, encounters with others, and primarily with other women, mark the progression of the text and the development of its narrative.

Four women in this text are central to Bettine's development. In the opening pages we encounter Bettine's grandmother, Sophie von La Roche, who initially appears as a figure who tries to keep Clemens's letters from his sister, perhaps because she seems to be aware of the erotic nature of their relationship.[8] As the text progresses, we come to see her as one of the mediators of the French Revolution to Bettine. The next person discussed is the Jewish seamstress Veilchen, who provides Bettine with the opportunity to act locally as a means of adhering to the ideals she ascribes to the French Revolution. Madame de Gachet, whom Clemens sends with a letter of introduction to Bettine, is a woman dressed in man's clothing who awakens in Bettine both an ambivalent erotic interest and a desire to travel throughout the world. Finally, we meet again in *Frühlingskranz* the figure of Günderode, whom Bettine often holds up to Clemens as an example of an individual with whom she can truly communicate. In addition to these women, the reader also encounters figures such as Achim von Arnim and the gardener, but they do not play a significant role in the development of the text's ideas. In contrast, these women provide models for Bettine, even though she remains selective about which of their traits she incorporates into her own identity.

This process of self-definition leads to an increasing distance between

Bettine and Clemens. Tracing a pattern familiar from *Briefwechsel* and *Günderode*, education leads both to individuation and to isolation.[9] Two-thirds of the way through the text, Bettine reports that Günderode has made clear to her why communication with Clemens is so difficult: "Ich hab der *Günderode*...(es mag Dir vielleicht nicht recht sein) Deinen Brief ganz vorgelesen—Sie sagte der *Clemens* spielt in einer fremden Tonart in der Du nicht bewandert bist, in die Du auch nie hinein kommen wirst" (197). Bettine and Clemens do not speak the same language. At the conclusion of *Frühlingskranz*, however, it is not Bettine but Clemens who strikes the reader as the more isolated of the two. Echoing the increasing isolation of the historical Clemens Brentano, his final words are a cry of loneliness:

> So eben kommt die Frankfurter Post. Ich habe keine Zeile von Dir und von Niemand. *Savigny* erhält die Briefe bündelweise; meine Einsamkeit erhöht sich so immer mehr, ich bitte Dich herzlich schreibe, ich bin traurig, wenn ich so meinen Herrn Baron seine Briefe verschlingen sehe, ohne mir etwas mitzuteilen, und ich habe gar nichts. Du hast ja auf der Welt nichts zu tun, schreibe mir doch oder ich glaube daß Du mich nicht mehr liebst. (293–294)

Bettine herself might argue that she still loves her brother but that she has plenty to do; yet it is clear that she has grown apart from him. She no longer finds any resonance, any echo, any mirror for herself in Clemens.

Unquestionably, however, Bettine has learned from their correspondence, for by the end of the text she comes away with newly defined roles for herself. The Bettine persona of *Frühlingskranz* wears many of the masks that she donned in Arnim's earlier texts—child, sister, friend, lover, woman, writer, and political activist—but because she interacts with a different partner, and because the final version of this text was written and edited at a different time in Arnim's life, the roles are defined differently.

Das Kind—Revisiting a Familiar Role

If one wishes to draw parallels between Arnim's life and that of her fictional Bettine, then Bettine is of course youngest in *Frühlingskranz*. Bettine Brentano became reacquainted with her brother in 1797, and they began their correspondence three years later. Describing the relationship of the historical siblings, Schmitz and Steinsdorff remark, "Clemens stilisiert

Bettine zur Inkarnation des 'Kindlichen' und des 'Weiblichen' zugleich, also der beiden Momente natürlicher Genialität, die Friedrich Schlegels *Lucinde* vorgestellt hatte" ("Kindheit und Jugend" 10). Clemens Brentano expressed his desire to define his sister Bettina in many of his letters. He wrote to his future brother-in-law Friedrich von Savigny, for example, "Lieben Sie die Bettine, sie wird mein schönstes Lied."[10] The relationship between the Clemens and Bettine personae of *Frühlingskranz* clearly corresponds to this dynamic, for Clemens often refers to his sister as *Kind*, and he portrays himself as Bettine's maker, her educator, the brother standing in for the deceased father.

In only a few instances, however, does Bettine appear as an *unmündiges Kind* in relation to Clemens. She depicts herself as a child, for example, when remembering her first meeting with Clemens and her time in the convent. But in contrast to *Briefwechsel*, Bettine never intentionally plays the role of the stammering child, and only rarely does she accede to her brother's wishes. Moreover, in contrast to the Bettine in *Günderode*, who acknowledges her older friend as her teacher, the Bettine of this text neither submits to Clemens's teachings nor accepts the rigid teacher-student dichotomy that he sets up for the two of them. Although this Bettine is chronologically the youngest of Arnim's Bettine personae, she seems in many ways to be one of the most autonomous and self-assured.

In this text, Arnim limits the role of the child to its metaphorical meaning. Here we witness Bettine as the child who is open to *Selbst-Bildung*, but who disregards the constraints others would place on her. The role of child allows for the poetic rebirth of Arnim's Bettine personae. At the same time, *Frühlingskranz* reveals the extent to which Arnim has actually left the role of the child behind her. Contrary to the emphasis placed on this role in the popular reception of Arnim and her writing, the role of the child is central only to *Briefwechsel*, giving way already in *Günderode* to an emphasis on youthfulness. In *Frühlingskranz*, as in the remainder of Arnim's texts, the role of the child continues to be invoked for its symbolic and associative value, but it takes a back seat to other, more central roles.

Sister and Intimate Friend

The complex nature of Bettine's relationship with Clemens changes over time. In *Frühlingskranz*, the reader sees her as adoring younger sister and friend who initially writes to her brother in the intimate tones of a lover, and who desires to achieve a union with him through heightened sociability. Simultaneously, and increasingly towards the end of the text, we see her as an independent woman who tries to convince Clemens that he misapprehends her: "Du siehst im Zauberspiegel die *Bettine* wie sie sein könnte, aber nicht ist!" (275). In fact, Clemens's pedagogical attempts vex Bettine to such a degree that she comes to criticize the notion of friendship, at least in the sense that he defines the term.

Throughout her correspondence with Clemens, Bettine tells stories of her past, a time when her affinity to Clemens was far greater than in the present. Upon their first meeting, she recalls, she tossed aside her doll—itself a symbol of her childhood—in favor of the attractive young man who had just entered her room. She recalls:

> Meine alte Puppe vor zwei Jahren!...*Clemente*! Du weißt noch wie ich sie geschwind unter den Tisch warf als Du hereintratst, und ich sah Dich an und kannte Dich nicht, und hielt Dich für einen fremden Mann, der mir aber so wohlgefiel mit seiner blendenden Stirne und Dein schwarz Haar so dicht und so weich, und Du setztest Dich auf den Stuhl, und nahmst mich auf einmal in Deine zwei Arme, und sagtest weißt Du wer ich bin? ich bin der *Clemens*! Und da klammerte ich mich an Dich, aber gleich darauf hattest Du die Puppe unter dem Tisch hervorgeholt und mir in den Arm gelegt, ich wollte aber die nicht mehr, ich wollte nur Dich. Ach das war eine große Wendung in meinem Schicksal, gleich denselben Augenblick wie ich statt der Puppe Dich umhalste. (40)

Initially, Bettine's love for Clemens is absolute, and his entrance into her life marks her discovery of the power of erotic attraction to inspire a desire for learning. Simultaneously, their encounter marks a rite of initiation. Bettine leaves behind her the world of dolls in which her identity remained unreflected because there was no one to challenge it, and she enters the world of social interaction in which identity becomes contested. Whereas the mirror-scene in the diary section of *Briefwechsel* represented Bettina's coming to an awareness of herself as other, this scene symbolizes her entrance into a world in which she must define herself vis-à-vis others. As we have seen in *Briefwechsel* and *Günderode*, this process of self-definition involves both a desire to become one with the other—here Bettine throws herself into Clemens's arms—and a need for individuation. Clemens, who wishes to see in his sister the romantic child, pushes the doll back into her arms, but Bettine insists on determining for herself the object of her affections. This moment of initial attraction thus paradoxically presents the first of what will become a series of instances that eventually drive a wedge between Bettine and Clemens.

Early in their correspondence, Clemens wishes to convince Bettine of the affinity of their thoughts and feelings, and he tells her that the more they share these ideas, the more intimate their friendship will be: "Je mehr Du mir ähnlich fühlst wo ich gut fühle, je mehr Du mir ähnlich denkst wo ich groß und edel denke je mehr bist Du mein Freund, je näher bist Du mir" (31). He requires Bettine for his sense of self and assumes the feeling is mutual. But in a surprising reversal of the understanding of friendship held by other Bettines, the persona in this text views friendship with suspicion and resists being assigned the role of friend:

> Die Freundschaft behauptet zwar, die edlere Natur im Freund hervorzurufen; wie aber kann dieser Adel des Willens sich bilden, wenn nicht in sich und durch sich selber? Raubt da die Freundschaft nicht die Kraft der höchsten Tätigkeit dem Freund, der dann nicht mehr den Willen in sich trägt des besonderen Seins.—Die Freundschaft hat ihn ausgelöscht. Held sein ist nicht befreundet sein, Selbstsein ist Held sein; das will ich sein. (114)

In her relationship with Clemens, friendship becomes not a space that facilitates mutual development but rather a constricting space that limits individual growth. In Bettine's relationships with Günderode and Frau Rath, and in the proposed relationship between the king and the people in *Dies Buch*, friendship is considered empowering and full of potential. Here, Bettine describes friendship as "Brudermord" (114), a case of fratricide in which a brother suffocates his sister's individuality and sense of self.

Yet Bettine does not reject friendship in and of itself.[11] Rather, she refuses to become the friend that her brother wishes her to be. "*Clemens!*" she writes to him, "ich glaub wohl es gibt Menschen die sich lenken lassen von dem Geiste anderer, ich auch, sobald dieser Geist in dem meinen wiederhallt, sobald also er den meinen zur Übereinstimmung weckt. Diesmal tut er das nicht" (197). Within this text, she finds an echo in her friend Günderode, in the Jewish seamstress Veilchen, and to an extent, in Madame de Gachet. She fails to find this same resonance in the correspondence with her brother because he uses her as a projection surface. The positions of mirror and autonomous individual are far more fluid (or, perhaps, more lined up in Bettine's favor) in her relationships with the women in the text.[12]

Bettine's realization of the impossibility of friendship with Clemens does not leave her feeling gleeful; far from it. Her letters waver between self-assertion and a sense of loss. In one of the most affecting passages of the text—a passage that disproves Schultz's claim, "Im *Frühlingskranz* ist es denn auch Clemens, aus dessen Feder die dichterisch ausgeformten Formulierungen fließen" ("Nachwort" 355)—she employs translation as a metaphor for communication:

> Ach wär es möglich, daß eine fremde Sprache eine andere fremde Sprache mit ihren Klängen und Wortarten so ganz decke, daß einer einen Roman in der einen schrieb, der andre in der Meinung es sei die andre Sprache in ihr diesen in der ersten geschriebnen Roman läse?—und kriegte da eine Geschichte heraus, von der keine Spur je geahnt oder gemeint war. So ists mit Dir, und ich muß Deine Hoffnungen alle niederschmettern, daß ich mich bemühen würde, "*allgemein liebenswürdig und geliebt zu werden.*" Du hast mich nicht in meiner Sprache gelesen; Du hast eine andre Natur herausgekriegt, die Dir nur *dann und wann* nicht gefällt, meistens aber doch. Wenn Du aber in der meinigen Sprache mich gefaßt hättest, so würde ich keinen Augenblick Dir gefallen, nein, davon nicht, von andern Dingen wär die Rede. Ein Gewimmel von Mißverständnissen. (199)

Arnim captures in this passage the complexity of language and, more importantly, of communication and friendship. The distance that Bettine felt already when writing to Günderode becomes accentuated here. She and Clemens speak languages so similar that they think they understand each other; in fact, each only comprehends what s/he reads into the other's words, and this leads to one misunderstanding after another. Clemens *reads* Bettine as a young girl, a child who is striving to be loved and lovable. But in contrast to the sisters of so many famous men who desired to please,[13] Bettine wishes neither to please nor to be expected to do so. She demands that Clemens love her more than he claims he does, for she wishes him to love the Bettine who does not please him rather than the sister of his imagination. Bettine's need for love is obvious, but her need for self-definition overrides it.

According to Schultz, Clemens's relationship with Sophie (Mereau) brings about "die endgültige Lösung und Befreiung aus der Ausschließlichkeit dieser erotisch gefärbten Geschwisterbeziehung" ("Nachwort" 352). Yet Bettine realizes long before the discussion of the impending wedding that she is outgrowing Clemens: "So gehts mit Deinen Briefen, sie sind meine Heimat, in ihnen bin ich geboren, aber die Heimat hab ich verlassen" (200). The lack of resonance that she finds in his letters, not the fact that he has found a new lover, impels her to move on.

Clemens did of course contribute to Bettine's *Bildung* through both his letters and his antagonism. Arnim acknowledges her debt to him through the title and the inclusion of his poems, which she sprinkles throughout the letters. This combination of distance from and tribute to Clemens makes it difficult to determine how Arnim intended her readers to view this relationship. Goozé has argued that the adversarial positions maintained throughout the text detract from it as a memorial to Clemens Brentano (*Bettine von Arnim* 41). French claims that "because of the lively and highly spirited exchange which goes on between the two siblings, there is no good and no bad person in the correspondence" (*Bettine von Arnim* 425). I agree with French insofar as the figure of Clemens is more to be pitied than criticized (Bettine, not Clemens, comes out of this narration with her sense of self intact). At the same time I believe that, as in all of Arnim's texts, Bettine (not the figure whose name appears in the title) takes center stage. In this and her following works Arnim begins, through her figures, to reflect more consciously on the complexity of human relations and the impossibility of locating the ideal friendship she is seeking. Her emotionally intense but also antagonistic relationship with her brother allows her to examine the mechanisms that limit sociability and friendship, a theme to which she will return in *Ilius Pamphilius und die Ambrosia*.

Struggles as a Writer

In his attempts to educate Bettine, Clemens encourages her to write and offers suggestions on how to write and on the meaning of writing. At times, Bettine respects his wishes. She writes to him of events from her past life, beginning her letter-autobiography in the manner of a fairy tale: "Es war einmal ein Kind das hatte viele Geschwister" (86). She chronicles events from her everyday life, such as a fire at the local dye works and the visits she and her grandmother receive. In the very act of writing letters to Clemens, she reinvents and gives meaning to her life.

On occasion, however, Bettine echoes the resistance to the act of writing that we have seen in other Bettine personae. She experiences two difficulties. On the one hand, writing involves an inevitable abridgment and truncation of events, experiences, and feelings. Following an attempt to capture her memories on paper she tells Clemens, "Es ist alles noch lebendig in mir, ich kann aber nicht die Blütenäste vom Baum abbrechen der ich selbst bin" (71). How does one recount a life? Bettine's solution is to offer a stream of narration that springs from one theme to another, thereby approximating the complexity of her life and the manner in which her memory transposes diachronic events into a synchrony of experiences.

In addition to her difficulty confining her life to written words, Bettine balks at writing the pleasing letters that Clemens demands of her, for he is receptive only to idyllic depictions of her childhood in the convent and sentimental tales of games she played with her siblings, i.e., to a severely limited version of her life. Recalling Frau Rath's insistence on *Rücksichtslosigkeit*, Bettine believes that writing involves straightforwardness. She states that, to be honest, she would have to write how ludicrous she finds much of what she sees: "Ich kann doch nicht auf jede Seite schreiben daß die Leute mir ganz närrisch vorkommen und sonst begegnet mir nichts jeden Tag, und ist mir von Jugend auf nichts begegnet als der große Gedanke wiederhallend von Stufe zu Stufe meines Ingeniums: *Alles was begonnen wird in der Welt sei närrisch*" (95). To an extent, then, Bettine cannot write for Clemens because he is incapable of understanding those aspects of her story that do not conform to his image of his sister. If writing and story telling involve both a teller and a recipient, the second part is missing on both sides of this relationship.

As occurs in *Briefwechsel* and *Günderode*, at the same time that Bettine resists writing, Arnim presents us with a written text that has a structure and explores in depth a given number of clearly demarcated themes. Whereas Bettine writes in respose to a letter in which Clemens tells her one can create his or her life through writing, "*Gar nicht*—tut es einem" (143), the author Arnim is clearly indebted to her brother for influencing her philosophy of writing. Indeed, one sees in her works a reflection of the very ideas that the Clemens of *Frühlingskranz* shares with his sister. In this text, Clemens instructs Bettine in the art of epistolarity, describing writing as the process of finding one's self in one's own words and in the mirror of the interlocutor. On the one hand: "Der Schreiber muß zugleich an sich selber schreiben, denn er selbst muß durch den Brief mit sich bekannt werden" (16); on the other: "Das Leben ist zwischen Zweien vollendet; jeder hat das seine im Sinne des Andern errungen; sie haben sich im Mute verwechselt, im Streben getrennt, und durchdringen sich nun im Errungnen, in der Ruhe des Bewußtseins, des *Ziels*" (105). Writing involves both individuation and finding one's self in the other. This paradox finds its way into Arnim's writing despite the fact that the Bettine of this text must resist Clemens's attempts to place her firmly in the role of his mirror. It is no coincidence that this discussion of writing and authorship reproduces the tension between the isolation of individuation and the threat of losing oneself in the other that is inherent in romantic sociability.

In his letters to Bettine, Clemens also posits that letter writing allows for exploration of the life of the mind or spirit: "Der gebildete Mensch oder der empfindendere lebt ein doppeltes Leben, er lebt das gesellige praktische Leben seines Standes, seiner Familie, und lebt das Leben seines Geistes, seiner Begriffe, seiner Empfindungen" (104). Bettine rejects his advice, refusing to draw a distinction between her actual and her ideal life. Her protests notwithstanding, writing allowed Arnim to draw this distinction, to create a world that, if not perfect, opened to her fictional Bettine possibilities that she herself did not necessarily have in the real world: possibilities for emancipation, influence, interaction, and resistance. In her texts, Arnim created a life that surpassed her biography, for the practice of her life seems to indicate that she would, to an extent, agree with Clemens's claim:

> Alle Menschen, die ihre eigne Biographie für ihr Leben halten, und so lange einen Menschen für lebendig halten, als seine Stelle nicht vakant ist, sind solche Handwerksburschen und ihr Leben sind blaue Montage.—
> Wir leben nur durch das Bewußtsein unseres Lebens, aber ohne alles Leben überhaupt haben wir kein Bewußtsein, und wir leben daher nur durch die Ewigkeit des Lebens, die alles Leben ist und jedes Leben.

> So gibt es denn nur ein Leben. Damit übrigens Etwas lebe, muß es im Momente erscheinen, und also von der Zeit gefesselt sein. (142)

The Bettine of *Frühlingskranz* resists the label of author and Clemens's attempts to define her as such. Yet the above passage tells us as much about the author as her literary protagonists. If one considers Arnim's life as a writer, then one can apply Clemens's words to her understanding of herself in this capacity. Like the Clemens of *Frühlingskranz*, Arnim refused to view her biography as her life, and the process of subject formation that continued into her adult years constituted an attempt to live by becoming ever more conscious of her present and her past. Writing was therefore an extension of living, and Arnim the writer used written words to transform her biography into her life. Clemens could not tell Bettine much about who she should become, but she did not ignore his advice in matters of *how* to become.

Women's Roles—Redefinition and Reassertion

All of Arnim's texts revolve around the notion of *Bildung*; in them we see her Bettine personae engaged in the process of educating themselves and others through their own and others' experiences. Under this rubric of education one also finds discussions of the education of girls and women. This discussion becomes most explicit in *Frühlingskranz*, in part because of its overriding importance to Bettine's interlocutor Clemens. Like the historical Clemens Brentano, who conducted a *moralische Korrespondenz* (*CBF* 1061) with his sisters Bettina and Gunda, this Clemens wishes to shape Bettine into an ideal romantic child-woman who would strengthen his sense of identity. That is, Clemens wishes Bettine to play Lucinde to his Julius. Bettine is of a different mind, however, and she feels just as entrapped by Clemens's wishes for her as by the ennui of her everyday life. Finding no resonance in her brother, she turns to women as role models and sources of strength, namely to Madame de Gachet and to Günderode. To a lesser degree she also turns to her grandmother Sophie von La Roche and to the Jewish seamstress Veilchen. In these characters, Bettine discovers a composite picture of a woman whose potential roles are far more diverse and contradictory than those Clemens would assign her.

From the first pages of the text, Clemens assumes the tone of a schoolmaster who has fallen in love with his pupil. His concern for Bettine's development extends from her intellectual growth to her daily life. Regarding the latter, for example, he inquires into Bettine's spending habits (34), instructs her not to allow herself to be brought down by others' low spirits (151), and asks her to knit socks and embroider a fire screen for him.[14]

Clemens also wishes for his sister to share in his middle class education. He expects Madame de Gachet to teach Bettine chemistry and expand her mind and spirit "durch ihre herrlichen Gedanken" (59). He recommends that Bettine read Schiller's *Briefe über die ästhetische Erziehung des Menschen* (77). And although he does not approve of his sister's interest in the French Revolution, he condones her writing of essays on this topic so long as exercising her mind prevents her from falling into melancholy (150).

Most importantly, however, Clemens wishes Bettine to adopt as her own the gender roles prescribed for middle-class German women of the early nineteenth century.[15] She should possess feeling but not be overly emotional. As an antidote to excessive *Empfindsamkeit* he suggests for example "viel Bewegung, Springen, Singen und Tanzen, Beschäftigung" (149). He tells her to accept the physical and geographical limits that have been placed upon her:

> So lange liebe *Bettine*, als die Einsamkeit dir noch anklebt als Widerwillen gegen die Gesellschaft, mußt Du Dich nach den Menschen umsehen, und alle Mittel anwenden Dich von allen Menschen geliebt zu machen.
> Das Leben des Weibes ist fester und unbeweglicher als das Leben des Mannes, das Weib berührt die Menschen näher und muß Segen über ihr Umgebung verbreiten. (195)

The ideal woman is eager to please, malleable, immobile, a source of security, and the bearer of blessings for whatever environment she happens to find herself in. Most importantly in this role Bettine could offer a sense of security to Clemens. He tells her:

> Weil Du nun einmal mein guter Engel bist so mußt Du auch Dein Amt mit Treue verwalten, mein guter Engel muß immer heiter sein und meiner mit Hoffnung und Segen gedenken und auch mich strafen mit Worten und mich anmahnen in Deinen Briefen daß ich mein Ziel nicht aus den Augen lasse, Du mußt mit Deiner Lebensfreude die meine anfachen, Du mußt Enthusiasmus die Flügel lösen, mit Deinem Ernst mit Deiner Güte und Wahrheit. (39)

It becomes clear as Clemens continues to write that he requires Bettine to play the role he ascribes to her because he needs a source of strength, because the weaknesses he warns her against are those he fears in himself. Indeed, Clemens projects his own weaknesses, his own need to please, and his own dependence onto Bettine, a point made more apparent by the loneliness that he exudes by the end of the text. In educating Bettine, Clemens not only tries to shape an ideal woman, he tries to shape his ideal self.[16]

Yet for every suggestion that Clemens makes, for every request, for every admonition, Bettine offers a response that indicates that she has no intention of striving to please him, for the desire to please runs counter to her understanding of sociability. The prerequisite for friendship is unconditional acceptance of the other:

> *Lieber Clemens*…Wär ich als Mädchen was die Apfelblüte ist, ich wär doch wohl alles Liebe und herzlich schöne. Was Du von mir denkst, dann könnt ich Dir verzeihen was Du mir und Dir weis machen willst. Ja es ist recht schön denn ich hab das Plaisir davon, und Dir schadets nichts. Aber sei nur nicht ängstlich daß ich keine Apfelblüte bin, weiß und rot und goldner Same darin, sondern daß ich vielleicht gar so eine Nessel bin oder Distel oder Dorn, wie Du meinst vor denen ich mich soll hüten…Ach *Clemens* wir wollen recht vertrauend einander schreiben, und nichts weis machen einander! (26)

Bettine refuses to play the role her brother intends for her, insisting that she is a thistle or a thorn rather than the apple blossom for which he takes her. She does the opposite of anything he asks or suggests that she do. Rather than remaining kind and passive, she describes herself as "Deine barbarische Schwester" (164). She tells him she has not read Schiller's *Aesthetic Letters* because she is too distracted: "ich kann nicht auf Komma und Punkt achtung geben" (84). She becomes enraged upon reading his prayer that God find her a suitable mate, assuring him, "glaube, daß ich keiner Stütze im Leben bedarf und das ich nicht das Opfer werden mag, von solchen närrischen Vorurteilen. Ich weiß, was ich bedarf!—ich bedarf, daß ich meine Freiheit behalte. Zu was?—dazu, daß ich das ausrichte, und vollende, was eine innere Stimme mich aufgibt zu tun" (213). Furthermore, she rejects Clemens's attempt to create a dichotomy between the ideal man and the ideal woman: "Mögen sich diese zwei beiden zusammen finden auf irgend einem glücklichen Stern, nur das einzige bitte ich mir aus, daß Du es mir nicht zu wissen tust; und ein für allemal will ich von diesem Heiligtum gänzlich ausgeschloßen sein!" (217)[17] Bettine's understanding of gender roles is informed by her brother's expectations and by early- and mid-nineteenth-century gender discourse, but she resists such admonitions and strives to define herself through her own education.

The pinnacle of Bettine's frustration with her brother occurs close to the middle of the text, following a letter whose source is one of the extant original letters from Clemens Brentano.[18] In Arnim's revision of the letter, Clemens instructs Bettine to avoid being a *Hans guck in die Luft*, to avoid *Empfindsamkeit*, to report to him all of her comings and goings, not to spend too much time with the gardener, and finally, to knit a half dozen boot socks for him. Bettine becomes so angry that she must write to him via Günderode. She begins her letter: "Lieber *Clemens*. Liebe *Günderode!* denn lieber *Clemens*, ich muß doch gewiß einen haben, bei dem ich Dich verklage, Dir ins Gesicht kann ichs nicht alles sagen was ich schlimmes von Dir weiß und aus Deinem Brief heraus sogleich entdeckt habe" (152). In this letter, Bettine inverts the concept of feminine duty, insisting that her duty is not to others but to herself and to her self-defined religion:

> Jetzt werde ich gleich einmal meine Pflicht überschreiten und werde ein bißchen zum Gärtner gehen, da es die Abendstunde ist wo er begießt, da hab ich ihm versprochen zu kommen und zwar nicht aus Pflichtgefühl, sondern aus Lust am lieblichen Geschäft, aus Lust an alle dem frischen Leben, was sich in dem schönen Schmelz der Farben regt...Ich werde mich da mit meinem Pflichtstrickstrumpf hinsetzen und etliche Pflichtmaschen stricken, ich werde aus Pflicht gegen meine Bildung in der alten Schweizergeschichte lesen, daß der Teutone keine Stiefelstrümpfe trug, als er noch ein freier Mann war, ich werde also aus Pflichtgefühl am Altar der Freia mein Strickzeug niederlegen und das Gelöbnis ihr tun, nie wieder Stiefelstrümpfe zu stricken, die dem freien deutschen Charakter Fesseln anlegen! (155)

In opposition to duty, Bettine poses the category of desire, stating that it is her duty to follow her desire, which is the center and source of her freedom. Traditional women's roles, in fact, run counter to her sense of duty. She therefore discards the socks that Clemens wants her to knit at the altar of Freya, the Germanic goddess of love and beauty whom she knows will bless her rebellion.

If one reads Bettine's actions and her emphasis on desire not only within the context of *Frühlingskranz* but also within that of *Günderode*, it becomes apparent that Bettine is engaged in more than the mere throwing of a temper tantrum. Rather she is struggling for her sense of identity; this, in turn, means fighting against the monotony and boredom of a woman's life and for an escape from this monotony that differs from the option of suicide chosen by her friend Günderode. Performing women's duties would mean resigning herself to the boredom of the life assigned to her. At times, she finds it difficult not to succumb to depression: "mich befällt oft eine tiefe Melancholie über mein Nichts.—Was kann ich dafür?—Die Sünden der Welt haben auch mir den Boden abgegraben" (98) and she protests against the "Sklavenzeit, in der ich geboren bin!" (240) Bettine finds one means of escape in her fantasies, a tactic familiar from the fantasy and dream sequences of *Briefwechsel* and *Günderode*. At a reading of *Hamlet*, she recites a scene between Hamlet and Ophelia,[19] sinking so deeply into the role of Ophelia that the others leave her alone in the room: "Was sie dachten weiß ich nicht. Auf mich hatte es eine glückliche Wirkung...Es weissagt etwas in mir, daß eine Kraft in dieser Welt sei, die mit Leidenschaft mich liebt" (240–241). By retreating into herself, by consulting with a power she elsewhere calls her genius, and by believing it loves her passionately and without reserve, Bettine finds a space in which she can be herself. At the same time, her development is more than a solipsistic exercise, for she also looks around her for role models and finds inspiration in other women. Although she never endeavors to imitate any of these individuals, she discerns in their examples possibilities for women other than those offered by her brother or by the gender discourses of middle-class German society.

The most ambiguous relationship in *Frühlingskranz* is that between Bettine and Madame de Gachet. Whereas Bettine stakes out a clear position with regard to Clemens early on in the narrative, her relationship with Madame de Gachet remains ambivalent, marked by admiration and fear, hope and resignation, attraction and repulsion, homosocial, and one might argue, homoerotic desire and fear of that desire. Gachet pushes the limits of Bettine's freedom but offers a model that, should Bettine follow it to the letter, would lead to a complete break between Bettine and the social world she inhabits, a move that Bettine is unwilling or unable to make.

Gachet comes to Bettine with a letter of introduction from Clemens who, in his first mention of the French woman, describes her as a beautiful warrior: "sie soll so schön sein, so vollkommen wohlgebildet wie ein Weib aus den Nibelungen, sie reitet das wildeste Pferd" (54). Impressed with Gachet's actions during the reign of terror in France, Clemens sends her to Bettine as a pedagogical measure:

> Sie ist ein Weib an dem die Vortrefflichkeit und Barbarei du jour, (das heißt wie es heute zu Tage hergeht) gescheitert ist, sie allein kann Deine Ideen über Revolution und Volksglück aufklären, o sie kann unendliches für Dich, sie ist ein Geschöpf aus Gotteshand, ein gewöhnliches Weib wie Eva und wie sie aus dem Herzen jedes Mannes heraus steigen soll. (56–57)

For all of Gachet's strength and autonomy, Clemens cannot, at least initially, imagine her as a woman separate from a man, as one who does not find her identity in a man. Yet the more he gets to know her and the more he thinks about the person he has met, the more suspicious he becomes of the potential influence Gachet may exert over Bettine. He soon admonishes Bettine to pay close attention only to Gachet's heart and soul, "die Narben aber, die ihr Erfahrung und Geschick geschlagen, das männliche Wilde ihres Seins und Verstandes sollst Du übersehen, überhaupt Dich ihr nicht hingeben; mein bleiben und Gott" (57). Clemens has come to realize that Gachet may become his competition for the role of Bettine's educator. This, in turn, poses the threat that he as a man may not be indispensable for his sister's development.

As it turns out, Gachet fascinates and frightens Bettine. Describing the arrival of the older woman, the younger writes: "Siehe da kam im Sturm daher gebraust ein Cabriolet wie ein abgeschoßner Pfeil vor die Haustür, herab springt der Wagenlenker, ein jugendlich voller schöner Mannjüngling mit klirrenden Sporen" (60).[20] This man turns out to be a woman, one who is clearly interested in and erotically attracted to Bettine. In contrast to the scene in *Günderode* in which Bettine kisses her friend's breast, here Bettine does not have the same control over the situation; whereas the earlier Bettine's embrace of Günderode arose out of the intense passion of a single moment, Gachet's interest in Bettine appears to be more reflected. Bettine wishes to maintain her sense of autonomy, but Gachet's arrival seems to shake up her sense of who she is. Bettine writes to Clemens: "Diese Frau hat mich in einem fortwährenden Schauerriesel erhalten, und denke Dir während ich in die Türe gelehnt sie ansah, verstummte sie oft mitten in ihrer Rede und sah sich nach mir um, keine Goldfrucht winkt lockender aus dem dunklen Grün, als ihr lächelnder Blick nach mir, ich fühlte mich beschämt" (68). This portrait of two women catching and holding each other's gaze, Bettine's dual sense of longing and shame conveys a far deeper sense of homoerotic attraction than her impulsiveness in *Günderode*. And reading further, one finds proof that Gachet was interested in sharing more than her wisdom with Bettine:

> Die *de Gachet* war auch noch am Sonntag Nachmittag hier…Sie redete von den Himmelskörpern, ihrem subtilen Ausströmen und von wechselseitiger Anziehung der Planeten in ihre Kreise, und vom innerlichen Sinn im Ozean der Gefühle, und ich war ganz betäubt. Wie komme ich ihr vor daß sie mir so was sagt!
> —Sie hielt mich fest in ihren Armen, ich hätte des Teufels werden mögen; ich schämte mich daß ich ihr zuhören mußte, gefangen in ihren Armen und nichts verstand; sie ließ mich los wie die Großmama hereinkam; ich, wie ein entwischter Vogel sprang in den Garten auf die Bank. (74)

Bettine flees Gachet's unfamiliar and unexpected advances. She feels inexplicably drawn to Gachet, but fears becoming trapped within the older woman's sphere of intellectual influence and her ocean of feeling.

Bettine is attracted to Gachet's independence, to her freedom, to the fact that she resists social constraints placed on women. Gachet is free to travel, she wears men's clothing that allows her to swing herself onto her horse "mit selbstgefälliger Anmut" (68), and "sie bekümmert sich gar um nichts" (85) other than what interests her; she decides to take up farming, for example. That such possibilities are in fact open to women fills Bettine with longing. Comparing herself to Gachet, she sighs, "Ach was kann ich großes tun? auf die Pappel klettern beim Gewitter daß es auf mich los donnert und blizt?—oder im Winter auf den Schneeflächen mich tummeln; dem Treibeis nachhelfen im Main?" (86) Her own sphere of action considerably limited, she views Gachet as the "Gegenteil…aller Verkehrtheit" (68), as the opposite of the folly that she sees in the world.

Despite Gachet's allure, Bettine does not accept either her suggestion that they travel together to Spain and Italy or her offer to become Bettine's mentor. The reasons for Bettine's rejection of an offer obviously so tempting to her are manifold. She is technically not of age and thus under the guardianship of her grandmother and her eldest brother Christian. In a concrete sense, then, the decision to travel is not hers to make. Indeed, in one passage she resigns herself to remaining at home, telling herself with little conviction that she should be satisfied with her relationship to Clemens: "Ich möchte nach Italien, ich möchte so gern reisen, die Sehnsucht ist gar zu groß; ich beschwichtige sie damit daß ich mir einbilde Dich bald zu sehen, diese Freude ist doch noch größer" (126). As the trajectory of her relationship with her brother would indicate, Bettine is hardly convinced by her own words.

In addition to external limitations, Bettine's sense of shame hints that Gachet's erotic attention makes her feel uncomfortable, in part it seems because she herself is attracted to Gachet. Her resistance can thus be read as an attempt to place herself closer to the heterosexual end of the "continuum of male or female homosocial desire."[21] Bettine is attracted to Gachet but finds her otherness overwhelming, threatening.

Bettine's resistance to Gachet cannot, however, be read solely as flight from other possible identities. Although Gachet offers a female role model that differs refreshingly from that presented by Clemens, Bettine fears that Gachet, like Clemens, wishes to shape her in her (Gachet's) own image. To achieve her aim of self-education, Bettine must ward off both of their advances. She resists those of Clemens because he cannot comprehend who she is, and those of Gachet because the French woman's personality is too strong to allow room for Bettine's growth:

> Morgen kommt sie wieder, sie hat mirs im Vorübergehen ins Ohr geflüstert, sie ist des Teufels aber ich bin auch des Teufels, ich will keine Freundschaft mit ihr, ich bin zu jung. Wär ich schon so wie es in mir werden will, dann ritt ich stehend auf zwei Gaulen und spränge dazu durch den Reif. Mit Kunststreichen und Übermut wollt ich ihren kühnen Ritt ausparieren. (72)

Intent on what she considers to be self-definition, Bettine does not feel ready for a friendship with Gachet, for such a relationship would—to her mind—lack the reciprocity that would facilitate her development outside Gachet's planetary sphere of influence. Unlike the relationships of Arnim's various Bettine personae with Goethe, Günderode, and Clemens, all of which develop (textually) through letters, this relationship holds the potential for close, physical interaction, a situation in which Bettine believes she would lose a degree of control.

Gachet does, however, offer a role model to which the younger woman aspires. Bettine writes to Clemens of Gachet's departure for Spain:

> Wie ich sah daß sie keine Tränen wollte fließen lassen, ging ich zurück hinter einen Baum und sah mich nicht mehr um nach ihr; sie stand bald auf von dem Stein wo sie gesessen hatte, sie sagte noch zum Abschied, ich solle immer bedenken daß jeder Mensch das Recht habe der größte zu werden, und daß darin die ganze Erziehung der Seele begründet sei,—und daß dazu nicht die äußere Größe und Anerkenntnis gehören, aber die Geschicke die seien der Tempel aller Größe, und ihr eignes Geschick beweise es, daß sie diesen Gedanken immer vor Augen gehabt, sie wolle Groß werden in ihrem Schicksal, Cette pensée est mon Pilote sagte sie, et il me menera par tous les Mondes et Cieux![22]—Ich vergaß Abschied zu nehmen ich sprang zwischen den Hecken fort. Wie ich mich nach ihr umsah stand sie noch da, ich winkte ihr mit dem Sacktuch, sie nickte mir und ging weg, und jetzt legte ich mich an die Erde und ließ mein Herz ausklopfen. (125)

Although the two figures could not be more dissimilar, Gachet serves in *Frühlingskranz* the function that the Jewish mathematics teacher Ephraim served in *Günderode*: she reassures Bettine that her desires and wishes are acceptable, and that not the opinion of others but rather her own history will serve as the measure of what she has achieved in her life. In other words, Gachet recognizes that Bettine must follow her own path. Like Ephraim, Gachet is an outsider for whom the society in which she lives has no place. Unwilling or unable to explore further her attraction to Gachet, Bettine nevertheless receives affirmation for her sense of self as an outsider from her encounter with the *Mannjüngling* from the Vendée.[23] This, in turn, helps Bettine to distance herself from her brother.

Another model of womanhood is offered by Günderode, for Günderode appears here to understand Bettine and, like Gachet, to accept her friend despite their differences. In *Frühlingskranz*, Günderode serves as Bettine's confidante, the friend to whom Bettine turns when she can no longer express her ideas to Clemens. As in *Günderode*, Bettine's friend seems to understand why communication between Bettine and Clemens is so fraught with conflict and thus becomes also a voice of understanding. Finally and most importantly, Günderode encourages Bettine to pursue her self-education: "Das Werden!—das große Werden—*ist und soll sein der einzige Genuß*, sagt die *Günderode, der wird aber nicht, der nicht göttlich wird*, sagt die *Günderode* auch noch" (182). Echoing the phrase borrowed from Schleiermacher that appears in all of Arnim's texts, Günderode— herself an outsider like Gachet—offers Bettine support in her pursuit of education and development.

Gachet and Günderode help to educate Bettine with regard to the possibilities open to women by playing roles that lie outside the boundaries assigned to definitions of feminine gender in the early- to mid-nineteenth century. Whereas Clemens wishes his sister to be educated but passive, to mirror him but to have no reflection herself, these women understand the importance of self-education and self-definition. They offer Bettine membership in a community of outsiders, a space in which she feels free to explore other possibilities and roles. Bettine claims to Clemens, "'*was kann ich, was kann ich dafür?*'—daß es mir um Freundschaft und Liebe nicht zu tun ist" (146). She requires love and friendship to further her education, but not in the confining forms that Clemens envisions. In the following section we encounter two additional women, Bettine's grandmother and the Jewish seamstress Veilchen, who help to educate her further.

Activist

Despite her protestations against her environment, the Bettine of this text remains confined to a small sphere, travelling between her grandmother's house in Offenbach and her family's home in Frankfurt. Unlike the Bettine personae in *Dies Buch* and *Dämonen*, she is the ward of various family members and has few opportunities to converse with kings and princes. Nevertheless, conversations with her grandmother about the French Revolution inspire Bettine to act locally, for she insists on a continuity between the public and the private spheres. Her involvement has not only political but also personal implications, because action means staving off the boredom and melancholy that she associates with traditional feminine roles.

She comes to her beliefs through the writings of the French statesman and revolutionary Mirabeau (1749–1791), from whose letters she on occasion reads to her grandmother. While reading one evening, her grandmother hands her a needle:

> Damit soll ich ins Heft stechen, welchen Satz ich treffe den soll ich als Gedenkspruch bewahren, sie hatte diese Sätze selbst alle gesammelt, und war überzeugt, ich werde mit der Nadel nicht unrecht stechen, aber ich stach in: "*Die Macht der Gewohnheit ist eine Kette die selbst das größte Genie nur mit vieler Mühe bricht*," und die Großmama stutzt ob ich den Satz nicht gar selbst erfunden hab. Nein liebe Großmama hier steht er, ich bin nicht *Mirabeau* aber sein Geist ist

mir ins Blut gegangen, er wird mich ewig mahnen nicht von der Gewohnheit abzuhängen. (22)

Bettine feels trapped by the ennui of normalcy, and she realizes with what she interprets to be the direct intervention of Mirabeau that it will take all of her efforts to break free. In response to the question, what should become of her life, she insists, "Viel soll daraus werden" (122). Yet she also views her situation realistically. Instead of wishing for more than is possible for her (as Günderode did), she decides to act whenever she can in the interest of those individuals who stand in harm's way.

Bettine's first step towards action is to educate herself. With her grandmother's encouragement, she follows the events of the French Revolution.[24] She also translates Mirabeau's analysis of state prisons, a topic that concerns Arnim in greater detail in *Dies Buch*. In addition to following the discussions that take place at her grandmother's house, Bettine transforms her enthusiasm for the French Revolution into action on behalf of those around her. When she hears, for example, that the hypnotist who lives in the house next door to her grandmother is in need of travel money, she takes the money she has been saving and throws it over the fence to him. When her grandmother decides to kill a hermaphrodite chicken that had been named "Männewei" Bettine distracts the cook so that the chicken can escape. Reflecting on this act, she writes:

> Abends beim Sternenschimmer, wo ich den Kopf weit aus unserm Mansardfenster streckte, um recht viele Sterne zu Zeugen meines feierlichen Schwures aufzurufen, tat ich das Gelübde, Alles dran zu wagen wenn ich einen Menschen in Gefahr sehe und wenn auch selbst das Messer schon über seinem Haupte schwebt.— Ein rascher Entschluß vermag viel, aber Zagen ist das Verderben aller Großtaten! (184)

Through this strangely touching anecdote, Bettine insists resistance must begin locally. In addition to the motto *es werde*, an emphasis on action and coming to the aid of others becomes part of Bettine's credo.

Bettine most defiantly expresses her desire to assist others in her decision to help the Jewish girl Veilchen sweep her front steps. Such an act violates class and religious norms—a young Christian woman of the middle class should neither associate with a Jew nor help her to sweep her front steps—and arouses the ire, first of one of her aunts, and then after she writes to him of the incident, of Clemens. In contrast to his sister,

Clemens concerns himself with what others will think:

> So habe ich jetzt zum Beispiel wieder gehört daß Du dem Mädchen, was Dich Sticken lehrt, Briefe von mir und Dir vorliest, und was hindert dies Mädchen, sie mag ein gutes Geschöpf sein oder nicht, das was sie gehört, herumzutragen?— Was Du selbst nicht verbirgst, wird sie auch nicht verschweigen, und hat es wohl nicht verschwiegen, sonst wüßte ichs nicht. So wie Du zu ihr mit Deiner Vertraulichkeit hinab steigst, steigt sie wieder hinab, und sofort ist der Weg sehr kurz, daß unser ganzer Umgang ein Gassenhauer wird. Das ist nun eine sehr verdrießliche Sache, das macht Dich und mich den Leuten lächerlich und mit Recht. (192)

Clemens disapproves of Bettine's actions and believes that, by confiding in Veilchen, Bettine is lowering herself. Most significantly, he concerns himself with what the neighbors will say, for he wishes that neither the content of his letters nor the fact that Bettine has shared them with a Jewish girl becomes public knowledge.[25]

Bettine does not allow herself to be swayed, either by Clemens's disapproval or by the opinion of others, insisting that she is not lowering but elevating herself by associating with Veilchen (200). Her insistence on helping Veilchen becomes an act of self-assertion; she chooses to valorize moral action and ignore the laws of custom and so-called decency:

> Für Einen zu sorgen oder Zwei, die mir grade in den Weg kommen, deucht Euch allen Extravaganz! Ihr verbietet mir mit einem armen Judenmädchen Umgang zu haben; und ich will Umgang haben mit allem was zugleich mit mir auf dieser Welt lebt. Oder sind dies etwa keine gerechten Ansprüche: daß ich bin; und der Hülfe bedarf, die Du geben kannst. Aber Sittlichkeit und Anstand, das sind zwei dumme Wächter, die dem menschlichen Sein und Willen den Weg verwehren. (212)

Rather than acting in accordance with the set rules of her bourgeois society, Bettine insists that actions grow out of individual circumstances and that one should offer help to the extent that it is possible to do so. Although frequently disheartened by the paucity of opportunities for action open to her, Bettine refuses to succumb to the melancholy that hovers on the fringes of her existence, using instead seemingly banal events such as the rescue of a chicken or her friendship with a Jewish girl to identify herself with the French Revolution. Arnim does not distinguish between revolutionary activity on a national level and the domestic protests of a twenty-year-old woman. Rather, she places both within the context of her moral law: "I exist, and someone needs help that I can give." In this sense,

Bettine's self-definition becomes the prerequisite for her political action. Möhrmann's assertion with regard to women's development before the women's movement—"Ohne einen übersteigerten Subjektivismus hätte sich das Individualbewußtsein der Frau vielleicht gar nicht artikulieren können. Ohne die Kenntnis ihres 'Ich' hätte ihr auch das Verständnis für das 'Wir' gefehlt" (*Die andere Frau* 44)—thus elucidates the relationship between Bettine's/Arnim's self-education and her political activism; it also helps to illuminate Arnim's position as a transitional figure between the female representatives of German romanticism and the leaders of the first wave of the German women's movement.

Summary: The Private Sphere as Provocation

On the surface, *Frühlingskranz* appears to be the story of a young woman's relationship to her brother, an impression strengthened by the seemingly innocent title. Yet both the text itself and Arnim's reputation at the time of its publication led to the confiscation of the book by the Berlin police. Although Karl August Varnhagen held the opinion, "das Buch hat nichts Verfängliches,"[26] there was plenty to arouse the suspicion of the censors: the brazen dedication to Prince Waldemar; the fact that the text's publisher, Edgar Bauer, was also publishing the provocative texts of the Young Hegelians; and the uproar provoked by *Dies Buch*. The censors did not prevail, however. Following a series of negotiations and a letter to Friedrich Wilhelm IV from Bettine, the king ordered the release of the text, which occurred on June 16, 1844.

It is telling that, whereas *Dies Buch* was banned in certain areas only after its publication, *Frühlingskranz* raised suspicion even before its appearance. This attests to Arnim's status but also to the text's contents. Although the French Revolution provides only an occasionally mentioned backdrop to *Frühlingskranz*, the text offers a defense of the individual and of the individual woman that must be regarded as revolutionary for the time in which it is written. Bettine asserts her autonomy as a woman, and she considers women to be no more and no less than individuals with the right to self-determination. When one reads this text, especially in its position between *Dies Buch* and *Dämonen*, one sees that Arnim has leveled the differences between the rights that Bettine has as an autonomous individual vis-à-vis her brother and the rights that the individual has vis-à-vis the king and the state. *Clemens Brentano's Frühlingskranz* offers a call for the emancipation of women and of the individual citizen. The text anticipates both the twentieth-century slogan that the personal is political and the contention that a free society cannot exist without freedom in the domestic and local spheres.

CHAPTER FIVE

"Motherhood" and the Perils of Autonomy: *Ilius Pamphilius und die Ambrosia* (1847)

The publication of *Goethe's Briefwechsel mit einem Kinde* in 1835 catapulted Bettina von Arnim into a position of prominence and influence among Berlin intellectuals and especially among students. With the publication of this text, she gained a degree of authority that enabled her to carve out a space for herself within the Berlin public sphere. Indeed, the success of this work licensed her to continue to write: she revised and augmented her correspondence with Karoline von Günderrode and Clemens Brentano and even ventured to dedicate *Dies Buch gehört dem König* to Friedrich Wilhelm IV. In addition to her textual production, Arnim strove to influence public opinion through her salon. Young visitors flocked to her apartments at Unter den Linden 21 (1834–1843), Hinter dem Neuen Packhof 2 (1843–1846), Köthener Strasse 44 (1846–1847), and In den Zelten 5 (1847 until her death in 1859) to visit and discuss their ideas with the woman they called, simply, "Bettina." One of the visiting admirers was Philipp Nathusius, son of an industry magnate from Althaldensleben near Magdeburg. A student in Berlin since 1836, he sought out Arnim after reading *Briefwechsel*, and their first meeting initiated a tension-filled friendship and correspondence that lasted until Nathusius's marriage in 1840. In this relationship, Nathusius assigned Arnim the role of mentor and she played this role willingly; she discussed with him the strengths and weaknesses of his poetry and tried to further his development as by allowing him to help edit the second edition of *Briefwechsel* and by trying, unsuccessfully, to persuade him to help the Grimms with her edition of Achim von Arnim's collected works. Nathusius was thus among the first of a number of young men who entered into and remained for a while within Arnim's sphere of influence. Arnim became acquainted with the law student Julius Döring and the medical student Moriz Carriere in 1839. Along with Wilhelm Levysohn, Bernhard Oppenheim, and Max Ring, Carriere was a member of the *Doktorenklub*, a society of older students and younger doctors who shared a deep admiration for Arnim and who presented her with an album of poetry in thanks for her dedication of *Die Günderode* to *den Studenten*.[1]

Arnim actively promoted this cult of personality, and she utilized it together with her publications to promote not only herself but also the political causes she supported. This was evident in her plan, following the publication of *Günderode*, to publish as her third volume a collection of the letters, poems, and drawings that she had received from various admirers. Bäumer notes in her article, "*Ilius Pamphilius*," that the author intended to use the proceeds from this collection to assist Jakob and Wilhelm Grimm following their dismissal from their university positions in Göttingen in 1837. Obviously, such a volume also would have underscored the prestige Arnim had gained over the past decade and would have shown how the mentor role that she played in her salon had extended beyond the walls of her Berlin apartment and into the broader public sphere.

Arnim became distracted from this project by her work on *Dies Buch* and never published this volume in the form initially planned, but she held on to the idea of a text that would depict her (or one of her Bettine personae) interacting directly with the students to whom she had dedicated *Günderode*. Revising her conception, she envisioned a project that would incorporate the letters she had exchanged with both Nathusius and Döring, and she planned to call it *Ilius, Pamphilius und die Ambrosia*. When Döring refused to grant Arnim permission to use his letters, she dropped the comma from the title and included primarily her correspondence with Nathusius, assigning him the name *Ilius Pamphilius* and herself the name *Ambrosia*. The purpose of the text was not primarily, however, to draw attention to Nathusius or his mediocre literary production (as with the poems of Karoline von Günderrode and Clemens Brentano, Arnim interspersed the poems of Nathusius throughout the text) but to help her regain her position at the center of public attention (Bäumer, "*Ilius*" 263). Following its peak just after the publication of *Dies Buch*, Arnim's popularity had begun to wane. In publishing a testimony to her relationship with and influence over a young poet, Arnim wished to remind her readers that she had been an apprentice to Goethe and to depict herself passing her poetic inheritance on to the next generation.

In comparison with her other novel-length texts, Arnim made few alterations to the original letters she exchanged with Nathusius before publishing them. Because *Ambrosia* remains so close to the original correspondence, Bäumer and Schultz suggest the generic designation of letter documentation:

> Die Grundlagenforschung Konstanze Bäumers hat ergeben, daß Bettina den originalen, zum Teil auf farbigen Briefpapier (in den Farben rosenrot, lindgrün und himmelblau) geschriebenen Briefwechsel mit Philipp Nathusius unmittelbar als Druckvorlage benutzte, indem sie die wenigen, ihr notwendig erscheinenden Textveränderungen in die Handschrift hineinkorrigierte. (77)

Perhaps because the socially engaged Arnim of the 1840s was too busy to engage in imaginative manipulation of the letters that served as her sources, or perhaps because she wanted to give her readers a very different picture of "Bettine," the development of Arnim's relationship with Nathusius determined the content and structure of this letter documentation. And yet, apparently due to the author's internalization of these ideas and roles, the by now familiar concepts of youth, friendship, motherhood, and activism that Arnim developed in her earlier works appear frequently here. This text thus documents five years in the life of Arnim and gives the reader both a sense of who she became in the wake of her interactions with her Bettine personae and a sense of the all-too-human difficulty of achieving the ideals that these figures represent.

As the Bettine persona of this text, Ambrosia is assuredly not the Bettine of Arnim's first work. Although Pamphilius and Ambrosia self-consciously mirror the Goethe and Bettine figures of *Briefwechsel*, here a younger man approaches an older woman, learns from her through the practice of pedagogical eros, and then moves on to stake out a space for himself. Pamphilius thus becomes the child and Ambrosia the genius, but as with the Bettine of *Briefwechsel*, the child in this text also tries to educate his mentor. Although Nathusius/Pamphilius reveals himself to be less than the inspired pupil his mentor initially believed him to be,[2] he accurately (and at times harshly) points to the extent to which Arnim/Ambrosia fails to live up to her own ideals of mutual development, sociability, and freedom of the individual.

In fact, at times in this text Ambrosia's words and actions resemble less those of earlier Bettines and more those of figures against whom those Bettines rebel. For this reason, Ambrosia is Arnim's most troubling persona. She can be startlingly domineering, and her acknowledged erotic attraction to the much younger Pamphilius is alternately mawkish and masochistic. To account for this ostensible inconsistency with Arnim's other works, Drewitz, in her biography, explains Arnim's actions as symptoms of menopause. Such an explanation not only wrongly perpetrates a myth that denies the legitimacy of older women's erotic feelings, it also ignores the fact that both the author Arnim and many of her Bettine personae feel and express erotic attraction to their counterparts in all stages of their lives. Attributing Arnim's/Ambrosia's feelings to hot flashes would therefore be to deny her sensuality and to explain away uncomfortable aspects of her writing as abberations rather than as a part of "Bettine's" development over six texts.

Ambrosia's actions are so disturbing because they challenge the image of Bettine that the reader has formed up until now. One can idealize a child and choose to understand what she says in a metaphorical sense, and one can admire a girl/woman struggling to assert her independence. But what does one do with an imperious woman who, regardless of her good intentions, seems to restrict the independence of others? To me, the fact that Ambrosia is so difficult is precisely what makes this text so fascinating. The reader does not find here an idealized past viewed through the filter of the present but rather aspects of Arnim's present viewed through the eyes of a woman who is resilient, but also as a result of her insistence on autonomy, and perhaps of the deaths of those closest to her, at times forgetful of others' needs for autonomy. Here, then, we see "Bettine," warts and all, a figure who, like the Bettine of *Frühlingskranz*, demands that we accept her as she is.

Unlike her first two texts Arnim does not begin this one with advice to her reader as to how to read the letters that follow. Nevertheless, a line tucked into one of Ambrosia's earliest letters to Pamphilius serves the same purpose:

> Ihnen deucht es seltsam, durch ein Buch sich aller Welt offen zu geben;—ist es nicht seltsamer noch, den Menschen insgesamt, oder jedem einzelnen besonders, für etwas zu gelten, was man nicht ist; mich deucht, jedem sollte es wichtig sein, die vorgefaßte Meinung anderer, die nicht mit seinem das Ideal bildenden Streben übereinstimmt, zu überwinden. Lange genug hab ich für etwas anders gelten müssen, als ich verantworten möchte. (426)

The very fact that this persona is so different from—while still so similar to—the Bettine personae we have encountered thus far makes it imperative to include *Ambrosia* in a reading of Arnim's works as an extended developmental text. Time and experience, as Lauretis defines the later term, have changed the positionality of Bettina and her Bettines significantly, and ignoring Ambrosia—as much scholarship has done—means neglecting a significant chapter in this development.

The opening letter of the text briefly evokes the Bettine persona of Arnim's first text, for here Pamphilius addresses a person, whom we will soon see is clearly an adult woman, with the appellation *Kind*:

> *Innigst verehrte Gnädige Frau!* Oder dürfte ich—wie viel lieber—das Kind beim rechten Namen nennen, mit dem es im Reich der Geister getauft ist, der allein dem Sinn der Anrede genügt, weil unter ihm das Geistesohr alles erfaßt, was Mächtiges und Liebliches aus einem unverschlossenen weiten lebendigen Märchenreich erklungen ist—Ambrosia! (411)

Pamphilius combines in this passage the epithet *Kind* with that of Ambrosia, the food of the Greek and Roman gods that bestowed upon them immortality. In this manner, he attributes to his letter partner the eternal youth foregrounded in both *Briefwechsel* and *Günderode* and anticipates that she will share the secret of this youth with him. At the same time, he indirectly equates Ambrosia with Goethe by assigning to her the same function that Bettine of *Briefwechsel* assigned to Goethe, namely that of genius and mentor. As did the protagonist of Arnim's first text, Pamphilius looks to his mentor for inspiration for self-development, the prerequisite to immortality. Throughout the text, Pamphilius places himself in Ambrosia's shadow by making references to *Briefwechsel*: he defends Ambrosia against her critics as Bettine defended Goethe (412); he claims that he sends her his letters without rereading them (573), and he describes his desire to write poems with out any regard for the rules (602). In this manner, he positions himself as child vis-à-vis Ambrosia and expects her to teach him to become the genius-poet he considers her to be.

As the text progresses, a vivid picture of two distinct personalities emerges. Unlike his model, Bettine, Pamphilius describes himself as weak and sickly. He is prone to illness and apologetic for his family and background. He also realizes that he is not the poet he wishes himself to be. In contrast, Ambrosia is energetic and vivacious; she is actively involved in political and literary affairs. At times, the two exchange mutual words of praise. Often, however, Ambrosia criticizes Pamphilius's poems and rebukes him for his emotional distance while Pamphilius balks at Ambrosia's attempts to control him and to come emotionally (and their letters would seem to indicate, physically) closer to him. Yet, at the same time, the two figures maintain the directness and candor, the *Rücksichtslosigkeit*, that Frau Rath held up as one of her values in *Dies Buch*. There is between them a pact of honesty, both with regard to their feelings about and responses to each other and with regard to themselves. Not surprisingly, this experiment in truth-telling will also lead to a clash of wills.

The first major conflict arises when Pamphilius decides to travel to Italy rather than accept Ambrosia's invitation to work on her new edition of Achim von Arnim's works. Apparently forgetting the difficulties earlier Bettines faced while trying to emancipate themselves from their educators and guardians, Ambrosia fears that Pamphilius will waste time better spent under her influence, and in a manipulative twist, she accuses him of selfish behavior. She describes the differences between them as follows:

> Das ist der Unterschied zwischen Dir und mir, ich mag nur sollen und Du magst nur wollen. Und in meinem Müssen kann ich alles beherrschen und alles zum Zweck meines Müssens benützen, und wenn Du willst, kannst Du nichts Deinem Willen entgegensetzen, sondern mußt Dich hin und her treiben lassen von Deinem Willen. (503)

Not wishing Pamphilius to leave for Italy, Ambrosia sends him on a guilt trip. Convinced of her authority as a pedagogue, she refuses to acknowledge Nathusius's wish to travel as anything other than the selfish yearning of an immature child.

Despite, or perhaps in response to, Ambrosia's emotional manipulation, Nathusius departs for his planned journey. Upon his return, he and Ambrosia continue their correspondence and he publishes a report of his experiences in which he describes what he considers to be the inferiority of the Italians in comparison to the Germans. According to his letters to Ambrosia the text received less than favorable reviews, but his worst critic by far must be Ambrosia herself, who is justifiably enraged by the self-satisfied, arrogant tone of his report. In her critique, she offers a plea for accepting other cultures on their own terms, and indirectly, for understanding the country of her ancestors: one is reminded here that Ambrosia/Arnim was the daughter of an Italian immigrant.[3]

Pamphilius criticizes the Italian practice of Catholicism as one based on superstition, argues that Italian architecture is inferior to that of the Germans, ridicules what he perceives to be the Italians' lack of a work ethic, and in general asserts the superiority of Germans over Italians. In response, Ambrosia suggests he take a second look at the results of the Germans' so-called progress:

> O Du schreitest über den Geist dieses Volkes wie über ihren Erdboden, von dem Du auch nicht weißt, was er in seinem Schoß verbirgt. Du verklagst ihre Nichtigkeit, wie Du einen Acker der Unfruchtbarkeit beschuldigst, den die Pflugschar noch nicht durchfurcht hat. Aber Deine Deutschen sind durchfurcht und geworfelt nach allen Seiten und rajolt, und bald haben sie ihren Sand untergegraben und tragen ihnen schlechten Hafer vor wie nach. Was kann es Dich doch kümmern, ob die Marktfrauen sich in der Kirche ausruhen, ob die Männer quer durch die Kirche ihren Geschäften nachgehen, ob die Kinderwärterinnen die Kinder zum Zeitvertreib darin herumtragen?—Ist nicht Christus auch unter allen umhergewandelt und hat so sich ihnen genaht, daß er sie belehrte? (585)

Foreshadowing discussions in *Dämonen*, Ambrosia argues for acceptance of the Italians on their own terms, for the potential of education as the source of all development, and for more modesty and less hypocrisy on the part of the German with whom she is corresponding. Now much older than the Bettine of *Frühlingskranz* who stood up for Veilchen, and recalling Frau Rath of *Dies Buch*, Ambrosia takes full advantage of the opportunities she has to influence the opinions of others and to point out to them their hypocrisy.

In addition to concerning herself with Pamphilius's writing, Ambrosia also sends him reports of her own literary work: her English translation and the second edition of *Briefwechsel*, her earlier correspondence with Frau Rath and Beethoven, and most importantly, her correspondence with Günderode, which she discovers and begins to rewrite in the course of her correspondence with Pamphilius. She tells Pamphilius how important Günderode was for her and how difficult it is to find partners equal to Günderode in their ability to inspire and support her.

Upon completing *Günderode*, Ambrosia sends a copy of the manuscript to Pamphilius, who finds it inspiring. In response to the dedication, however, he offers a sobering assessment of the students (and with them, perhaps, of himself):

> Deine Widmung an *die Studenten* hätte mich lächeln gemacht, wenn ich mir die Studenten vergegenwärtigte, wie ich sie kennengelernt habe, wenn sie mich nicht zugleich so gerührt hätte durch den großartigen Glauben, den Du an die Menschen hast. Und gewiß, der Glaube an sie ist ja auch das einzige, was Großartiges aus ihnen wecken kann. Wie sie sich angesprochen sehen, so müssen sie zu werden sich bestreben, das zeigt überall das Edle der Natur im Menschen. (688)

For the reader familiar with *Günderode*, Pamphilius's skepticism about the discrepancy between Ambrosia's perceptions and the real human beings he knows sums up the tension between the ideal and the real that pervades both this earlier text and *Ambrosia*.

The break between Ambrosia and Pamphilius comes when the latter decides to marry. Pamphilius broaches the topic gingerly:

> Die Leute sagen, ich habe mich verlobt, sie haben sogar darauf bestanden, Karten zu drucken, wovon Du hier eine erhälst; ich weiß davon nichts, ich habe weder gegen die, die sie meine Braut nennen, noch gegen die Ihrigen, noch gegen die Meinigen ein Wort darüber verloren, aber ich lebe in einem innern vereinigten Leben, von dem ich fühle, daß es für alle Zeit und darüber hinaus—für ewig ist! (689)

He is happily in love but fearful of expressing to Ambrosia any sense of commitment to another—theirs is, after all, an emotional and erotic attachment.

Pamphilius tries to reassure Ambrosia of his loyalty by insisting that his fiancée reminds him of her, "Dasselbe, was mich zu Dir geführt hat, hat mich zu ihr geführt" (699). Ambrosia refuses to listen, however, and makes the same argument that she made when Pamphilius expressed his wish to travel to Italy: his decision is a form of betrayal because he is willingly departing from her sphere of influence and thus cutting short his apprenticeship. Indeed, the only bride she can imagine for her charge is an imaginary one who, astonishingly, recognizes not Pamphilius but Ambrosia as her lover:

> Ich erhalte Deinen Scheidebrief in diesem Augenblick, was soll ich Dir da noch vorschwindeln von Glückwünschen allenfalls? Dies fällt mir gar nicht ein; ich habe noch nie gegen Dich gelogen und wünsche Dir daher nicht Glück. Alles, was Du mir über Deine Gefühle schreibst, rührt mich nicht. Eine andere Braut habe ich im Sinn, eine himmlische, hoch in Lüften schwebend über mir und die Fahne schwingend, daß sie mich als den Geliebten erkenne; ja und ich werde sie einholen, trotz dem, der nicht bekennen wollte, ich sei ein starker Krieger mit kühnen, mit heiligen Kräften, sie zu erringen. Ja, guter *Pamphil*, was sollte ich Dir Glück wünschen?—Glück ist ein so geringfügiges Ding, daß der mir nichts gilt, der danach greift, oder darauf hofft oder baut. (691)

Here, Ambrosia's dream of success in her project of pedagogical eros becomes the fantasy of a pedagogical threesome. If Pamphilius will not recognize her as teacher in the sense of *Mittler* and *Dämon*, she wishes him a bride who might do so, and she suggests that she play the male role in order to seduce this woman of her dreams to join them. As a continuation of earlier Bettines, we can surmise that Ambrosia is unable to feel happiness for Pamphilius because she has been forced to take leave of so many of her interlocutors, and because she has had so much difficulty finding someone to live up to her standards for sociability. While the reader cheers for the Bettine of *Briefwechsel* as she asserts her genius as equal to that of Goethe, Ambrosia's self-assurance seems desperate and saddening.

The final three epistles of this letter documentation are written by Pamphilius. Like the Bettine of *Briefwechsel*, albeit perhaps without her strong drive to challenge social conventions and strive for political change, Pamphilius the child is now on his own in the world. Like the Bettine of *Frühlingskranz*, who must ward off both Clemens and Gachet, he has pulled himself out of the gravity field of the planet to whom he was attracted and he hopes "mit der Gunst der Götter" to prove to Ambrosia "daß die Ehe der Poesie nicht den Hals bricht" (707). Yet the conclusion of the text is as much about Ambrosia as it is about her student. She has, after all, been his mentor all this time, and he has learned many the lessons she wished to teach him better than she might have wished for. In his final lines, Pamphilius also alludes to *Dies Buch*: "Von andern hörte ich, Du schriebest ein Königsbuch, und habe eine heimliche Freude darauf" (707), thus again drawing attention to Ambrosia/Arnim as author.

The text concludes with four Hölderlin poems that Pamphilius received during a visit to the poet and then sent on to Ambrosia. By 1841, Hölderlin's mental illness was in an advanced state. As Pamphilius writes,

> nur irre Töne kommen aus seinem Mund, und jede Gegenwart der Menschen verschüchtert und beklemmt ihn. Nur die Muse vermag noch mit ihm zu reden, und in einzelnen Stunden schreibt er Verse, kleine Gedichte auf, in denen sich die frühere Tiefe und Anmut des Geistes spiegelt, aber jäh unmittelbar in dem Verstande unzugängliche Wortrhythmen übergeht. (706)

Recalling Bettine's defense of Hölderlin in *Günderode*, Arnim concludes her text with the words of this poet with whose marginal status she so closely identified. In that text, Bettine identified as the source of Hölderlin's *Wahnsinn* the fact that he could find no echo in anyone else. At the end of *Ambrosia*, we see a woman writer who, although perfectly sane, has lost her dialogue partner, her own source of resonance.

Like its predecessors, this text deals with education, and here Ambrosia tries to educate Pamphilius in both the art of sociability and the skill of political thought and action. She serves as a model for him in her roles as child, activist, writer, and individual. For Arnim, however, education is based on interaction with another, and this text addresses more directly than any of Arnim's other texts the difficulty of a truly reciprocal relationship. In her roles as mother, friend and lover, and educator, Ambrosia switches into a dominant mode that earlier Bettines struggled to resist, but this very dominance is a response to the isolation that, in turn, is the price of her independence.

Writer and Activist—Without Apologies

The Bettine personae of *Briefwechsel*, *Günderode*, and *Frühlingskranz* often resist the appellation of writer, even as one sees them developing as writers and formulating theories of writing. The girl sitting at Frau Rath's feet in *Dies Buch* and the narrator of *Dämonen* both claim to be no more than scribes, of Frau Rath and the King's genius respectively. At least on the surface, all of these texts appear to de-emphasize authorship. In contrast, *Ambrosia* foregrounds Ambrosia/Arnim as a writer whose skills give her license to play the master to Pamphilius's apprentice. I agree with French that this text contains some of Arnim's most forceful statements on her life and work and especially her writing (*Bettine von Arnim*). Indeed, the role of writer is Ambrosia's most important, and her assertiveness in this role contradicts Daley's claim that "confident self presentation" is to be found in the nineteenth century only in men's letter writing (106).

Ambrosia describes herself as incessantly active. She writes for example of her English translation of *Briefwechsel*:

> Meine englische Übersetzung von dem Buch, von dem die Engländer behaupten, daß es nicht übersetzt werden könne, macht mich ganz dumm, weil sie gescheuter ist wie ich; und wie jene Zauberlehrlinge über die Großtaten der zitierten Geister erstaunten, so erstaune ich mich über diese Übersetzung; und alle Menschen erstaunen mit, aber am meisten darüber, daß ich die Kühnheit habe, immer siebentausend Exemplare von meinem Brouillon ziehen zu lassen. (497–498)

Here, we find no frustration with the difficulty of confining thoughts in written language. Rather, Ambrosia finds pleasure in writing and is proud of the results.

Now an adult, the difficulties that plague Ambrosia as a writer have nothing to do with the wish to present herself as a child, nor with self doubts nor questions as to the adequacy of the written word. One hundred pages after the above citation, she describes her difficulty selling the second German-language edition of *Briefwechsel*. She also laments the time she must put into publishing Achim von Arnim's collected works and her frustration with her sense of obligation to others:

> Die Gesamtwerke, deren Druck heute begonnen hat, nehmen mir viel Zeit. Angelegenheiten andrer Menschen, denen ich mich berufen fühle zu dienen und zu helfen, nicht weil sie mich interessieren oder mir's Dank wissen, sondern weil sie sich selbst nicht zu helfen wissen und mir's verargen, liegen mir auch wie eine Last auf, die ich nur mit Energie zu bestreiten vermag. Dabei ereignet sich's denn, daß man glaubt mir widersprechen zu müssen, Steine in den Weg zu legen; kurz eine Laufbahn mit Hindernissen. (529)

The young Bettine who made a vow to help those in need has, in this text, become a person to whom those in need turn for help, which of course takes time away from her writing and publishing efforts. This passage reveals the exhaustion Ambrosia feels after having tried to accommodate their needs but also her awareness that writing has become her career, albeit one frought with difficulties.

Ambrosia's activity does have its rewards, as indicated by the pleasure she takes in her translation of *Briefwechsel*. She feels equally elated after completing *Günderode*:

> Du kannst mir Glück wünschen, gestern habe ich nach einer Reihe von Tagen, die mit angestrengter Arbeit überfüllt waren, die *Günderode* beendet...Den Tag vorher war ich ganz schwindlig geworden über ein Brief der *Günderode*, wo sie mich erinnert, daß ich im Traum habe wollen mit einem, der hingerichtet wurde, aufs Schafott steigen, und daß ich verzweifelt aufgewacht sei, weil der Scharfrichter ihm den Streich gegeben habe, noch eh ich meinen Kopf mit auf den Block legen konnte. (677–678)

Ambrosia expresses no insecurities about whether or not her text says what she wants it to say. She has finished it and asks only that Pamphilius congratulate her. Her project completed, however, Ambrosia is also reminded of Günderode's prophecy that she/Bettine would be unable to realize all of her ambitions. Perhaps it is for this reason that Ambrosia is so adamant about assuming the role of Pamphilius's mentor.

Now an established author, Ambrosia feels free to give Pamphilius advice about his writing. Her suggestions are, however, often contradictory. On the one hand she tells him, "Das Urteil, ob Sie Ihre Gedichte drucken sollen, muß aus Ihrer Überzeugung hervorgehen" (427). On the other hand, she writes of one of his collections of poems, "erstens sind sie nicht rein geschrieben, es würde zu tausend Mißverständnissen Anlaß geben, sie so abdrucken zu lassen...man gibt niemals Gedichte, ohne sie ganz rein und frei von jedem Fehl, so wie sie im Geist sein sollen, auch in der Abschrift" (533). This second passage indicates that Ambrosia/Arnim was more concerned about the form of her writing than many critics give her credit for being, that she did not merely write into the wind. At the same time, these contradictory statements reveal the difficulty of Arnim's conception of genius in general. How does one know when to trust one's genius? Should Pamphilius trust his instincts as to when to publish his poems, or should Ambrosia trust hers in telling him that they are not ready for publication? How does one know when to play the pupil and when to play the teacher? It is the struggle of trying to negotiate these positions that ultimately leads this pupil and his teacher to grow apart.

Closely related to Ambrosia's role as writer is that as public activist. For her, writing represents one part of a multifaceted life and she devotes herself whole-heartedly to all of her commitments. She points to the extent of her connections throughout Germany by offering to write letters of introduction for Pamphilius to use in his travels. She describes her engagement with the trial of the Göttingen Seven and her frustration with her brother-in-law Savigny for failing to support the Grimms. And she writes of her work during one of the repeated outbreaks of cholera in Berlin. Seemingly immune to all illnesses, she spends days and nights with the sick and dying. She writes in one passage, "Also drum schrieb ich nicht, weil Särge zu bestellen waren, russische Totenfeier zu halten und nachts zwischen Schlaf und Wachen kaum Deiner zu denken" (508), and in another:

> Noch kommen tausenderlei Dinge mir in den Weg, von Briefen, die eine Antwort erfordern, von Forderungen, die ich abschlagen muß—ich bin bis jetzt schlaflos gewesen und hab also in der Nacht manches abgemacht, wozu am Tag keine Zeit war,—dies versetzt in einen so nüchternen Zustand, daß man sagen möchte, man sei des Lebens satt; da ich aber nie hungrig darauf war, so kann ich's auch nicht satt werden; es zieht so hin, schimmerlos. (531)

These passages offer no glimmer of the youthfully optimistic Bettine who appears in Arnim's other texts, but rather of a woman who must battle incessantly to realize her dreams: to come to the aid of others, to publish her writing. She must watch people die despite her efforts to help them, and following the appearance of *Dies Buch*, she must struggle with Prussian censors over the publication of subsequent texts; the title page of *Ambrosia* had to be reprinted three times before the censors would release the book. Finally, she is confronted with family members—her brothers and sisters (including her brother-in-law Savigny) and many of her children—who disapprove of what she is doing: "Familienleben ist von mir abgesondert, ich bin allein…man duldet mich nur, der Anteil, den man an mir nimmt, ist Tadel, daß ich mich solcher Dinge annehme, die mich nichts angehen" (531). Although Arnim's Bettine personae proclaim repeatedly that one should pay no heed to what others think but rather only to one's own conscience, Ambrosia's experience seems to indicate how wearing it is for the individual to go her own way. In this text, then, Arnim depicts Ambrosia as writer, and above all activist, but she also points to the toll that such activism takes despite her emphasis on youth and eternal life.

Child

Giving the lie to those who would see Arnim's "Bettine" as *das ewige Kind*, the role of child in this text belongs not to her Bettine persona Ambrosia but to her interlocutor. In his first letter, Pamphilius compares himself to the childlike Bettine of *Briefwechsel*, effectively positioning Ambrosia in the role of Goethe, i.e., in the role of mentor. In response, Ambrosia expresses satisfaction with this division of roles:

> Im März also bekamen Sie ein Buch, dessen Titel Ihnen Geheimnisvolles über *Goethe* und das Kind anzudeuten schien. Sie dachten: "Was mag das sein?"—und die Überzeugung, Sie seien Kind so gut wie jenes, um mit dem größten Dichter unbefangen sich zu messen, mußte Ihnen Ihr heiliges Recht an diese Briefe bewähren; das hab ich auch mit diesem Titel gewollt: listig das Jünglingsalter locken, ein rascheres Tempo dem Hymnus der Jugend in ihren Herzen wecken und so die Frühlingslüfte mit süßen Seufzern befrachten, und es ist mir gelungen, Sie schreiben mir's...wie freut mich's! und noch, daß Sie gern über ihm einschliefen am stillen Mittag—und daß Sie gern nicht mehr denken wollten, lieber träumen. (415–416)

Pamphilius compliments Ambrosia with proof that her text has had its desired effect, and she clearly wishes to continue to wield influence over him.

In *Ambrosia*, Arnim continues to employ the figure of the child to represent an ideal person open to influence and growth, and she assigns Ambrosia the role of the figure who inspires this growth, thus equating her with Goethe. Nevertheless, the male mentor of a child takes on far different valences from those of the female mentor. Whereas Goethe, "the father" of the child Bettine, struggled to maintain a distant relationship to his pupil, Ambrosia "the mother" assumes a far more possessive, one could even say domineering stance towards her "child." Together with the fact that Pamphilius seems far less willing to embrace life than was Bettine, this affects how he plays his role.

Bettine delights in her meetings with Goethe and extends these meetings into fantasies about him while at the same time feeling free to criticize his literary works and especially the female characters in them. In contrast to this spontaneous child, Pamphilius seems more like a moody adolescent.

He wishes to bask in Ambrosia's light but then complains that he feels limited in her presence. She responds that the problem lies in his lack of spontaneity and inner freedom:

> Der junge *Ilius* [here: Döring] hat mir auch über Deinen Besuch geschrieben, und daß Du geäußert: mir gegenüber habest Du Dich stets unfrei und wie des eignen Willens beraubt gefühlt, und daß in Gesellschaft anderer mit mir zusammen zu sein Dich befange. Das hast Du mit dem Fürsten P. gemein, der mir oft darüber klagte, aber ob es bei Dir denselben Grund hat wie bei ihm, der mir offenherzig gestand, er schäme sich, in meiner Gegenwart mit den Leuten seine gewöhnliche Rolle zu spielen, das weiß ich nicht.—Aber das weiß ich, daß es vergeblich ist, mit Dir der Aufgabe nachzustreben: werdet wie die Kinder,—denn die Harmonie der Offenherzigkeit wird uns nicht gegenseitig durchströmen, was hab ich also für ein Verhältnis zu Dir?—keins, das mich ergreifen könnte. (547)

Ambrosia attempts to understand Pamphilius by recalling a similar difficulty with Pückler-Muskau, whose discomfort stemmed, he claimed, from his fear of resisting middle-class expectations. She finds no answers, however, and comes only to the realization that Pamphilius is incapable of playing the child that he claims he is and that she wants him to be. The difficulty comes from two sides. On the one hand, Ambrosia is so controlling that she leaves little room for free and creative development. She forgets that Goethe as *Mittler* and mentor was more a figment of Bettine's imagination than an actual person telling her how to write and be in the world. On the other hand, Pamphilius lacks the will, the inner genius or daemon, to make creative use of his relationship with his mentor. He does play the child in this text, but in comparison to Bettine he lacks imagination, and his growth therefore seems stunted.

Mother/Lover

Referring to a role also articulated in *Dies Buch*, and later in *Dämonen*, Ambrosia plays in this text the role of mother to Pamphilius. Whereas in the other two texts the role of mother is a positive one, representing an attempt to transfer the constructive attributes traditionally assigned to women (those of nurturance, support, and understanding) to the public sphere, in this text the role of mother is more disturbing. The mother we see here is sometimes nurturing but often demanding, imperious, and controlling; at the same time, she depicts herself as passive and incapable of directing her "child" Pamphilius. It is hard to know what to make of such a figure. Is she merely living out her own philosophy of acting according to what her genius commands? Is she lonely and therefore incapable of understanding how her wishes affect others? Is her behavior understandable considering who her partner is? Has she forgotten her own/Bettine's earlier struggles for self-definition against others? Waldstein supports the latter hypothesis:

> In the epistolary novels Bettine von Arnim comes full circle. None of her fictional correspondences with men completely reaches the goal of total communication. The epistolary partners are never equal. A paternal attitude toward the female correspondent restricts the exchange in *Goethe's Briefwechsel mit einem Kinde* and *Clemens Brentano's Frühlingskranz*, and the maternal posturing of the female character in *Ilius Pamphilius und die Ambrosia* reflects a similar relationship to the one in *Goethe's Briefwechsel*, only with the gender roles reversed. (58)

Yet the dynamics of *Briefwechsel* and *Ambrosia* do not mirror each other exactly, for the distribution of the number of letters between the two partners is more equal in *Pamphilius*, and Ambrosia is both more engaged with her partner than was Goethe *and* more aware of her own failings at the practice of sociability. One can assume that, since Arnim spent very little time revising this text, it reflects the vicissitudes of an imperfect human being rather than those of an idealized literary figure. At the same time, this text reveals perhaps more than any of Arnim's other novel-length works the near impossibility of achieving the ideal of sociability for which all of Arnim's Bettine peronae—and presumably also the author herself—strove.

In many respects, Ambrosia's letters sound like those of the stereotypical mother hen. She concerns herself with Pamphilius's health and recommends homeopathic cures for his ailments[4] while also pointing out to him the relationship between psychic and physical well-being: "Zweifel ist Krankheit, Zuversicht ist die Gesundheit dafür.—Haben Sie keine Krankheit" (462). She complains when he doesn't write, worrying that he has found someone else to take her place (476). She says she wishes to help him in his development: "das Schicksal spielte mir Fäden in die Hand, die mir für dich gesponnen schienen, ich wollte Dich auffordern, sie zu durchweben und so Dein Verhältnis mit Deiner Zukunft zu beginnen" (509). In many ways, these tasks are similar to those that are recommended to rulers in *Dies Buch* and *Dämonen*: the ruler should strive to heal the ills of the people and further their development to insure that they continue to respect the ruler and not depart in search of another.

There is in this text, however, another aspect of the mother, one in line with early- and mid-nineteenth-century conceptions of the role[5] but seemingly at odds with the insistence of earlier Bettines on self-determination, namely the self-sacrificial aspect of the role. Comparing herself to the Egyptian goddess Isis, for example, Ambrosia writes: "Dieses symbolische Frucht der Mutter Isis, die so stolz aus tausend Brüsten die allgegenwärtige Natur tränkt und doch so demütig sich unter den Fuß einer zukünftigen Generation schmiegt, beweist, mit welchem Recht die Nachkommen ihren Vordern den Fuß in den Nacken setzen" (435). That one generation must give way to another is clear already in the dedication of *Günderode*, but the masochistic language of this passage causes the reader to pause and wonder why all of the sudden we see such a submissive Bettine persona, one who also writes, "ich [will] lieber lieben als geliebt sein" (509). In her review of 1849, Fanny Lewald praises "den tiefen selbstverleugnenden Liebesdienst der Frauenseele" (681) revealed in the text, but today's reader has difficulty reconciling Ambrosia's self-assertion with this self-denial.

In part, the reason this depiction of a mother figure strikes us as so disturbing is because it meshes with that of the lover. Unlike the relationship of Frau Rath or the narrator to the king in *Dies Buch* and *Dämonen*, respectively, in which motherhood had no erotic overtones, here Ambrosia's attraction to Pamphilius is not only that of a mother to a child but also that of the pedagogical eros seen in *Briefwechsel* and *Günderode*. To achieve the relationship of romantic sociability that she considers the foundation of education, Ambrosia tries to get as close as possible to her partner, or so it seems to Pamphilius. In one of his harshest and most direct letters, Pamphilius writes that the more Ambrosia seems drawn to him, the more he resists her advances:

> Ich will wagen, Dir zu mißfallen, um aufrichtig gegen Dich zu sein und Dir vielleicht einen Dienst damit zu erweisen.—Ich habe nämlich bemerkt: je einladender Deine Briefe zur Antwort sind, je zuvorkommender und herzlicher, desto langsamer tritt der Zeitpunkt ein, wo meine Antwort reif wird, je gleichgültiger sie sind, desto eifriger schreib ich wieder…Überall, wo man auf etwas dringt, fordert oder nur dem Ähnliches tut, regt man in den Göttern und in den Menschen ein ge-

wisses widerstrebendes Prinzip gegen sich auf. (493)

In keeping his distance Pamphilius wishes to have a relationship with the Ambrosia he imagines, and he fears that Ambrosia wants to control him, to deprive him of his own individuality. He therefore insists in words that echo those we have heard many times from Bettine, "Sollte man nun den Menschen nicht auch für den Künstler seines eigenen Lebens halten können?" (515) He wishes to be an artist, and he wishes his life to be more than his biography, but on his own terms.

Ambrosia's response to Pamphilius's reluctance to come closer to her is curious in its ambivalence, for she both maintains an ideal of love based on the mutual give-and-take and describes as her own form of love one that is astoundingly narcissistic. She recalls for example the moment when she first saw herself in the mirror, a scene recounted in *Briefwechsel*. Just as the Bettine personae of *Briefwechsel* and *Günderode* reassess their readings of Mignon, here we see a Bettine persona—Ambrosia—reassessing her reading of herself. Whereas in the earlier work the mirror scene represented a triumphant moment of individuation, Ambrosia recalls this moment of separation with a sense of loss. In seeing herself in the mirror, Ambrosia now claims, she realized how alone she was in the world:

> Die *Ambrosia*, die als Kind im Spiegel erkannte, daß sie alles mit *sich* abmachen müsse, der war nichts an andern gelegen; einen Augenblick vielleicht, solang es nötig war, die Befruchtung in den Geist aufzunehmen, aber ein solcher Augenblick verschlingt sich in der eignen Tiefe, und ob er auch dem andern zu verdanken ist, so ist er ihm doch nicht mitgeteilt und also gleichsam unabhängig—und was hätte ich endlich davon, daß mich einer lieb hätte?—Bedenk's und sage selber!—Hier auf diesem Erdenrund, wo die Menschen auseinandergleiten, als ob es mit Glatteis überzogen wär; wo sie nicht Macht haben, einen Atemzug lang aneinander zu halten, und doch immer von der Macht der Leidenschaft schwindeln. Wär Liebe wahrhaftig, so zeigte sie sich nicht als Gespenst in Form von Leidenschaften, sondern sie wär unser Element, und da wär denn freilich nicht die Rede von Ansichthalten. (512)

Arnim's Bettine has changed over time, and this touching passage reveals Ambrosia's new sense of the futility of a truly reciprocal love. The ideal of love between two autonomous individuals in which there is a balance between give and take, domination and submission, appears to be a chimera. Ambrosia herself questions the validity of passion. Yet if one looks back at the texts preceding *Ambrosia* and reads them as one continuous developmental text, one finds a possible explanation for her stance. With the exception of *Dies Buch*, all end on the note of loss. In each work "Bettine" has achieved autonomy but is left standing alone, either because her partner refuses to communicate or commits suicide, or because she has outgrown her partner. With this experience behind her, it is no wonder that Ambrosia has become skeptical about the potential for *Geselligkeit*. In this text, she remembers the intimacy she shared with Günderode and Schleiermacher (she includes among her letters an obituary she wrote upon the theologian's death), but these events are long past and the reader knows that even the relationship with Günderode lacked the complete reciprocity for which Arnim's figures (and certainly the author herself) were searching.

Her experience has made Ambrosia skeptical about love. At one point, she even pokes fun at her own passion for Pamphilius by writing him in language that even for Arnim is exaggeratedly melodramatic in order, so she claims, to keep him from writing her when he travels to Italy:

> Und damit Du mir ja nicht mehr schreibst, so sage ich Dir hier: *Pamphil*, ich bin von Herzen in Dich verliebt, und Oh! und Ach!—Und sage Dir nochmals: Ich küsse Deine Hände und Füße. Und sage Dir nochmals: Ich möchte Dich in meine Seele begraben!—Das wird Dir das Scheiden leicht machen. (514)

Although Ambrosia is obviously attached to Pamphilius and although her claims to him often seem unjustified, this passage strikes an ironic tone found in no other place in the text: here Ambrosia uses her language to become the maternal lover Pamphilius fears. She does this in part to make him feel guilty for travelling to Italy (she wants no letters from him while he is there) but also to prove to him she is not who he thinks she is.

Indeed, when Ambrosia writes of her love, she writes of a self-love, one that requires others for inspiration but is not dependent on them:

> Ich liebe nicht, ich tue aber alles andern zulieb; und wo ich's nicht tue oder gar um Liebe werbe, mit dem, was ich andern zuliebe tue, da tritt der einzige Freund, der Genius, aus dem Spiegel auf, in seiner ganzen mächtigen Schönheit und zeigt sich mir und fragt: "Wie kannst du mich verleugnen und nach der Liebe von andern fragen, da du mich darum verscherzest, die ich allein schön für dich bin?"—Ja guter *Pamphil*, für jeden gibt es eine alleinige Schönheit, der er treu

> sein soll, und diese ist *das eigne Ideal*. Und mein Ideal ist diese Ironie in der Liebe, die dazu lächelt, daß sie es nicht erreicht, nicht aber "klagt" (wie Du schreibst), daß sie verlassen ist. (512)

Ambrosia, then, is fixated not on Pamphilius but on herself, on her genius, but requires him for confirmation of her ability to inspire, to share her genius with others. This may explain her jealousy when he travels to Italy and when he decides to marry, for if in loving him as her child and lover she is loving the person she wishes to be the mirror of herself, loss of him means loss of self. It is hard to tell whether such jealousy results from genuine loss or whether it merely reveals her narcissism. Perhaps the best explanation is that she is capable of love but unable to find an object for it: "ich [war] nie in meinem Leben verliebt...aber meine große Anlage ist *Lieben*, das ist was anders.—Meine Energie ist, diese Liebe trotz der mißlichsten Umstände lebendig zu erhalten (wirksam), aber manchmal kommt mein Dämon und bläst mir's Licht vor der Nase aus, das muß ich mir auch gefallen lassen" (678). Ambrosia's emotional attachment to Pamphilius is thus a product of both love (that of a woman and of a mother) and loneliness.

Friendship and Autonomy

As we have seen in earlier texts, the role of lover is closely related to that of friend, and in this text Ambrosia not only refers to Pamphilius as child and lover but also tries to win him over as a friend. Just as she wishes to see herself mirrored in him and his development, she also presents herself as a mirror to him, thus offering him the reciprocity of romantic sociability:

> Der junge *Pamphil* hält einen Spiegel in der Hand und schaut hinein, und der ist schön, der aus dem Spiegel ihn ansieht.—Wessen Seele ein Spiegel ist, die ist klar und da kann das Bild im Spiegel ja auch nur schön sein, drum liebe die Bilder deiner Seele, des Bild ist es, den du lieben sollst als dich selbst, und Gott, der in dir ist über alles, drum leg die Hand aufs Herz, so legst du's auf den größten Schatz, auf den dir nächsten und auf den Gott. (482)

Although Ambrosia wishes to play multiple roles with him, he interprets her actions as confining and insists upon using words that recall those of earlier Bettines: "Treu kann man nur dem sein, was uns eigen ist. So sind uns auch die Gedanken treu, die uns eingenommen haben; wenn man sie haschte, hätte man sie nicht" (438). With this, we have an explicit discussion of a tension that has run as an undercurrent throughout Arnim's texts, namely that between the desire for sociability, for communication and union with another, and the desire for individuality and freedom from the influence of others in order to follow one's inner voice. In earlier texts, Bettine used interaction with others as a springboard from which to develop a sense of self, but she had little power to influence or change others' lives. As a result of her prominence and self-assurance, the situation is now different. Now it is Pamphilius who must assert his individuality, telling her: "Ich kann auch nicht versprechen, daß ich gegen Sie immer derselbe bleiben will, nur ich will sich's entwickeln lassen, so naturgetreu wie möglich" (447). In contrast, Ambrosia appears only to want to control him, to tell him when to travel and how to write and with whom to associate.

Ambrosia is imperious, but she also knows how her words and actions influence others:

> *Pamphilius!* ich muß Ihnen schreiben, was mich schon mehrere Tage bedrückt. Ich glaube, meine Nähe ist Ihnen unbequem; was auch die Veranlassung dieses sonderbaren Resultats unseres Umgangs sein mag: es war von meiner Seite kein böser Wille; seien Sie so großmütig, es zu glauben und das Unwillkürliche zu verzeihen. Ich bin durch lange Erfahrungen darauf gefaßt, wo ich mich angezogen fühle, abzustoßen, und habe mich bloß zwischen Zurückweisenden durch das Lebensgewühl gedrängt. So kömmt's, daß ich in der Einsamkeit den einzigen Zeugen meiner Gesinnung deutlich vernehme, nämlich ihren Widerhall, dieser ist's, dem ich alles zulieb tue, um ihn schöner auf mich zurückströmen zu lassen. Wenn denn so einer wie Sie eine Weile bei mir aushart, da kann ich ihn nur lieben als jenen Widerhall; ich sag ihm alles und empfinde es aus ihm auf mich zurückströmen, dann kann ich nur gar zu geschwind vergessen, daß er noch etwas anders sein könnte, als bloß mir zugewendet; ein geheimes Bewußtsein, daß ich in ihm lebe, und daß er mich jeden Augenblick empfinde, begleitet mich, es macht mich feurig, gleichsam, als sei mir ein neues Element angewiesen, in dem die Geister sich um mich her tummeln; ich fühl's, daß nicht ich mich ihrer bemeistern werde, sondern diese sich meiner. (441)

Here Ambrosia reveals her awareness of the narcissistic nature of her wish for friendship. She sees that, by loving, she engages in the activity that many of Arnim's other Bettine personae have opposed when they sensed it in others: her form of sociability imposes limits on others, on who they can be. Unlike Clemens of *Frühlingskranz*, however, Ambrosia is fully aware that she reads Pamphilius in a language different from the one in which he reads himself.

Summary: The Challenge of Agency

In many ways the main characters of *Ambrosia* act out the roles of Goethe and Bettine in *Briefwechsel*, but as a sure indicator of her maturation, it is now the female character Ambrosia who "plays Goethe." One can also read this text within the historical bookends of Bettine Brentano's reacquaintance with Clemens and her first encounter with Philipp Nathusius. Although the correspondences that served as the basis for *Frühlingskranz* and *Ambrosia* respectively occurred more than three decades apart from one another, the texts that developed out of these correspondences were remarkably similar. Both dealt with the limits of sociability and both begged the question as to whether deep intimate friendship on the one hand and development of the individual on the other were, for Arnim's Bettine personae, compatible with one another. In *Frühlingskranz* Clemens treats Bettine as no more than an extension of himself; the Bettine figure of *Ambrosia* does the same with Pamphilius. And whereas in *Frühlingskranz* Bettine attempts to free herself from prescribed gender roles, *Ambrosia* reveals not only that women are capable of agency, but that agency brings with it both the responsibility to respect others' individuality and the potential for disregarding that individuality.

In this text, Arnim had little distance to her source material. She therefore had less opportunity for idealization of her Bettine persona, whom we see here with many flaws. Despite these weaknesses, I suggest that this figure can be distinguished from a figure like Clemens through the words she uses and the sensitivity she displays in the passage cited above. Ambrosia is not immune to the perils of autonomy, but standing in a line of personae who must constantly fight for a degree of self determination, she is capable of seeing her own weaknesses and of realizing that the other just may be someone other than she believes him to be. As we will see in the next chapter, Arnim turns in her final work, *Gespräche mit Dämonen*, to a discussion of the repercussions and responsibilities of autonomy as they relate to the role of the king and his understanding of *das Volk*.

CHAPTER SIX

The Genius Speaks:
Gespräche mit Dämonen (1852)

Arnim's texts reveal the extent to which for her the personal was political; her writing developed out of a confluence of personal development and the political events of her day. *Goethe's Briefwechsel mit einem Kinde*, bears the mark of both the Tyrolean uprising of 1809 and the tensions of the *Vormärz*. At the same time, with this first published work the fifty-year-old author began a narrative account of her literary Bettine that ran parallel to her own adult self-fashioning. Fittingly for such a beginning, she depicted her *Doppelgänger* as a child, passionately in love with and desirous of learning from arguably the best known figure in German letters. Subsequently, throughout Arnim's remaining major works, this figure grows, changes, adopts new roles and alters others, fragments into a number of different, complementary figures, and comes to reside again in a figure named Bettine, then Ambrosia, responding always to her conversation partners and to broader political events. In *Gespräche mit Dämonen*, Bettine transforms into a daemon, an apotheosis of her previous self/selves.

The central event that informed Arnim's final work was the revolutionary upheaval of 1848. Arnim witnessed the rebellion in Berlin firsthand and she followed with concern reports of the suppression of uprisings in Poland and Hungary. Although by this time Arnim no longer wielded the same influence as after the publication of *Dies Buch gehört dem König*, she remained a radical and controversial thinker who maintained contact with the leading liberal thinkers of the period. In fact, her associations with revolutionaries led to a small feud in her own household as she, together with her more liberal daughter Gisela, was forced in the summer of 1848 to establish a salon separate from that of her more conservative daughters, Maximiliane and Armgardt. As Maximiliane later wrote:

> Auf die Dauer ging es aber doch nicht an, daß unsere Freunde [von Hof und Adel] in Bettinas Saal mit den Revolutionären zusammentrafen, ohne daß Reibungen oder doch Verstimmungen drohten...So wurde—schiedlich, friedlich—die weise Einrichtung getroffen, die noch lange...bestanden hat: im Hause Arnim gab es zwei Salons, einen demokratischen und einen aristokratischen. Links vom Saal in unseren Räumen empfingen wir unsere Freunde, rechts in ihren Zimmern Bettina ihre "edlen" Weltverbesserer. (Arnim, *Die Andacht zum Menschenbild* 337)

Yet Arnim's activity was not confined to the limited realm of her salon. In the years directly following the revolution, she continued to strive through personal intervention for influence over public events and opinion. She anonymously published "An die aufgelös'te Preußische National-Versammlung. Stimmen aus Paris," a brochure sharply critical of the events in Poland. She corresponded with the Hungarian writer Karl Maria Benkert, who had translated the poetry of the revolutionary poet Petöfi, and in 1850 she wrote her own poem, "Petöfy dem Sonnengott," dedicated to this poet and the memory of the Hungarian revolution. She followed with keen interest ongoing discussions of the emancipation of the Jews, and most importantly, she continued to strive to influence public affairs through her correspondence with Friedrich Wilhelm IV. She wrote to him, for example, to encourage him to release the revolutionary Gottfried Kinkel from prison.

Arnim's final work both represents the author's final attempt to effect political change through the written word and presents the reader with an apotheosis of Arnim's Bettine personae in the form of a daemon. Notably, the self-assurance of her character provides a stark contrast to the hopelessness of her endeavor and to the lack of attention given the book upon publication. Whereas Arnim may have been sure of her message, and whereas she remained active in the service of the poor and oppressed until physical debility forced her to discontinue her work,[1] she had by this time lost her status as a public figure to be reckoned with. Her efforts found little resonance, little reflection in the way of others' reception of her ideas, in other words, little of what she required for her own productivity. In the wake of the revolution of 1848 and the publication of Marx's

Communist Manifesto the same year, Arnim lost her hold on public interest altogether. This by no means implies that we should discount Arnim's final work. As a document of one—for the time and place in which she was writing uniquely public—woman's belief in enlightened and romantic conversation as well as of the culmination of her sense of identity, the text deserves considerably more attention than it has received thus far.

In *Dämonen* Arnim turns from epistolarity back to the conversational form she employed in *Dies Buch*, a move required by the message she wished to convey. As Schmitz notes,

> Im Alterswerk [wird] ganz aus dem Formgedanken des Gesprächs entwickelt— vom "inneren," erinnernden Selbstgespräch über den Dialog mit dem König, dessen "innerer Sinn" im Traum aufnahmefähig ist, bis zum Vision einer Mitteilungsgemeinschaft der Welt, wie sie zuerst im Republikanismus der Frühromantik formuliert worden war. ("Die freie Kultur," 143-144)

This conversation therefore expands beyond the dialog with the king and a world community to include the reader "in an attempt to achieve a completed act of communication, in which artistic and political visions can inspire efforts to help shape the future" (Baldwin 226). Such communication encourages process-oriented thinking and individual development, both of which have as their goal political enlightenment.[2] Arnim thus aims in this work not to offer specific answers to the social and political problems she so relentlessly criticizes, but rather to suggest conversation as a space— and as she believed after the failure of the revolution, the only space—in which to discover directions that might lead to viable change. Yet despite the emancipatory nature of this realm of conversation, the conversations of this text cannot be read as free-floating, spontaneous interaction. As with her earlier works, Arnim structures her conversations with daemons in order to highlight specific themes and to direct her text towards a distinct conclusion.

Like its thematic predecessor, *Dies Buch*, *Dämonen* begins with a monologue and progresses to a conversation first between two and then among multiple partners. But whereas Arnim used the title *Dies Buch gehört dem König* to dedicate the work to Friedrich Wilhelm IV, she dedicated her final work to a spirit embodied by another ruler: "Dem Geist des Islam vertreten durch den großmütigen ABDUL-MEDSCHID-KAHN

Kaiser der Osmanen." This dedication to a non-European, non-Christian ruler surely expressed to Arnim's readers, especially to those familiar with her oeuvre, her frustration not only with the Prussian king, but also with the Prussian state and Christian religion in general. In addition to leading the Crimean War against Russia (1853–1856) towards the end of his reign, Abd al-Madjîd I (Ottoman sultan from 1839 to 1861) became known for continuing the reforms instituted by his father Mahmud II. These measures included further centralization of the government, educational reforms, and the construction of hospitals, the first depository for state archives, and the first theater. He also strove to establish equality among all Ottonian subjects. Abd al-Madjîd thus offered a model for the type of ruler that Arnim hoped she could inspire Friedrich Wilhelm IV to become.[3]

The reader familiar with Arnim's earlier works has by now come to expect that the introductory sections of her work suggest a standpoint for her reader. In this text she employs two brief sections, one untitled and the other dated 4 April 1808, to remind her readers of the intertextual links between her works and to encourage a reading of this work as a continuation of her previous publications. She achieves this in part by once again reminding her reader of her relationships to the king and to Goethe.

Like the figure in *Dies Buch* who serves as scribe for Frau Rath, the narrator of this text remains unnamed, while at the same time clearly being a continuation or another facet of Arnim's Bettine personae. The narrator begins by situating herself between two representatives of (potential) genius, a representative of political genius on the one hand and of poetic genius on the other. She muses:

> Es ist schon manches Jahr her, da stand ich vor einem König voll huldreichem Willen zu mir. Sein guter Dämon stand neben mir und schloß meine Lippen vor törichten Schmeichelreden, aber anderer Lobreden verleugneten diese Ehrfurcht der Pietät, die mich schweigen hieß.—
> Und nach längerer Zeit—es war im Jahr, wo alle Huldigungen dem großen Dichter galten, der hundert Jahre früher dem deutschen Volk geboren war—da sammelte auch ich verklungne Laute seinem Gedächtnis.—Zu derselben Zeit gelangte dieselbe Königsstimme zu mir, sie hat aber nicht mehr so freundlich geklungen. (259)

In the year of the 100th anniversary of Goethe's birth, while she continued to work on her monument to him, Arnim's relationship to the king was unraveling. Reflecting on this situation, the narrator admits that she no longer wields the influence over the king that she once had. Saddened by the temporal and emotional distance that has arisen between herself and the king, the narrator searches for comfort and finds it in the king's daemon. At this point in the text, the narrator and this daemon appear to be two separate entities, but as I will demonstrate, the narrator soon merges with and assumes the identity of the daemon. Still distinct from the narrator, the daemon reminds her that spirits are more reliable than great men and advises her to turn to yet another spirit: "Hab ich dich nicht oft gewarnt, mit großen Herrn ist nicht gut Kirschen essen? Es war der Geist des Islam, den die bedrängten Völker aus diesem Weltteil scheidend grüßten, und er beschwichtigte sie. Rede auch du mit ihm" (259). In a surprising combination of cynicism and hope, Arnim gives voice in this passage to her lack of faith in rulers in general and to her hope that a spirit, daemon, or conscience will guide her, her literary narrator, and in turn, her readers.

It becomes clear that the narrator has no doubt that she receives guidance from this positive force when she receives her absolution from the spirit of Islam, "Da redete der Islam zu mir: 'Suche keine Verteidigung, denn das Gute überlebt dich, und der Nachlebende wird's erkennen!'" (259). By echoing a phrase from *Günderode*—"ich geh mit meinem Dämon um, der sagt: *Du sollst dich nicht verteidigen*" (*G* 409)— the narrator lets the reader know that the spirit of Islam is *her* daemon and reveals at the same time an unshakable faith in the goodness and truth inherent in her work.

The next brief section, which recalls *Briefwechsel*, is dated 4 April 1808, Arnim's twenty-third birthday. Here the narrator expresses a wish for power: "Ich will der große Geist werden, der alles umfaßt!" (261) And addressing Nature she exclaims:

> Ach du, heb mich hinaus über ihre Formen und Bräuche. Aber wenn's gilt, dann löse mich von der Gewohnheit heimlicher Umgarnung, der Sitte, der Menschenfurcht. Entkleide mich von ihrer Tugendlehre Fastnacht-Gewanden, hülle mich in dein Erz, lasse meine Gefühle hineinwachsen in den Harnisch deiner Wahrheit und lasse mich nicht mutlos werden, wenn das Herz so voll Sehnsucht ist! (262)

This narrator wishes to escape the emptiness she sees around her—in the church, in politics, in daily life—in order to remain in contact with her own genius. Nature provides the enabling space for this: "Heute ist mein Geburtstag, *Goethe*, da habe ich mit der Natur geredet von dir, sie soll mich heben zu dir hinauf, die ich geboren bin so tief unter dir" (262). At this point, the narrator places herself, as did the Bettine of *Briefwechsel*, in Goethe's shadow in order to establish a position for herself as his equal, but as becomes evident in the remainder of the text, the figure who emerges bears little resemblance to the stammering, insecure child we encounter at the beginning of *Briefwechsel*. Rather, this narrator possesses a self-assurance that anticipates her transformation into (or union with) the daemon of the king.

The following section, the only narrative section in the text, is dated 28 August 1808 and bears the title, "Die Klosterbeere. Zum Andenken an die Frankfurter Judengasse." Recalling the discussions of history between Bettine and Günderode in Arnim's second work, the narrator reveals here how, through reflection and personal engagement, one's personal history informs one's present. In this section the narrator moves, seemingly without transition, from an anecdote about her childhood in a convent to a conversation with a "Du," who from the immediate context could be Goethe, but from the broader context of Arnim's oeuvre could also be Schleiermacher. She then vaults into a conversation with Primate Dalberg, a minor figure in Arnim's earlier works, who here stands in as a strong believer in the narrator's potential, even if not always in agreement with her ideas about the status of Jews in German society, with her claim, for example, that Orthodox Jews should be granted equal rights without being forced to assimilate. By tracing this trajectory from her life in a convent to conversation with the primate, the narrator reveals stages in the process of her own development.

Initially, the narrator tells us, she considered her life in the convent idyllic. She recalls an episode in which she tried to ascertain why gooseberries were called *Klosterbeeren*:

> Ich konnt in die Frucht hineinsehen, wie sie, von der Sonne durchsichtig gereift, kleine Zellen bildet mit Bogenfensterchen, in deren jedem ein Korn sich hält, darunter dacht ich mir Nönnchen, die hier im nährenden Element wie in wohnlicher Herberg für ein späteres Leben reiften. Ein Kloster dacht ich mir wie eine Frucht, die für die Gottheit reife. (263)

While living in the convent, she accepts the view that the nuns are preparing themselves for an existence beyond their earth-bound lives. But eventually, she tells us, she comes to consider her beliefs childish—"da hat ich Betrachtungen, wie ein Kind hat, die waren zum Lachen" (263)—and begins to see a contrast between the emptiness of the nuns' existence within the confines of the convent walls and the liveliness they exhibited when working outside in the fields and orchards. She cries out to them in her dream-memory: "Auch *ihr*, Nönnchen, die ihr starr in eurer Klause euch nicht mehr dreht und wendet, dem Leben abgestorben, nichts mehr auf Erden vorhabt als mit gefalteten Händen die Paternosterkugel drehn, wenn ihr die Hülle sprengt, dann werdet ihr ins Meer der Freiheit wieder fliegen" (264). The process of ripening, of spiritual and emotional development towards freedom—a central concept throughout Arnim's works that is symbolized by the apple in *Dies Buch*—cannot and does not take place in isolated detachment from the world. Rather, it requires visceral contact with nature, interaction with others, and direct involvement in human affairs. In contrast to the nuns, the narrator eventually breaks out of her cloistered existence. Indeed, reading *Dämonen* within the context of Arnim's six major works, one sees the development of a Bettine who moves from a predominant preoccupation with her own development to a figure involved with broader issues concerning the place of the individual, and especially the outsider, within the broader society. Thus the role of the child, while still useful for establishing intertextual links between the works and for symbolizing an openness to individual development, becomes overshadowed by roles such as that of the protector. The narrator of *Dämonen* recalls a conversation with a figure that bears strong resemblance to the "Du" whom Bettine addressed in the diary section of *Briefwechsel*:

> Oft hat dein Wort mich getroffen und zu manchem bewegt, und am letzten Abend, wo wir sprachen von der Weisheit des Nathan und es sei Heldennatur, den Unterdrückten zu lieben, da wollt ich, deiner Rede getreu, aus feuriger Liebe zu dir ein Held sein—Weil du gesagt hast, in des Helden Krone sei der Unterdrückte ein Kleinod und das höchste Ziel sich strecken sei das Einfachste, denn man könne nie es aus dem Auge verlieren; ich dachte, wäre das mein Ziel, *Beschützer der Unterdrückten*, das wollt ich so gerne sein. (266)

The narrator is inspired by love, a force that creates in her a desire to take up the cause of others. In turn, assisting others leads to individual development. Within the context of this brief section, we see how love inspires the narrator to move from the sheltered life of the convent to the streets of the Jewish ghetto in Frankfurt.

Following the conversation about *Nathan der Weise*, the narrator has gained a new awareness of her surroundings, in particular of the living conditions of those inhabitants of the *Judengasse* whom she often sees as she wanders through the narrow, cramped streets of this ghetto street:

> Nun gehe ich nicht mehr gleichgültig schüchtern an des weisen Nathan Brüdern vorüber, ich betrachte mit Verwunderung die engen dunklen Häuser; alles wimmelt, kein Plätzchen zum Alleinsein, zum Besinnen. Manch schönes Kinderauge und feingebildete Nasen und blasse Mädchenwangen füllen die engen Fensterräume, Luft zu schöpfen, und die Väter in den Haustüren fallen die Vorübergehenden an mit ihrem Schacher. Ein Volksstrom wogt in der Straße, da laufen so viele Kinder herum in Lumpen, die lernen Geld erwerben, und die Alten, Tag und Nacht sind eifrig, sie in Wohlstand zu bringen, das wehrt man ihnen und schimpft sie lästig.
> Wie wunderlich ist's, daß alles sich zankt um den Platz auf Erden, ja, wie schauerlich ist dies!—So grausam ist der Dornenweg, auf dem die Menschheit sich ein Eigentum der Sorge erwirbt—und neiden's einander!—
> Vom Höchsten bis zum Niedrigsten ist alles eifersüchtig um den Zankapfel des Lebens. (267)

Clearly, the narrator idealizes the individuals she sees, and one cannot help but wonder whether her attempt to invert the often demeaning depictions of the physical characteristics of Jews might imply less acceptance for facial features not so finely formed or cheeks not quite so pale. Yet underlying this idealization one also finds a sincere effort to understand the motivations behind behavior such as aggressive peddling, which was frowned upon by members of the German, Christian middle class, and to point out that not only the Jews but also Christians made no secret of their interest in securing possessions in order to maintain their well being. Through both her conversation with an unnamed "Du" and her own peregrinations, then, the narrator gains experience and insight previously unavailable to her.

The narrator carries her new-found knowledge into her conversations with Dalberg. At this point, too, she begins to move towards her transformation into the king's daemon. In the middle of a concert, she strives to convince the primate that any faults the Jews may have as a group are no worse than the faults of their oppressors—"Schlechter als ihre Unterdrücker sind die Juden nicht" (268)—and that the Jews have a right to self-determination and education even if they do not choose to assimilate into German society. This does not, however, mean that she proposes the continued separation between Jews and Christians as it existed in Frankfurt at the beginning of the nineteenth century. Rather, she draws on the—by now familiar—concept of mutual interaction and friendship, *Geselligkeit*, as a model for the relationship she envisions between the two groups:

> "...So würde der Christ durch des Juden freie Bildung Fülle freier Anschauung gewinnen, eine Entwicklung würde die andere steigern und endlich durch den goldnen Frieden sich ins goldne Zeitalter verwandeln, wo Jude und Christ gemeinsam fühlen, Gott sei unter ihnen!"
> *Primas*: "Sie würden also die Juden nicht bekehren wollen?"
> "Nein, aber sie bewegen, die Wahrheit zu erkennen!"
> *Primas*: "Ist denn das Christentum nicht die Wahrheit?"
> "Für den Primas, aber nicht für den Rabbi!" (270)

The narrator bases her argument on two premises that all of Arnim's main characters have held essential for human development: each individual (or group of individuals) possesses a daemon, conscience, spirit to whom she must listen in order to develop fully; and individuals (and groups) must develop friendships so that they may come to know themselves more fully by using the other as a mirror. This is the model that various Bettine personae have used for their development throughout Arnim's works. In the above passage, the narrator applies it to the development of Jews and Christians, and later in the text she applies it to the development of the king and of different peoples of Europe. With regard to the Jews, she argues that the ruler (here, the primate) bears responsibility for insuring that they have the basic conditions necessary for this development. As she tells him, "Das Anrecht freier Entwicklung seiner gesunden Anlagen kann um keiner Voraussetzung willen einem vorenthalten werden, noch weniger ist's denen abzusprechen, deren Naturanlagen nicht in heiteren Lebensbächen dahinzurauschen vergönnt ist. Gebt erst Luft, wie bald wird dann Licht leuchten!" (273) It is a telling indicator of the limits on the narrator's ability to effect change directly that crashing drums end the conversation between the narrator and the primate before she can persuade him to express a willingness to alter his policies toward the Jews. The narrator has a plethora of ideas but must rely on a man to implement them.

When the narrator and the primate take up the conversation at another date, she expresses her wish to converse with the king as she does with the primate, to transform herself into a spirit who could fly into the king's chambers and share with him her wisdom:

> O wär ich ein Geist! unsichtbar—und könnte meine Flügel schwingen, fort durch den stillen Äther, durchs dunkle Gewölk der Nacht, auf seines Thrones Fußschemel mich niederlassen und ihm verdünken die reifenden Zwecke alle, auf die Gottes Wille hindeutete, als er ihn erschuf! (287)

The primate believes she is up to the task. Yet he also warns her—and here we find a sobering and more explicit assessment of the narrator's chances of truly influencing the king—that, instead of listening to what this daemon has to say, the king will probably view her as a bothersome mosquito and try to shoo her away or even swat at her. This warning fails to dissuade the narrator. Like earlier Bettine personae, she possesses a sense of mission that allows her to hold on to hope. She insists that it is up to her to tell the king "Er soll *revolutionär* werden," to which the primate replies, "So muß das Mückchen Regententugenden in ihm wachsummen, die er im Traum selbst für Traum hält, und wenn er auch daran glaubt, wahre Ideen sind Kontrebande für Fürsten, die sie nie verwirklichen" (289). Fully aware that her chances of having any real impact on the king's thinking are slim, the narrator nevertheless transforms herself into his daemon in the hope that, while the king is sleeping and free of the close watch of his advisors, he might be open to what she has to say.[4] At this point, if one takes grammatical gender at face value, the narrator—who through intertextual references is associated with the feminine Bettine—becomes masculine: *der Daemon*. Yet because Arnim does not attribute male gender attributes to this figure, indeed it even assumes the role of mother, I have chosen here to refer to the daemon with the gender-neutral pronoun "it."

When the daemon arrives, it finds that the sleeping king is willing to listen and proceeds to convey its ideas about justice and equality and its criticisms of the death penalty and war. It refers to the Bible to expose the actions of those who would call themselves Christians as decisively unchristian; and it suggests to the king that placing trust in his subjects would be more effective than his current version of politics based on what he considers to be reality. These admonitions soon prove too much for the king. As the primate predicted, he comes to call the daemon a "kleine Mücke" (304) and threatens to put an end to what he considers to be the daemon's flights of fancy: "Ich werde gleich dich haschen und deine Flügelkraft lähmen" (354). Then, as if to rescue the daemon, other spirits begin to appear: the spirit of genius, the spirit of the people, the spirit of the ancestors, the spirits of the Poles, the Hungarians, the Lombardians. At one point, the most promising in the text, the king is so overcome by these apparitions that he calls out to his genius (translating from Arnim's parlance: to his conscience) to guide him. But in the wake of their conversation up until this point, the daemon has doubts that the king will really listen to this voice:

> *Schlafender König*: "Hört Geister!—Genius, komme herab zu mir!"—
> *Dämon*: "Du rufst ihm?—und wenn er zu unsterblichen Taten die Fackel dir zündet, wirst du nicht zagen?" (398)

The king appears to wish to continue listening to the voices that surround him, and these spirits tell him they desire nothing other than friendship with him, in other words, the chance to mirror and be mirrored by him:

> *Genius*: "Willst du um ihre Urkraft, deren Erzeugnis du bist, die Völker betrügen?—Willst du nicht ihre fruchtbare Fülle, von Gottes Gnaden dir eingeboren, herabströmen wieder zu ihm und wolltest lieber, daß es seiner eignen Erhebung sich begebe in dir?"
> ...
> *Völker*: "Gütig warst du uns einst und gewährtest, was die Zeit verlangte, und wir vergaßen nie, daß des Freundes freiwilliges Geschenk der schönste Gewinn dem Liebenden sei." (402)

Using the language of love and friendship, the text proposes a relationship of mutual guidance, mutual giving, and mutual submission to the other. The ultimate role model for this absolute friendship is that individual who gives his life for another.

In the final section of the text, the voice of Islam speaks again. It tells the story of the noble-spirited Kaab been Mame who became lost with his tribe in the desert. Among this group was a man from another tribe to whom Kaab gave his daily ration of water and for whom he sacrificed his life. The Spirit of Islam summarizes this parable as follows:

> Wenn zum Gericht Gott in Schirm der Wolken erscheint und die Völker umstehen ihn, der die Kreatur richtet und die Odemzüge der Welt hat gezählt und dem kein Grab das Anvertraute versagt, so hofft auf Erbarmen, der aus Liebe alles hat getan, und Gottes Gnade ist sein Trost, da, wo sein Werk ihm Feind ist. (407)

Addressing the king's fears that, although he sees the rightness of the parable's moral, its solutions would never obtain in the real world, the spirit of Islam proposes that the rewards of immortality far exceed any earthly rewards the king might receive for acting in the interests of power rather than love. The spirit then ends its speech with an admonition: "Gewähre, solange es Zeit ist. Es wird eine Zeit kommen, wo du gewähren möchtest, aber keinen findest du, der es annehme. *Wärst du gestern gekommen, heute bedarf ich [Dich, bzw. den König] nicht*" (407). The king must act now, while there are still people ready to listen to him. Through the spirit, Arnim predicts that the time for kings is nearing an end, that a day will come when the people have no need for monarchs, "Wärst du gestern gekommen, heute bedürfen wir nicht," they will tell him. With this, the conversation with the daemon(s) is over. The daemon transforms back into the narrator who returns to the primate:

> "Wo bleibt der Primas"—
> *Primas*: "Hier—im geistlichen Ornate, besessen vom Dämon, den ich als heidnisch verdammen muß, und hingerissen von seiner Weisheit, die ich als ketzerisch dem ewigen Feuer preisgebe!"
> "Ja, ewiges Feuer lodert im Busen dem, der dieser Weisheit frönt." (407)

With this the narrator, and through her Arnim, asserts the eternal value and validity of what she has to say.

The action of Arnim's final published text, then, moves from the isolation of a convent, to the streets of a Jewish ghetto, to a concert hall, and then to the king's chambers. The narrator moves from a secluded space out into the world to acquire knowledge and then into the ideal space of conversation.[5] As in the case of *Dies Buch*, however, the conversations in the text tend to be unidirectional, with the comments of the king and the primate serving merely as sounding boards for the ideas of the daemon. In contrast to the multiple roles that Bettine plays in *Briefwechsel* and *Günderode*, or to the manner in which Bettine fragments into various personae in *Dies Buch*, the central and dominant role that Bettine assumes in this text is that of the daemon who speaks in a unified voice but who also leaves room for the other voices that speak towards the end of the text. At the same time, however, the reader catches glimpses of roles Bettine has played in earlier works: child, friend, writer, and a role that has grown in importance throughout her work, mother. In comparison to Arnim's earlier works, the valences of these roles have changed significantly. The role of the child serves largely as a means of establishing an intertextual link with Arnim's earlier works and reaffirming Arnim's authority to her readers. The role of the friend now extends to serve as a model for the relationship not only between Bettine and her interlocutors but also between state and religious authorities and the people. Finally, the roles of mother and daemon are now foregrounded as the ones that this Bettine persona most assertively claims as her own.

Roles in the Shadows: Child, Friend, Writer

The title of *Briefwechsel* points to the centrality of the role of the child in Arnim's first published work. One can discern a development of her original Bettine persona away from this role. The narrator of Arnim's final work presents herself as a child at only two points in the text: in the early section dated 4 April, in which she recalls Goethe's appellation of her as child, and when she remembers her childhood years spent in a convent. Significantly, the narrator does not refer to herself as a child in the present tense, but instead places her childhood firmly in the past in both of these sections. In contrast, allusions to Friedrich Wilhelm IV situate the present of the text in the late 1840s. While pointing to a distance between the present and past of the narration may be stating the obvious, the chronology of the text discloses a development not always recognized in secondary literature on Arnim, namely that her Bettine moves far beyond the role of the child, indeed, outgrows it. As mentioned above, at one point she laughs at the foolish ideas she held as a child. Certainly the narrator has characteristics that remind the reader of her predecessors; especially when speaking with the primate, she is as impudent and self-assured as only a child can be. Furthermore, youth and youthfulness remain key terms here as throughout Arnim's works. Nevertheless, the narrator's childlike actions and the direct references in the text to the role of the child serve primarily to situate this text within the context of Arnim's other works, to show where Bettine has been, and I would argue also, how far she has come. Bettine assumes the dual roles of child/pupil and adult/mother/teacher in all six of the works discussed here, but in her final text the balance between these two roles shifts significantly towards emphasis on a mature Bettine.

In contrast to the role of child, that of friend remains central to this text. The daemon not only suggests that the king develop a friendship with the people, it considers itself to be a friend of the king (328). Yet the friendship between the daemon and the king is not the same as that which the daemon envisions between the king and the people, for as in *Dies Buch*, we see the Bettine persona (here, the daemon) promulgating the main ideas of the text to a more passive respondent (the king). At one point the king appropriates the daemon's ideas in order to criticize the daemon for its failure to recognize all that a king's station entails:

> *Schlafender König*: "...Ich glaube, es steht nicht richtig mit dir, und viel hab ich von fremden Zungen erfahren müssen, daß du nämlich mich mancher Dinge fähig hältst, vor denen mir grauelt.—Aber ich habe deine Verleumder abgewiesen. Nein! ich hab nicht beachtet, daß du gleichgültig gegen mein Leben meine Mörder bemitleidet hast, lange hab ich mir geleugnet, daß du Könige verabscheust und doch *den* anrufst, der nach deinem Sinn das Gute soll durchsetzen. Hierüber stehe mir Rede—in diesem Augenblick, wo du selber so beredsam dich zeigst, mein inneres Leben mir darzulegen."
> *Dämon*: "Um wenigstens es zu retten vor dem Untergang deines äußern Wirkens. So glaube du von mir."
> *Schlafender König*: "Du willst recht behalten. Aber dich verantworten, dazu hast du nie Zeit—und führst auf Bahnen überraschender Wendung mich hier und dort zum Ufer, wo der Schein dir Recht spricht. Ob ich als Herrscher dem mich fügen könne, danach fragst du nicht." (353–354)

Angered because the daemon sympathizes with individuals who, because of their political alliances, would rather see him dead, and because despite its general criticism of kings, the daemon continues to come to him for assistance, the king tells his daemon that talk is cheap. In its position outside the public sphere, the daemon must bear no responsibility for any actions carried out within that sphere. Such a turning of the tables may appear an empty defensive gesture on the part of the king. His words also serve, however, to remind the reader both of the difficulty that Arnim's main characters tend to have attaining the reciprocity they seek and of the impediments to a complete understanding of the other. In the above passage, the reciprocity of friendship breaks down on two levels: it collapses structurally because the daemon controls the conversation, and it breaks down on the content level because, just as the king and the daemon are incapable of stepping into one another's shoes, so too are the chances for a rapprochement between the king and the people slim, if not impossible. As in Arnim's earlier works, ideal friendship remains a central value but an unattainable goal.

The third role that is central to Arnim's oeuvre but not really foregrounded in *Dämonen* is that of writer. We encounter none of the complaints that Bettine expresses in *Briefwechsel*, *Günderode*, or *Frühlingskranz* about the difficulty of writing, in part because of the conversational structure of the text. As such, this structure offers no opportunity (in contrast to the letter books) for reflecting on the process of capturing ideas on a sheet of paper. And yet, at the beginning of the text the narrator explicitly calls to our attention her role as writer. At this point she is still a separate entity from the daemon, and she describes herself as the recorder of this daemon's conversations with the king as well as the censor of the sections of which the daemon disapproved:

> Nun vernahm ich sein [des Dämons] Gespräch mit jenem König—das mußte ich nach seinem Willen hier aufzeichnen. Dann hieß der Dämon mich alle Stellen streichen, die seinem Geist nicht zusagten. Dies sind *die Lücken* eigner Zensur.—Auch diese kann jeder wahrnehmen, der dieses Buch durchblättert. (259)

In contrast to the manner in which earlier Bettines recorded the words of Frau Rath or Günderode, this narrator makes no indication that she alters what she hears as she records it. I believe there are two reasons for this. First, by this point in her writing career Arnim has become certain of what she wants to write, and this is mirrored in the self-assurance of her figures. Second, although the narrator and the daemon still stand apart at this point in the text, the daemon (like Frau Rath and the magpie in *Dies Buch*) must be read as an extension of Bettine, for the narrator merges with the daemon in order to gain access to the king. The daemon is unequivocally certain of the truth of what it says, and because it is really an extension of the narrator, its command to erase part of what it has written can be read as a form of self-editing as well as a satirical comment on censorship.[6] Although *Dämonen* does not underscore the role of the writer in the manner of *Ambrosia*, there can be no doubt that the narrator of this text has no hesitation about writing.

Mother/Demeter

In comparison to the roles of child, friend, and writer, all of which receive less emphasis here than in earlier works, the role of mother is far more pronounced in *Dämonen*, and to a greater extent than in *Ambrosia*, this mother is of divine provenance. Expanding on one of the roles played by Ambrosia, the daemon stylizes itself as an idealized mother of the king. It compares itself to Demeter, the ancient goddess of fertility and the harvest who bestowed immortality on her children by dipping them into ambrosia and then holding them in fire until only their immortal essence remained. As it tells the king, "Himmlischbeauftragt wie Demeter, ins Feuer der Unsterblichkeit dich zu halten, wehrte ich aller witzlosen Satanstheorie deiner Schmeichler" (308). Its approach to insuring the king's immortality is to transform him into a "good" king, to guide and educate him, to nurture him to productive growth. When, for example, the city councilors plan to honor the king with a tower on which likenesses of his ancestors are painted, the daemon criticizes this gesture as inappropriate for a festival intended to honor the city's inhabitants. As an alternative, it suggests that the tower honor these citizens: "Bemalt euren Turm mit Völkern aller Zonen, mit Menschen aus dem Mond, ja aller Sterne Wesen, die, seines Zepters Freiheit huldigend, ihren Göttern dienen. Malt den Genius der Zeiten...aber nicht den volkswidersinnigen, transluziden Baum verblichner Ahnen" (309). To achieve immortality, then, the king must create a monument not to himself and to his individual past but to the peoples of his country and the world; the daemon considers the people to be the true ancestors of the king. In its capacity as mother and Demeter figure, the daemon steers the king towards actions that it believes will live beyond the king's regency, thereby insuring his immortality.

As in *Dies Buch*, the role of the mother is not limited to women or to duties in the domestic sphere. As with friendship and genius, motherhood is reciprocal. Not only the daemon is capable of assuming this role, for it views the king and the state as mothers to the people *and* the people as mother to the king. To articulate the responsibility that the king bears for the well-being of the people, the daemon makes reference to the Book of Revelations and the manner in which the figure Mary appears there:

> Das Weib in der Offenbarung, prächtig umkleidet mit der Sonne, ihre Füße ruhend auf dem Mond, ihr Haupt funkelnd unter einer Krone von zwölf Sternen!—sie geht schwanger—sie schmachtet in Kindsnöten, sie ahnet den lauernden Drachen, der ihr Kind verschlinge.—Was ist die Majestät der Könige?—Mutterangst, durch Sorgen, Schützen, Retten und Opfern ihren Glanz ausbreitend und ihre Macht über die Völker.—Zwölf Sterne—wie herrlich funkelnd über deinem Haupt, wenn jeder ein geschütztes, ein gerettetes, ein angefeuertes, ein versöhntes Volk dir spiegelt. (320)

In her own version of a revelation—and Arnim uses biblical references and cadences throughout the text—the daemon makes a plea for a feminized king, one who gives birth to the people, who creates and shapes them through his treatment of them. Recalling the narrator's attempt to convince the primate that the behavior of the Jews reflected their rulers' treatment of them, this passage implies that the king bears responsibility for the education and development of the people. He achieves greatness through his concern and sacrifice for and protection of them. In turn, they become part of him, the very jewels in the crown he wears.

Arnim's emphasis here on the role of king as educator would appear to recall Novalis's depiction in *Glauben und Liebe* of the role of the king as *Erzieher des Volkes*. Yet by feminizing the king, by imputing to him the role of mother, Arnim breaks with Novalis. Whereas her romantic predecessor conceived of a monarchy necessarily comprised of a happily married royal couple, of separate masculine and feminine parts, each assuming distinct roles, Arnim's vision collapses the queen/mother and the king/father into one person. In this manner she implies that the feminine duties that Novalis deemed appropriate for "einen häuslichen Wirkungskreis" (297), those of nurturing and caring for others, are appropriate duties for the king in the public sphere as well.

Arnim's text also differs from *Glauben und Liebe* insofar as there is no queen and no marriage within which the king receives his education through the love of the queen. Rather, in *Dämonen* the king's genius stems from "die Muttererde der Menschheit" (332). In the daemon's view, one becomes kinglike neither because of divine provenance nor through the love of a queen but rather through the will of the people who must decide to be ruled by the king: "Ist das Volk schlecht, so ist der Herrscher ruchlos; läßt es sich von dir regieren, so ist dein Genie die Verklärung des Volkes; dein Atem kann Feuer aus ihm wecken; oder auch sein Feuer ist, was dich zur großen Seele macht" (332). In contrast to Locke, Arnim would argue that a social contract can exist within a monarchy and that it is founded as much upon emotional ties as upon reason. Bound by a symbiotic need, the king and the people cannot, according to the daemon, exist without each other: "jedes hängt vom andern ab, wie von der Mutter das Kind abhängt; jedes ist volle Schöpferkraft des andern" (323). As many times before in Arnim's work, there is here a reciprocity in the roles of mother and child. The king and the people depend upon one other and each bears responsibility for educating and for learning from the other.

In addition to portraying her daemon as mother vis-à-vis the king, then, Arnim also transforms the king from stern and rational representative of the *Vater-Staat* into a caring mother, thereby feminizing not only the king but also the relationship between the king and the people. The king no longer looks to a queen to mother him, i.e., to guide his development, but rather to the people. Such an emphasis on a maternal state hints at the manner in which the author Arnim perceived herself as well. As a woman Arnim appears only to have been able to imagine herself (her fictional selves) standing on the sidelines of the public sphere—as a daemon offering advice to the king. The real author thus may have taken the advice, which the fictional Günderode gave to Bettine, to content herself with being a woman. And yet this gesture may be more than one of resignation, for in her texts she significantly redefines the role of the king and reshapes the relationship between the king and the people. Rather than accepting a state system based on tradition, on the right of the king to rule, and on the unquestioning subservience of the people, Arnim suggests a state based on mutual concern and the mutual wish to nurture and educate—idealistic, yes, impossibly utopian and thus unachievable, yes, unprogressive in comparison to other political texts of the period, yes, but nevertheless a resounding indictment of the masculinist model of government with which she had been forced to contend throughout the 1840s. Furthermore, with this assertion of the role of the mother in her final work, she makes a convincing argument for a transformation of the public sphere according to models taken from traditional women's roles. In so doing, she redefines these roles and their political import.

Teacher/Philosopher/Daemon

The central role of this text and the one to which—if one considers Arnim's texts together as an extended novel of development—her literary Bettine has aspired all along, is that of daemon. This role can be understood in its myriad connotations and within the various traditions outlined in the chapter on *Briefwechsel*—daemon as conscience of another, daemon as one's own conscience, daemon as a god—for all three valences inhere in the main figure of *Dämonen*. Arnim's Bettine achieves this position as genius, one in which she considers herself capable of advising the king, through her development of a sense of self and conscience. Not surprisingly, then, the daemon repeats in this text the motto espoused by various Bettines throughout Arnim's works in order to assert this status:

> "Gott sagte: *Es werde!*—und da ward!—und glauben Sie denn, daß die Schöpfungskraft bloß in dem Wort lag!—und daß da sogleich alles geworden, bloß aufs Kommandowort?"—
> *Primas*: "Das müssen wir allerdings in der Allmacht Gottes liegend uns denken."
> "Nein! das denke ich mir nicht so!—Und das weiß ich auch ganz anders, durch prophetisches Ahnen, durch meinen Scharfsinn; daran zweifeln wollen, wäre nicht klug vom Primas." (271)

Asserting a pantheistic belief in the godlike nature of all creation, the daemon does not assert here that a higher being spoke creation into existence. Rather, it insists that humankind has created itself through self-knowledge and makes the tautological claim that its source for this knowledge is its own understanding. The individual who is free to listen to his/her own conscience, his/her daemon, is free to create him- or herself and the world, to become daemon to others. This belief in one's own conscience is a form of religion, one that the daemon of this text claims will eventually subsume all other religions: "die Religion des eignen Gewissens, die Mittler ist zwischen ihm und dem Göttlichen, die ist Überwinderin aller Religionen" (277). Just as her own conscience has become the mediator between herself and that which is godlike, the narrator of this text, by appropriating the role of the king's daemon, proposes to mediate between the king and godlikeness. Yet, as both the title and the conclusion of *Dämonen* make clear, this religion is not monotheistic. The individual learns from his or her inner conscience, to be sure, but also from external daemons, from contact with others. Within the context of this work, not only the narrator as daemon but also daemons representing different nationalities serve as a collective conscience from which the king can learn and in which he can see himself reflected.

Both *Dies Buch* and *Dämonen* offer pointed criticism of Prussian state and church policies. In contrast to *Dies Buch*, *Dämonen* offers not only more in the way of suggestions for solving the problems it illuminates but also a psychological study of the king as a means of helping the reader (and the king) to understand the origins of these problems. In Arnim's view, not institutions but individuals make up a state, and one must begin with the individual if one wishes to transform that state. For this reason, the daemon of this text addresses individual responsibility for the mistreatment of the Jews and for violence in the form of war and state executions.

In the foreground of the text's critique stands the narrator's discussion of policies towards the Jews. Although the section entitled "Die Klosterbeere" is set in the early-nineteenth century, it addresses the treatment of the Jews in mid-century Prussia.[7] In discussing the situation of the Jews with the primate, the narrator admonishes him to understand the Jews of Frankfurt on their own terms while emphasizing that any problems the primate may have with the Jews most certainly stem from the state's mistreatment of them.

It is however misleading to apply the appellation of Arnim's Bettine as protector of the Jews to Arnim herself, for even in her later years, the author did not fully reject the stereotypes frequently associated with Jews in the nineteenth century. This becomes evident when the daemon makes a reference to *The Merchant of Venice*:

> Weißt du, der Jude, der dem Schuldner ein Pfund Fleisch wollte ausschneiden, selbst wenn es mit seiner Seele solle aufgewogen werden. Da sprach der Richter: "Fleisch kannst du nehmen, aber Blut darfst du nicht vergießen, und mehr als ein Pfund darfst du nicht nehmen." Da mußte der Jude ablassen vom Schein des Rechts. Wenn aber unerleuchtete Gesetze ins Fleisch schneiden dem Unmündigen, der, alles Trostes bar, rachgierigem Blutdurst fortan sich hingibt, strahlt da nicht göttliche Weisheit in dich: du sollst die Gesetze niederschlagen, die deinen

Stern verdunkeln, und die Macht deiner Verheißungen soll klar hervortreten aus ihrer Verschattung? (325)

The daemon does not refer in this passage to Jews per se, but rather presents Shylock as a figure of comparison against whom it measures the king's injustice. At the same time, the choice of a Jewish figure as object of comparison reveals a lack of reflection on associations and deep-seated stereotypes, which Sander Gilman claims "reflect a crude set of mental representations of the world" (*Inscribing the Other* 12).

The above-cited passage notwithstanding, I agree with Baldwin that this text represents Arnim's "most focused literary effort on behalf of the Jews," and that she develops here "a sustained argument for their legal emancipation and acceptance in society" (213). In her literary treatment, Arnim does, to an extent, rely on stereotypical depictions of Jews, but at the same time her text moves towards the recognition of Jews (and of all people) as individuals.

In addition to offering Arnim's strongest statement in support of Jewish emancipation, *Dämonen* also presents a sustained criticism of violence, be it in the form of war, compulsory service to the state, or state-sponsored execution. As the daemon insists, "Alles gewaltsame Töten ist Brudermord" (301). Citing the Bible as its source of authority, the daemon recounts the story of Cain and Abel to indict the role that kings play in inciting both the murder of and murder among their subjects. Although it does not condone such actions, the daemon tempers its indictment with an analysis of the motivation behind this brutality. It views state-sponsored violence as an act of aggression engendered by the perpetrator's bad conscience: "Und immer noch schlägt der *Kain* den *Abel* tot, weil er sich rächen will am eignen strafenden Gewissen…. So fluchte damals der erste Mörder seinen Ahnen!—so flucht heute noch der Herrscher dem Volk, aus dem er hervorging" (301). According to the daemon, when the king curses the people, he directs his sense of guilt into his anger towards them. This is tantamount to saying that the king bears responsibility for their insubordination. The king then decides to silence the voice of his conscience by violently silencing the voice of the people. But as the daemon points out to the king, a state order that is forced upon the people lacks authority: "Der Staat, der mit Gewalt der Vernunft Herrschaft will erzwingen und nicht den freien Flug dem Genius sichert, der ist nicht kraftvoll, sondern nur mächtig; nicht wohltätig, nur wohlexerziert und nur auf Sand gebaut" (342). Any ruler who forces his will upon the people will eventually come to find that he has built his realm on sandy ground.

The daemon asserts that the weaknesses of the king, that is his political inability to establish a relationship of mutual respect and inspiration with the people, and his psychological inability to come to terms with his conscience, reveal themselves in the pursuit of foreign wars and in the king's support of the death penalty. As it tells the king, the state of war, which forces one brother to kill another, violates the moral principle that one should not destroy one's own flesh and blood. The daemon even goes so far as to claim that, given a free choice, individuals would choose not to engage in such killing:

> Es ist die Todesqual des eignen Willens, der dem göttlichen Ebenbild abstirbt, wenn er noch vor Einbruch des Jüngsten Gerichts den Zorn Gottes über sich nimmt und durch Kriegszucht zusammengekoppelte Sklaven zwingt zur Hinrichtung ihrer Brüder. Frage einen, ob er's lassen würde, wär's ihm freigestellt; und ist er nicht Sklave der Furcht, so wehrt er sich, aus einem menschlichen Keim ein teuflisches Tier zu werden, das aus dummer Blutgier seinen Bruder mordet. (326–327)

Murder—here the killing of war—is a sign of a reduced, enslaved personality, for killing is the act of a slave rather than of a free individual. If the king kills (generally through inciting others to kill for him), then he too becomes enslaved by his will to power, his illusion of control, and his fear of losing that control.[8]

The king's illusions, indeed his blindness, lead him not only to make war but also to advocate state executions. The daemon tells him that by supporting such violence he not only violates moral laws, he also neglects his duty as ruler to maintain order in the state. For this reason, the daemon proposes, it would be no surprise should the people, imitating the behavior of their leader, rise up in violence against him. The daemon therefore implores, "Siehst du ein, daß Gewalt, der des Gewissens Trieb muß weichen, verfemt ist? und daß Volksaufruhr göttliche Mahnung ist, zu meiden, was ihn errege?" (376) Recalling Locke, the daemon maintains that, rather than upsetting the established order, revolution and people's uprisings maintain and restore it by reminding government of its duties towards the people.

According to the daemon, the duties of the king include establishing a humane state in which human violence against humans is minimized.

In addition to educating the king about the dangers of tyranny and violence, the daemon analyses both his roles and attitudes as well as those of the people in order to suggest an ideal form for the relationship between king and people. Like *Dies Buch, Dämonen* questions the reliance of the king upon the counsel of his advisors, advice which, as the narrator tells the primate, serves as a crutch that hinders the king from walking on his own (286), from aspiring to the ideals that the daemon lays out before him.

Not only his advisors but also his own fear hinder the king in his development and prevent him from listening to the daemon. At one point the king announces his wish to climb onto "das hohe Pferd" of the daemon's ideals, but he then recoils when he comprehends the risk this might entail: "Wie? dies Roß ist beflügelt!—Und ich soll es besteigen, da es schon flatternd mit seinen Feuerhufen auskratzt—und mit seinen Nüstern die Wolkengebirge anschnaubt und die Winde zerpeitscht mit seinen ungeduldigen Schwingen—und keinen Augenblick zur Besinnung mir läßt?" (291). When compared to the daemon, who is willing to risk being swatted like a fly in order to talk to the king, the king—who has far more power than the mosquito-like daemon—appears a coward. In contrast to the daemon and its insistence on the right of individuals to self determination, the king is consumed by his fear of losing control, a fear that ultimately leads to the desire for revenge, that is, to the very loss of control that he fears.

Rather than succumbing to his fear and to the impulse to take revenge, the daemon suggests that the king listen to his own spirit, conscience, daemon. This inner voice will guide the king towards humane treatment of others, something that it considers to be not only possible but necessary in a less than perfect world:

> *Schlafender König*: "Könnte diese Dämondichtung zur Wahrheit an mir werden, so müßte der ganze Weltenzustand ein vollkommenerer sein, als den wir begreifen."
> *Dämon*: "Es ist nicht dein Beruf, dies Erdenleben gegen ein künftiges geringer zu achten. Du mußt Trieb haben, diese Welt zum Himmel umschaffen zu können."
> (335)

This passage points again to two of Arnim's key principles: the emphasis on becoming, or on perpetual self-education, and the importance of remaining in the present. Rather than espousing a teleology that anticipates some distant future, this text insists on the possibility for change in the present. Individual acts of kindness and the humane treatment of others outweigh any idea of a cumulative perfection to be achieved sometime, somewhere, a perfection, which as Arnim knows all too well, can be found no place on earth. This implies that, rather than waiting for a more enlightened moment in time, the king must accept the responsibilities as educator and nurturer of the people in the here and now.

Staff has indicated that the term "Volkskönigtum" implies a valorization and realization of the will of the people (11). Yet the king can arrive at a more accurate understanding of this will only if he can abjure his present conceptions about the people. The king, convinced that he does understand the people, echoes the primate's arguments from earlier in the text by claiming that the source of their problems lies in their own unruliness: "leiden muß [das Volk] von Geschicken, die es selbst über sich verhängte" (345). Refuting the king's argument, the daemon turns the table by insisting that the king bears responsibility for the sufferings of the people, and that in their actions, they hold up a mirror to the king: "Das Volk ist der Zauberspiegel euerer Mißgriffe. Es offenbart durch sein Verzweifeln, durch sein Verwildern und Wildwerden euere Fehle und auch die Gefahren, die ihr damit heranbeschworen habt" (315). Here again we encounter the mirror motif that runs as a red thread through Arnim's texts. Maintaining that individuals in relation with each other necessarily mirror one another, the daemon implicitly takes up the theme of responsibility explored in *Günderode*. The king is accountable to and responsible for his subjects, and when he shirks his responsibility he finds the consequences reflected in the magic mirror of the people and their actions.

The daemon also sees the people as a source of strength for the king. For this reason, it introduces towards the end of its conversation with the king the spirits or daemons of various peoples. These spirits criticize previous actions such as the invasion of Poland, but they also express their desire to be treated as individuals and to respect the king as an individual:

> *Völker*: "Wir wollen keinen Maschinengott zum Schirmherrn, der Herrscher sei des Volkes Gesamtausdruck, der sich in ihm offenbarende Volkswille und die nach allen Seiten hin sich fühlende Volksnatur."
>
> ...

Germane: "Also Friede mit unserm eignen Selbst im Herrscher, solange er der unsre will sein und nicht Maschinengötze."
Volk: "Denn der muß ja geschehen lassen, was seine Imperative angemessen finden."
Magyar: "Die Philisterrotte, die kein Herz hat für der Völker Befreiung, hält ihm den Geist gebunden."
Volksgeist: "Ein geistig Gefürsteter ist, der den Volkscharakter in sich trägt."
(387)

Echoing Kant's assertion that the human being is "mehr als Maschine" ("Was ist Aufklärung?" 61), the spirits of various nations join together to insist that the king be more than a machine, that he judge individual persons and individual nations according to their specific needs rather than according to how they fit into the king's designs. In so doing, they inform the king that, should he find it possible to do this, they will recognize and support him. With the arrival of these spirits it also becomes clear that neither the king (nor anyone else) has simply one daemon, that he must be open to all of those with whom he has contact and for whom he has responsibility. Whereas the personal ties of friendship require one only to look to the mirror of those whom one considers one's friends, the ties of a ruler to the people require a greater degree of responsiveness and responsibility.

As the above-cited passage makes apparent, *Dämonen* proposes that the ideal relationship between the king and his subjects is one in which the king both subjects himself to the wishes of the people and respects their subjectivity. Indeed, Arnim's vision of a monarchy is one in which the king eventually becomes superfluous. Here again, Arnim appears to echo Novalis, who writes in *Glauben und Liebe*, "Alle Menschen sollen thronfähig werden. Das Erziehungsmittel zu diesem fernen Ziel ist ein König. Er assimiliert sich allmählig die Masse seiner Unterthanen" (294). Püschel has, in fact, gone so far as to say that *Dämonen* is not really about a king at all, and she points out that the term *Volkskönig* appears only once in the text. For Püschel, "das General-Thema des letzten Buches ist das Volk—seine Lage, seine Rolle im gesellschaftlichen Organismus, sein Recht auf Revolution" ("Charakter hat nur der...," "...*wider die Philister und die bleierne Zeit*" 291). Taking Püschel's argument into consideration, I contend that *Dämonen* performs an inversion: although on the surface a text about the king and his duties, a closer reading reveals that the text is about the people; it is a justification of their right to revolution should the king ride roughshod over their education.

While I agree that the people play a central role in this text, I am not convinced that they receive the main emphasis. Although Arnim's belief in Friedrich Wilhelm IV has been shaken, and although the daemon's goal is to encourage the king, through "Menschenliebe," voluntarily to make himself superfluous (Schmitz, "die freie Kultur," 142), the daemon directs its efforts towards addressing the king. And because the text maintains as its working model a constitutional monarchy with a king at its center, the possibility of emancipation in this text hinges on the king's willingness to listen to his genius, to accept the new roles set before him. In other words, although Arnim's text anticipates a more democratic state form, it remains situated in the present in which she is writing.

This is not to say one should discount Arnim's words, for the daemon's criticism of the king and suggestions for a more humane state still obtain today. In the opinion of the daemon, the ruler has only two choices—to serve in the interests of the people or to destroy them and, thus, himself:

> Sich selber leben im Volk, das ist absolutes Herrschen, und Regieren ist, der Völker Segnungen teilhaftig ihnen gebieten. Welcher Herrscher nicht Fleisch geworden in ihnen, der ist Verwüster der Nationen, ihre Trümmer fremdem Gewürm überlassend, das an ihrem Verderben sich mästet; wie Skorpione kalt verfolgend die Eingebornen; blutdürstige Ländergeißel, den Fuß im Nacken der Übriggebliebenen. Bruder ist ihm der Wolf. Gefängnisse und Richtstätten in seiner Nähe, ohne Sporn zu edlen Taten, ohne Kraft, Held zu sein den Nationen, die wie dampfende Brände aus dem Vaterland geschleudert, außen gelöscht, innerlich fortglühend, die Luft verpesten mit Brandgeruch verwesender Völker, gekreuzigt statt gesegnet. (366)

In this passage, the daemon again takes recourse to apocalyptic language to describe what might happen should the king refuse to listen to the voices of the people. The daemon's voice is prophetic insofar as it insists that the monarchy will not be able to continue in its present form, that revolutionary changes will be required for the king to maintain his role within the state. As the text makes clear, the possibility of maintaining his role as king depends upon his willingness to give up his position of power and to assume the role of moral authority. Because the text focuses on the king and the necessity for him to make such a decision, *Dämonen* remains very much about the monarchy and the king. Simultaneously, it prophesies the coming end of the monarchy: either voluntarily through a radical shift in the king's actions or involuntarily through violent revolution. In a sense, Arnim is writing in the tradition of Enlightenment thinkers such as the early Kant who advocated transformation of the state from above, i.e. through institutions of the state. Instead of appealing to the transformative power of reason, however, Arnim appeals to the affective power of love, friendship, and motherhood.

Clearly in the tradition of the Enlightenment, the daemon suggests that positive radical change will occur not only through a transformation of the roles traditionally assumed by the king. Rather, this change will be brought about by the dual practices of doubt and education: by questioning the world and educating one's self through openness to the lessons gained from living immediately in that world. The only secure means of assuring positive change is to remain open to doubt and to resist the urge to maintain control and order: "Zweifel sind keine Irrtümer und Glaubensgelübde kein Verbrechen an der Liebe, sie verklären den Geist und scheitern an ihm, der das Göttliche umschreibt im Meere der Erzeugungen und taucht unter in ihm, alles Gewand abwerfend, frei, nackt, unbefleckt zu sein—und alles Forschen ist Religion" (266). The daemon rejects the security blanket of religious and legal/political dogma. True religion consists not of following prescribed rules but rather of examining and investigating the world, one's responses to it, and the manner in which the world mirrors the individual. This explains why the king must banish his advisors, whose very positions require them to whisper dogma into his ear, and learn to think on his own, to listen to the voices of other daemons waiting to be heard.

Grand Illusion or Grand Experiment?

So what has become of Bettine in *Gespräche mit Dämonen*, at the end of her years of apprenticeship? How do we assess her? How do we evaluate Arnim in light of the development of her Bettine personae over the course of her six lengthy prose texts? Certainly no one paid attention to the text in

Arnim's lifetime. Neither the German nor the Turkish monarch ever read it, no copies of it were sold, and it did not, as was the case with *Dies Buch*, create a stir among the educated reading public of Berlin. More contemporary criticism of the work falls into two camps. One, more traditional camp acknowledges Arnim's efforts on behalf of the socially underprivileged in one breath but then emphasizes that, in comparison with enlightenment and romantic thinkers, her work lacks both philosophical and artistic value (Staff, Hahn, Wyss). In contrast, others have read the text outside of canonically established norms for aesthetics and intellectual history and tend to be more favorable towards Arnim. Yet even many of these critics consider the work something of a failure. Within the context of their readings of Arnim's work as *kontinuierliche Partnerautobiographie*, for example, Bäumer and Schultz explain Arnim's difficulty composing her final works as follows: "Einerseits war es Bettina (noch) nicht möglich, beim Schreiben von sich selbst abzusehen; andererseits war es ihr nicht (mehr) möglich, Texte zu verfassen, in die sie sich selbst mit 'hineinschreiben' konnte—sie hatte den Stoff ihres Lebens literarisch aufgebraucht und ausgeschöpft" (159). In secondary literature only Schmitz, Püschel, and Baldwin give Arnim credit for her original attempts to write outside of traditional aesthetic and philosophical norms. Püschel, for example, attributes the weaknesses "Im sprachlichen Gestaltungsniveau" to "die Anspruchsvollen Gegenstände und die Traditionslosigkeit für ihre Erörtung" ("Charakter hat nur der...," "...*wider die Philister und die bleierne Zeit*" 294).

If one considers all six of Arnim's texts as the story of the figure Bettine, then *Dämonen* must be read as a culmination of what has come before. In a development rare for female characters in nineteenth-century texts, Bettine has transformed herself from child to friend to lover to mother to daemon, an apotheosis of her former selves. Compromises are made along the way: Bettine decides to settle on womanhood and to accept that, in this role, public engagement will remain off limits to her. Yet if one considers Kant's definition of the public and private uses of reason in "Was ist Aufklärung" and "Streit der Fakultäten," the Bettine of *Gespräche* also follows in the steps of many thinkers who came before her, choosing to push for change through her influence and personal connections rather than through direct intervention in institutions where she would be subject to the dictates of others. It can certainly be said of both Arnim and her Bettine figures that, had they been in the employ of the state, they would have been far more restricted in voicing their opinions than when standing behind the masks of child/ mother/ daemon.

In Arnim's final works, her Bettine personae become less nuanced, the roles they play more fixed. They listen to others less and do more to insure that others are listening to them. This is especially true in *Ambrosia* and *Dämonen*. Yet one cannot overlook Bettine's insistence on her own subjectivity, on her right to shape herself through experience, feelings, and interactions with others, and on her right to influence others. This Bettine describes herself not as muse (a term long associated with women and unfairly considered as being "less than the artist") but as daemon, conscience, spirit, guide, and writer, a status she has achieved through a long process of self-incurred apprenticeship with mentors of her choice. The boundaries between her sources of inspiration and the ideas they inspire are fluid in these texts, and Bettine never claims that her genius arises out of herself as an individual separate from the world. Rather, her development, that of her subjectivity and possibility for agency, arises out of contact with and experiences in the world. In this regard, Arnim's final work must be considered the last chapter of a developmental text that limns a praxis for transforming the public sphere through development of the self.

Conclusion

In all six of her novel-length works, Bettina von Arnim's Bettine personae lay claim to the idea of becoming (*Werden*) as both a personal and a political motto. By tracing both the various roles assigned to these personae and the manner in which these roles change over the course of Arnim's writing career, I have tried to sketch a collective portrait not of the historical Bettina von Arnim, but of the personae and their respective roles that the author created as her textual mirrors; for in writing the life of her textual Bettine(s), Arnim recorded the story of a life that ran parallel to her own. This story developed out of the confluence of her life experiences (shaped by interactions with others, discourses on gender, and her own agency) and out of the roles played by its main characters. It was not merely a product of Arnim's life; it also contributed to the shaping of her life.

Because of the importance that becoming plays in these works, I have chosen to read them as an extended developmental text. Arnim scholarship has long acknowledged that the author played a number of *Lebensrollen* over the course of her life, but scant attention has been paid to how the author defined these roles in her six texts, to the nuanced meanings she attached to these roles, and to how the intertextual links between these texts and Arnim's life created a context within which one can read them. Arnim's early works, *Goethe's Briefwechsel mit einem Kinde* and *Die Günderode*, are texts of awakening and development, and in them we see Bettine developing through interaction with others. Although the first of her texts if one considers its sources, Arnim's fourth publication, *Clemens Brentano's Frühlingskranz*, presents a Bettine who now defines herself against her primary interlocutor, her brother. In Arnim's other three texts,

Dies Buch gehört dem König, Ilius Pamphilius und die Ambrosia, and *Gespräche mit Dämonen* we see Bettine personae who increasingly assume the adult roles of mentor, teacher, and daemon (genius or conscience). In *Ambrosia,* Arnim inverts the roles of *Briefwechsel,* allowing Ambrosia to play the role of mentor and Pamphilius to assume that of child and pupil. In *Dies Buch* and *Dämonen,* Arnim suggests that romantic sociability, the form of interaction that allowed Bettine to develop a sense of her self, be applied to the relationship between a king and his people. Although she works within the framework of constitutional monarchy, her suggestion that the king and people become friends, i.e., that they assume mutual responsibility for one another, suggests that the author was indeed in favor of breaking down social hierarchies in order to establish a more democratic form of government.

The roles that Arnim assigned to her Bettine personae shift and change throughout her texts. In all of Arnim's texts the role of the child represents spontaneity and openness to experience. At the same time, her textual personae quite literally grow up to assume the roles of lover, mother, old woman, and eventually genius. In this process, the fluid boundaries between teacher and pupil, which were envisioned especially in *Günderode,* tend to become more rigid. As Bettine distances herself from the role of child, she gains increasing authority to influence others but also becomes more imperious in her insistence on doing so. This becomes particularly evident in *Ambrosia.* The price of autonomy seems to be forgetting, at times, that others require their own autonomy and space for development.

In addition to the roles of child, mother, and old woman, Arnim's Bettines also assume the often erotically nuanced role of friend and the role of girl/woman. As friend, lover, and even as daemon to the king, Arnim's Bettine personae seek out others in whom they can see themselves mirrored; but they also offer themselves as a mirror to others. This process often proves difficult for the various Bettines, whom family members, in keeping with nineteenth-century mores, insist on seeing as the demure and passive woman they wish her to be. Although Bettine cannot escape her gender—indeed she seems to accept her femininity from *Günderode* on—she does try to redefine feminine gender roles, thereby insisting that she prefers to be a thorn to a rose.

Arnim's Bettines grow and change, acquiring along the way an increasing sense of autonomy and agency, a development that was influenced by and influenced the author's own life. But the cost of this autonomy is an increasing sense of isolation, thus revealing the paradox inherent in romantic sociability. With one important exception, we see "Bettine" standing alone at the end of Arnim's texts. Her partner (Goethe, Günderode, Pamphilius) has left her, or she has outgrown her interlocutor (Pamphilius), or her partner (the king in *Dämonen*) has grown wary of her. Arnim's Bettine personae inevitably come to the realization, familiar to many early romantic philosophers and authors, that the individual stands alone in the world, that the possibility of union with another exists only in a utopian realm.

In four of her works, the epistolary structure reinforces this sense of isolation. The letters serve not only as bridges to the other but also as barriers that hinder understanding, for each figure reads the letters of the other in his or her own language. An epistolary structure requires an exchange between two or more partners, and as we see in Arnim's works, in those instances when one of her personae forgets that her partner is an individual (this is especially true in *Ambrosia*), communication breaks down. Finally, like the portrait of "Bettine" that these texts present, the epistolary structures are fragmented, offering us a series of glimpses rather than an entire portrait of Arnim or her literary personae. Arnim's conversational texts, *Dies Buch* and *Dämonen*, are equally fragmented, but as a result of the conversational structure less distance exists between the characters. The friendship between Bettine and Frau Rath is the only one that does not end with the two figures going their separate ways, and in *Dämonen* Arnim creates a space of hope, albeit an imaginary one, in which her daemon actually appears to have some influence over the king. This conversational form is only possible once Arnim's Bettine figures have developed a sense of their own individuality. Before that, they require the space provided by the epistolary form.

Bettina von Arnim's texts differ from other developmental texts written by nineteenth-century women insofar as the heroines do not die, renounce the world, fall ill, or go insane by the end of the texts. Indeed, her personae grapple with many of the issues of individuality and autonomy explored by early-nineteenth-century male writers. Her texts offer a rare example of nineteenth-century female characters who have found a sense of autonomy and agency, if only in the ideal space of a written text. Yet they also challenge the essentialist view that women, because of their experience, are less prone to domination and hierarchical thinking. If one ventures to make the journey through all six of Arnim's texts, one finds not only admirable but also disturbing personae, figures who are socially engaged and figures who seem only to dominate those around them. The collective picture that one takes away from this journey is not one of an ideal Bettine, but of a complex and multifaceted figure who asks her interlocutors and also us as readers to see her not as "Bettine wie sie sein sollte," but rather as a woman whose life is a work in progress.

NOTES

Introduction
Dichtung und Wahrheit: Life as Text

1 Loeper's biographical overview in the *Allgemeine Deutsche Biographie* provides one of the earliest tripartite divisions of Arnim's life. In his useful *Chronik*, Heinz Härtl divides her life into: "Das erste Leben: Kindheit und Jugend (1785–1811);" "Das zweite Leben: Ehejahre mit Arnim (1811–1831);" and "Das dritte Leben: Schriftstellerin und Demokratin (1831–1859)." In her biography Ingeborg Drewitz offers two subdivisions of Arnim's "third life": "Das Ich Bettina" and "Erkennen und Altern."

2 Rather than employing Waldemar Oehlke's term *Briefromane*, which emphasizes the fictionality of Arnim's four epistolary novels (*Briefwechsel, Günderode, Frühlingskranz*, and *Ambrosia*), Lorely French argues in her dissertation for the term *Briefbuch*: "The designation *Briefbuch* describes the amalgamation of fiction and non-fiction, of art and life, and of author, narrator, and character found constantly in Arnim's epistolary works" (195). Extrapolating from this term, I will employ the term "letter book" to refer to the texts based on Arnim's correspondence with Goethe, Günderrode, and Brentano. I will use the term "dialogue book" to refer to the conversational texts *Dies Buch* and *Dämonen* although, as will become apparent, all of Arnim's texts manifest characteristics of epistolarity. For reasons discussed in Chapter Five, I will refer to *Ambrosia* as a letter documentation.

3 This passage is quoted in the critical apparatus of Bettina von Arnim, *Werke*, ed. Härtl, vol. 2 835. Piautaz helped raise the Brentano children following Maximiliane Brentano's death in 1793.

4 Bettine Brentano, "[An Savigny]," um Neujahr 1823, letter 152 of *Die Andacht zum Menschenbild: Unbekannte Briefe* 233.

5 Ann Willison Lemke writes that during this time Arnim also worked to develop her skills as a musician and composer.

6   Among other collections of Arnim's letters, both her correspondence with Achim von Arnim and the collection of letters, *Die Andacht zum Menschenbild*, point to Arnim's textual production during her "second life" as well as to the sense of confinement she felt during this period.

7   See especially the third volume of Lewald's autobiography, *Meine Lebensgeschichte*.

8   As Schormann notes, "Eine Auflistung von Bettines Familien-, Freundes- und Bekanntenkreis nimmt sich—leger formuliert—wie ein Who-is-Who der deutschen Geistesgeschichte zwischen Aufklärung und Jungem Deutschland aus" (*Bettine von Arnim* 17, footnote 49). Arnim's most important acquaintances included: Achim von Arnim, Franz von Baader, Bruno and Edgar Bauer, Beethoven, Clemens Brentano, Moriz Carriere, Hoffmann von Fallersleben, Goethe, Jacob and Wilhelm Grimm, Karoline von Günderrode, Heinrich Heine, Alexander von Humboldt, Heinrich von Kleist, Sophie von La Roche, Rahel Levin, Franz Liszt, Karl Marx, Heinrich Bernhard Oppenheim, Prince Hermann von Pückler-Muskau, Johann Sailer, Friedrich Karl von Savigny, Friedrich Wilhelm Schelling, Karl Friedrich Schinkel, August Wilhelm Schlegel, Friedrich Daniel Schleiermacher, Germaine de Staël-Holstein, David Friedrich Strauß, Ludwig and Friedrich Tieck, Karl August Varnhagen van Ense, and Christoph Martin Wieland.

9   Lemke reveals that, as in the period before her husband's death, Arnim directed much of this activity towards her song compositions.

10 Gersdorff writes of Arnim's talents as a healer: "Bettinas medizinische Befähigung wirkte, als [1831] Cholera ausbrach, ebenso großartig wie ihr soziales Pflichtbewußtsein. Sie scheute sich nicht, Kranke und Befallene in ihren Elendsquartieren aufzusuchen und die Arznei, die sie für die beste hält—den Tollkirschenextrakt Bella Donna—eigenhändig an Bedürftige zu verteilen. Mit Schleiermacher organisiert sie Geldsammlungen, kauft auf dem Wochenmarkt alle vorhandenen Schuhe, läßt in ihrer Wohnung weitere Schuhe nähen und an Arme verteilen. Nach Abklingen der Seuche zogen die Gilden der Stadt vor ihr Haus, um ihr zu danken" (182-184).

11 Arnim began in 1822 to conceptualize a larger-than-life-size monument to Goethe—including a representation of herself as Psyche—and she worked throughout her life to finance and complete this project. Although Arnim was not entirely pleased with Steinhäuser's rendition (Schorn 26), the monument was placed in the *Tempelherrenhaus* of the Weimar Park on December 12, 1853 and was then moved to the newly-constructed city museum in 1865. Severely damaged during World War II, the museum is being renovated for public access.

12 Arnim also expresses this concern in texts beyond the scope of this project: For her *Armenbuch*, a collection of reports on poverty in Germany that she was advised against publishing in 1844, Arnim completed several drafts of an epilogue criticizing Prussia's

social policies and neglect of the poor. In the proceedings of *Der Magistratsprozeß*, published by Gertrud Meyer-Hepner in 1960, she mockingly documented her trial for treason (1846–47), and in *Die Polenbroschüre*, published under a pseudonym in 1848, she criticized the partitioning of Poland and made a plea for Polish self-determination.

13 See Johann Wolfgang von Goethe, *Briefe Goethes an Sophie La Roche und Bettina Brentano nebst dichterischen Beilagen*, ed. Gustav von Loeper.

14 See, for example, Ludwig Geiger, "Goethe, Bettine und die Frankfurter Juden;" Margarete Susman, "Bettina," *Frauen der Romantik* 120; Hirsch, "Jüdische Aspekte im Leben und Werk Bettina von Arnims" and "Zur Dichotomie von Theorie und Praxis in Bettines Äußerungen über Judentum und Juden;" and Heuberger and Krohn. In his review of *Briefwechsel*, Börne wrote that Goethe was upset, "als er erfuhr, die Frankfurter Juden forderten Bürgerrechte, und er geiferte gegen die 'Huminatitätssalbader,' die den Juden das Wort sprachen. Ja, der Gott ärgerte sich und geiferte, und das Kind Bettina mußte ihm weiche Umschläge auf sein gichtisches Herz legen und ihn beschwichtigen wie einen leidenden mürrischen Onkel" (857–858).

15 See Bäumer, *Bettine, Psyche, Mignon*; Hoock-Demarle, "Bettinas Umgang mit Außenseitern;" Hock, " 'Sonderbare,' 'heißhungrige' und 'edle' Gestalten." My own reading notwithstanding, I disagree with Gerhard Lauer's assessment of *Gespräche mit Dämonen* as "protoantisemitisch" (315). Lauer bases his claim primarily on one passage in *Gespräche* and on anti-Semitic comments made by Arnim in her early twenties. His article takes into account neither the development in Arnim's thinking over the course of her life nor the emancipatory function that Jewish figures, especially Ephraim, serve in her texts. Peter-Anton von Arnim's article on Jewish aspects in Arnim's writing provides new documentary information—based on the holdings in Arnim's library—about her keen interest in Jews and Judaism. At the same time, he unnecessarily idealizes the author in his use of a quote from Varnhagen to describe Arnim—in regard to her dealings with Jews—as "die einzige wahrhaft freie und starke Stimme" of her time. I find Arnim and her Bettine personae intriguing because of their desire and ability to change and grow over time; I find them courageous because of their honesty: they never make the claim that they have achieved the utopia(s) for which they are striving. They are not perfect but they are strong enough to bear criticism.

16 See, for example, Edith Waldstein, *Bettine von Arnim and the Politics of Romantic Conversation* and Elke Frederiksen and Monika Shafi, "'Sich im Unbekannten suchen gehen.'"

17 Gustav von Loeper, "Bettina;" Moriz Carriere, "Bettina von Arnim;" Reinhold Steig, "Bettina." See also Anna Sonnenfels, "Die Erhebung der Frau in ihrem Zusammenhang mit der Literatur."

18 Christa Bürger, "Nachwort," *Bettina von Arnim: Ein Lesebuch* 317.

19 With the term "traditional autobiography" I refer to a genre whose formal aspects, as Felicity Nussbaum writes, have since the mid-twentieth century been "frequently codified as narrative with a beginning, middle, and end which purports to be true, is told retrospectively, and whose author is the same historical being as the first-person narrator and protagonist" (*The Autobiographical Subject* 4).

20 See "Der echte und der unechte Briefwechsel zwischen Goethe und Bettine von Arnim" 3275. A century later, Christa Wolf reappropriates the adjective "Bettinisch" positively, referring to Arnim's writing as "das unklassifizierbar Bettinische, das in kein Raster paßt" ("Nun ja!" 323).

21 See Katherine Goodman, *Dis/Closures*; Biddy Martin, "Lesbian Identity and Autobiographical Difference[s];" Martin, "Feminism, Criticism, and Foucault;" Michèle Barrett, "Ideology and the Cultural Production of Gender."

22 For further explanation of this term and its significance for Arnim, see Katherine R. Goodman and Edith Waldstein, eds., *In the Shadow of Olympus*.

23 Other texts that address this problem include Diana Fuss, *Essentially Speaking: Feminism, Nature & Difference* and Diamond and Quinby, *Feminism and Foucault*.

24 Elke Frederiksen and Katherine Goodman, "Introduction," *Bettina Brentano-von Arnim: Gender and Politics* 29. They quote in this passage from Christa Wolf, *Im Dialog* 15.

Chapter One
The Child Speaks: *Goethe's Briefwechsel mit einem Kinde* (1835)

1 Loeper published fourteen of Goethe's original letters in 1879, and Steig published the complete extant correspondence 1922. Waldemar Oehlke was the first to analyze the similarities and differences between the original correspondence and *Briefwechsel* in *Bettina von Arnims Briefromane*. In contrast to Oehlke's study, which compares the original correspondence with *Briefwechsel* in order to discern what Arnim fabricated in the latter, Marjanne Goozé's dissertation examines Arnim's early letters and then her published texts in order to chart the trajectory of Arnim's development as a writer. Konstanze Bäumer was working on an analysis of the correspondence that served as the basis for *Ambrosia* before her untimely death in 1993.

2 The first version of Arnim's Teplitz fragments begins: "Es war in der Abenddämmerung im heissen Augustmonat, in Töpplitz er saß am offnen Fenster, ich stand vor ihm und hielt ihn umhalst und mein Blick wie ein Pfeil scharf ihm ins Aug gedrückt blieb drinn haften bohrte sich tiefer und tiefer ein. Vielleicht weil ers nicht länger ertragen mochte frug er ob mir nicht Heiß sei, und ob ich nicht wolle daß mich die Kühlung anwehe, ich nickte so sagt er: Mache doch den Busen frei daß ihm die Abendluft zu gut komme" (*GB* 800). Presumably, such explicit eroticism was too

risqué for publication.

3   According to Helene von Kügelgen, "Frau von Arnim" spread the story throughout Weimar: "es wäre eine Blutwurst toll geworden und hätte sie gebissen" (Wilhelm Bode, ed. "Helene von Kügelgen an Friederike und Wilhelm Volkmann," 12 October 1912, letter 1793 of *Goethe in vertraulichen Briefen seiner Zeitgenossen*, vol. 2 573).

4   See Ludmilla Assing, ed., "Briefwechsel zwischen Pückler und Bettina von Arnim" and Bettina von Arnim and Hermann Fürst Pückler-Muskau, "Pückler und Bettina von Arnim." For analyses of Pückler's influence on *Briefwechsel* see *GB* 859–864; Bäumer and Schultz 61–63; and Enid Margarete Gajek's analyses: "Die Bedeutung des Fürsten Hermann Pückler für Bettine," and "'Das gefährliche Spiel meiner Sinne,' Gedanken zu Bettine und Pückler."

5   To date, Sabine Schormann has written the most detailed analyses of the influence of Schleiermacher on Arnim's thinking and writing. See *Bettine von Arnim: Die Bedeutung Schleiermachers für ihr Leben und Werk* and "'Was ich nur ahndete, das machte er mir zur Gewißheit.'"

6   Because Arnim's texts demand recursive reading, I take issue with Kittler's interpretation, in his essay "In den Wind schreibend, Bettina," of Bettine's/Arnim's claim that she "wrote into the wind." While such a claim may serve to support poststructuralist assertions of the opacity of language, it also trivializes Arnim's work by ignoring both the dialogic nature of her texts and the complex relationship between and development of the author and her protagonists.

7   Arnim and Pückler-Muskau, "Pückler an Bettina," 20 March 1832, letter 6 of *Frauenbriefe von und an Hermann Fürsten Pückler-Muskau* 17.

8   See the poem and Erich Trunz's related comments in the first volume of *Goethes Werke* (36 and 602). Schmitz and Steinsdorff compare Goethe's poem with Arnim's rendering of it in *GB* 970.

9   In 1809, Austria and Tyrol rose up against Napoleon, whose army was supported by Bavaria. With the Peace of Schönbrunn in the same year, Austria was forced to cede Tyrol to Bavaria.

10 Ruth–Ellen Boetcher Joeres describes the complexity of the "mask of [Arnim's] womanchild" as follows: "Eccentricity can mask radicality and make it acceptable, even in a less than cordial environment. Sometimes shields are needed for rebellion; overt performances can provide a mask behind which the masked woman writer gets to say what she wants to say. She may be crazy—but she is crazy like a fox" (*Respectability and Deviance* 100).

11 With regard to the historical Bettina Brentano, it was actually her brother Clemens who suggested the role of child to her and who attempted to confine her within his under-

standing of its parameters. As is clear throughout her writing, Arnim did everything she could to define the roles she wished to play.

12   "In der Epoche der Romantik hat der Kult um die Kindlichkeit wohl seinen Höhepunkt erreicht...Zahlreiche literarische und populärwissenschaftlich-philosophische Werke und Traktate der Zeit zentrieren sich um Darstellung und Lob der Kindheit...Die Romantiker haben zudem mit Nachdruck die Interdependenzen zwischen Kind und Künstler betont. Kindlichkeit galt vielen romantischen Autoren mithin als 'conditio sine qua non' der Kunstausübung" (Bäumer, *Bettine, Psyche, Mignon* 123).

13   Note further treatments of the theme of the child in Clemens Brentano's *Godwi* and Hölderlin's *Hyperion*.

14   *Ordnung im Chaos* 16. Liebertz-Grün is careful to point out that the Goethe of *Briefwechsel* is Arnim's projection and does not necessarily bear any resemblance to the historical figure: "Goethe erkennt das Künstlertum in Bettine und fordert sie auf, nicht länger nur eine Kunstbegeisterte zu sein, sondern sich durch Kunstwerke als Künstlerin zu realisieren...Während der historische Goethe wie Schiller, Fichte, Kant, Hegel nicht wenig dazu beigetragen hat, Genialität bei Frauen im Keim zu ersticken und Frauen die Menschenrechte vorzuenthalten, ist der fiktive Goethe für die junge Künstlerin eine allgütige Mutter."

15   One can assume that this holds true for Arnim's grandmother Sophie von La Roche, who never appears in Arnim's texts as a writer, but whom Arnim certainly knew in this capacity and whose works, such as *Das Fräulein von Sternheim*, must have influenced her choice of the epistolary genre.

16   See Becker-Cantarino, Duden, and Hausen for discussions of female gender roles in the nineteenth century.

17   See Waldstein, Goodman, Dischner, and Goozé.

18   Note 19,7 in *GB* 973.

19   As Krimmer notes in her engaging dissertation, "Offizier und Amazone: Frauen in Männerkleidung in der deutschen Literatur um 1800," it was not uncommon in the period around 1800 for women to don men's clothing while travelling: "Hier stellte eine männliche Erscheinung eine bedeutende Erleichterung und Schutzmaßnahme dar" (13). With regard to *Briefwechsel*, Krimmer writes, Bettine's pants "leiten neue Zeiten ein und verschaffen Zugang zu neuen Weltteilen...durch ihr Tarnung als Mann vergrößern sich Aktionsradius and (phallische) Wehrhaftigkeit" (221). While I agree with Krimmer's overall analyses of *Briefwechsel* and *Frühlingskranz*, one must keep in mind that her claim, "[Bettine] beansprucht mit männlicher Kleidung auch Männerprivilegien" (194), holds true for only one instance in *Briefwechsel* rather than for all of Arnim's Bettine personae in the six works I am discussing here.

20   In his article on Bettina Brentano's experiences with the Bavarian *Erweckungs*

bewegung and especially with the theologian Johann Michael Sailer around 1810, Bernhard Gajek argues that Arnim's concept of *"Werden* als Veränderung und Verwandlung, die wirklich und sinnenhaft zu erleben sind und ohne die das Neue nicht eintreten kann," date from this time (Gajek, "Bettine von Arnim und die bayerische Erweckungsbewegung" 268). The notion of becoming remains a central theme throughout Arnim's works.

21 Klaus Gille writes, "Mignons Leiden an der Welt kann nur im Tode aufgehoben werden. Der 'Schein des Lebens,' erzeugt durch die Kunst des Einbalsamierens, enthebt den Leichnam dem Leben und transzendiert es zugleich in der Kunst. Bettinas Mignon zeigt die Aufbrechung der Ichverschlossenheit; endet Goethes Mignon als Artefakt, vom Leben geschieden, so erlangt Bettinas Mignon die Künstlerschaft *im* (geträumten) Leben. Das bedeutet gesellschaftliche Anerkennung, Anerkennung auch durch den 'Meister,' Selbstbefreiung durch die Kunst und durch das weiße Kleid, das jetzt nicht mehr den Tod, sondern das Künstlertum symbolisiert" ("'Der anmutige Scheinknabe'" 281).

22 As Gisela Dischner writes, the romantics believed, "in der Liebe wird diese Diskontinuität des abgeschlossenen Individuums, seine 'Identität,' aufgesprengt, so wie sie im Tod aufgelöst wird" (*Bettina von Arnim* 67).

23 For detailed discussions of the role of Psyche in Arnim's life and work see Bäumer, *Bettine, Psyche, Mignon*; Ulrike Landfester, "'Da, wo ich duldend mich unterwerfen sollte, da werde ich mich rächen,' Mignon auf dem Weg zur Revolte, Stationen einer Rezeptionsgeschichte;" Gille, "'Der anmutige Scheinknabe;'" and Monika Shafi, "The Myth of Psyche as Developmental Paradigm in Bettina Brentano-von Arnim's Epistolary Novels."

24 Both the fictional and the historical break-ups were preceded by Günderode's affair with the married philologist Georg Friedrich Creuzer (referred to as Kreuzer in *Briefwechsel*).

25 This passage provides the most convincing proof of Steinsdorff and Leitner's assertion of the physical nature of Bettine's love: "Bettine denkt die Vereinigung u.E. ganz metaphysisch und ganz physisch in einem. Es kommt ihr auf die körperliche Intimität ebenso an wie auf die geistige—eine Dualität äußerster Spannweite also und nicht eine Enthebung oder 'Entschwebung' des Körperlichen durch das Geistige. Es geht nicht um Dezenz und elfenhafte Spiritualität. Die körperliche Liebe zwischen Mann und Frau ist für Bettine das Beschreibungsmodell der Annäherung des fiktiven Ichs an den zu Verehrenden (Goethe)" ("'...wunderliche Bilder...'" 192).

26 Grimm, *Deutsches Wörterbuch*, vol 4, part I, section 2. See columns 3396–3450.

27 See *GB* 107–109 and 580–583.

28 Bäumer correctly notes that Arnim eliminates here the "Seitenhiebe auf die Juden"

present in the original correspondence between Bettina Brentano and Goethe (*Bettine, Psyche, Mignon* 239).

29 Molitor was Catholic board member of and teacher at the Frankfurt *Philanthropin zur Hebung der Judenschaft*.

Chapter Two
Youth and Ideal Friendship: *Die Günderode* (1840)

1 Arnim wrote to Caroline von Egloffstein in 1838: "Dies Buch hat mir viel Bekanntschaften zugezogen…viele Gedichte sind mir zugeflogen aus allen Ecken Deutschlands, namentlich aus dem Harz; viele schwärmerische Bekenntnisse, Offenbarungen von Gemütszuständen…Sechs dicke Bücher sind mir von verschiedenen Seiten zugeschickt in dunkelrotem Samt oder in Grün mit Gold gestickt…voll Gedichte an mich, voll philosophischer Anmerkungen, Schauspiele, Auszügen aus meinen Büchern in Verse übertragen" (Hermann Freiherr von Egloffstein, ed. "Bettina von Arnim an Line," 9 April 1838, *Alt-Weimars Abend* 501).

2 Bäumer discusses the development of Arnim's salon and the changes in the types of people visiting it in her article "Interdependenzen zwischen mündlicher und schriftlicher Expressivität: Bettina von Arnims Berliner Salon."

3 For a detailed discussion of Arnim's relationship with and her efforts on behalf of the Grimm brothers, see Hartwig Schultz, "Bettines Auseinandersetzung mit Friedrich Karl von Savigny um die Einstellung der Brüder Grimm in Berlin," as well as his edited volume, Bettina von Arnim and Jakob and Wilhelm Grimm, *Der Briefwechsel Bettine von Arnims mit den Brüdern Grimm. 1838–1841*.

4 Members included Moriz Carriere, Heinrich Bernhard Oppenheim, and Max Ring. Bäumer describes their adulation of Arnim in: "Die Rezeption Bettina von Arnims in der Berliner Kultur und Literaturgeschichte."

5 Dischner and Schormann have explored in depth the influence of German Romanticism on Arnim's writing. For studies of the influence of the political and philosophical movements of the 1830s and 1840s on her work, see Härtl, "'Dies Völkchen mit der vorkämpfenden Alten,' Bettina von Arnim und die Junghegelianer;" Hahn, *Bettina von Arnim in ihrem Verhältnis zu Staat und Politik*; and Wyss, *Bettina von Arnims Stellung zur deutschen Romantik und dem Jungen Deutschland*.

6 See, for example, Bäumer and Schultz 34; French, diss. 354; Waldstein, "Goethe and Beyond" 111; and Dischner 10.

7 Edith Waldstein explores the communicational aspects of Arnim's body of work in *Bettine von Arnim and the Politics of Romantic Conversation*.

8   "Finality is actualized in epistolary terms by motivated renunciation of writing, the death of the writer, the arrival of the addressee, whereas enigmatic silence realizes the letter form's potential for open-endedness" (Altman 187).

9   See Roetzel, "Acting Out: Bettine as Performer of Feminine Genius."

10 Here one has to wonder whether, in Bettine's insistence on youth and life, Arnim is not herself responding to the deaths of numerous loved ones. As both Gersdorff and Baumgart note in their respective accounts of the relationship between Bettina and Achim von Arnim, death was a significant part of Bettina von Arnim's youth as well as of her adult years. Her mother died in 1793, followed by her father in 1797. Karoline von Günderrode killed herself in 1806; Clemens Brentano's wife, Sophie Mereau, died in childbirth later the same year. Sophie von La Roche passed away in 1807, and Catharina Elisabeth Goethe died in 1808. In 1831, Bettina von Arnim had to face the deaths of both her husband Achim and her good friend Amalie von Helvig. Goethe died in 1832, Rahel Varnhagen in 1833, and Schleiermacher in 1834. Within this context it becomes difficult not to read *Die Günderode* as Arnim's attempt to assert and preserve life in both the figurative and the literal senses of the word.

11 Sabine Schormann has convincingly analyzed the connection between the feeling that drove Günderrode to her early death—and that Arnim and her Bettine figures constantly combated—and the nihilism common to many romantic writers in her article, "Bettines Rezeption der frühromantischen Philosophie" as well as in her monograph, *Bettine von Arnim*. She notes in the latter: "Die existenzielle Langeweile ...ist Ausdruck einer nihilistischen Lebenserfahrung, die mit dem Zeiterleben zusammenhängt, und erst vom Zusammenbruch der ontologisch fundierten Seinsordnung ausgelöst werden konnte. Seitdem die Zeit nicht mehr durch ihr Zulaufen auf die Ewigkeit Sinn erhält, wird sie als mechanische, sich ewig um sich selbst drehende Bewegung erlebt, deren leere, dumpfe Sinnlosigkeit zuerst Langeweile und dann Angst erregt" (106).

12 Whereas the historical Karoline von Günderrode did suffer in her relationships with Savigny and Friedrich Creuzer, and while Bettine does discuss the breakup with Creuzer in the *Briefwechsel*, it is not mentioned in *Günderode*. This can be read either as a lack of understanding of her friend's problems on Bettine's/Arnim's part or as an attempt to assert a potential for female agency that does not stem from an intimate relationship with a man (a desire that Günderrode herself often expressed in her letters and poems). I believe that both readings are accurate and will address them throughout this chapter.

13 "Vor der Philisterwelt die meinen Geist doch nicht begreift, schäm ich mich nicht für sie nicht Jugend zu sein, die von den heiteren Frühlingstagen nichts weiß welche der Geist durchlebt" (700). This passage reflects the dichotomy of student and philistine that had a long tradition in German territories and that became a central

concern both of the German romantics and of the Young Germans. For a detailed discussion of the term, see *G* 895–900.

14   This is true not only of the text itself but also of Arnim's process of remembering her relationship with Karoline von Günderrode. As Roswitha Burwick accurately observes: "Erinnerung und Beziehung zum anderen färben das Bild subjektiv, machen es zum Spiegel, in dem man das eigene Ich erblickt, zum Echo, dem Widerhall der eigenen Stimme" (66).

15   Arnim echos Schleiermacher, who writes in "Versuch einer Theorie des geselligen Betragens" that his model of social interaction is an ideal that can never be achieved in entirety: "[Es] braucht also eigentlich nicht ausdrücklich gesagt zu werden, daß die darin aufgestellten Ideen Ideale sind, welchen sich die Ausübung nur nähern soll. Das ist denn auch der Fall mit dem hier durchgeführten Begriff, daß jede Gesellschaft eine Einheit, ein Ganzes sein soll. Eine jede wird unvermeidlich nicht nur Augenblicke haben, wo sie eigentlich in mehrere Teile geteilt ist, sondern es wird auch für die vortrefflichste ein besonderes Glück sein, wenn sie sich auch nur eine Zeitlang als ein wirkliches Ganzes erhalten kann" (91).

16   Heukenkamp has convincingly shown how Arnim's concept of God and Christ as moral authorities has as its model the teachings of David Friedrich Strauss, who writes in *Über Vergängliches und Bleibendes im Christentum* (1838): "So geht die Richtung dieser Zeit dahin, die Offenbarung Gottes in allen den Geistern zu verehren, welche belebend und schöpferisch auf die Menschheit eingewirkt haben. Der einzige Cultus—mag man es nun beklagen oder loben—aber läugnen wird man es nicht können—der einzige Cultus, welcher den Gebildeten dieser Zeit aus dem religiösen Zerfalle der letzten übrigbleiben, ist der Cultus der Genius" (Quoted in Heukenkamp 16). As Heukenkamp notes further, the cult of the genius can only be worshiped through an active life: "An einem wesentlichen Punkt aber erweist sich die Religionsauffassung Bettina von Arnims als radikaler als die Strauß, denn das erste Grundgesetz ihrer Religion gebietet dem Menschen das *Handeln*, also das aktive Befördern der eigenen Entwicklung zur göttlichen Selbstvervollkommnung gegen die Widerstände der 'verkehrten' Welt" (16).

17   As Wuthenow argues, in Bettine's eyes not Hölderlin but *die Philister* are the ones who are truly ill: "Die Erstarrung der Sinne wie des inneren Lebens, deren sich die Menschen nicht bewußt sind, das ist in ihren Augen die eigentliche Krankheit, der eigentliche Wahnsinn—und schlimmer als der jenes Dichters, dessen Geistesflamme 'im trüben Regenbach zusammengelaufner Alltäglichkeit' erlöschen mußte" (324). Lemke makes the fascinating argument that Arnim's interest in Hölderlin extended to her musical settings of his poems. Here, Arnim attempts to depict the poet "as a musical, misunderstood soul with whom her own soul resonates." Lemke explains further: "The handwriting is very small, sometimes leaning backwards, and Bettine squeezed in many notes and accidentals...She wrote thick chords, some of them

stacked up seven notes high" (130).

18 Underscoring a function of epistolary exchange also discussed by Altman, Heukenkamp notes: "die dialogische Grundstruktur [regt] den Leser zu aktivem Verhalten gegenüber dem Text [an], da er den Part des jeweils zuhörenden Gesprächpartners übernimmt und nun seinerseits dessen mögliche Antworten entwirft" (116). I would argue that Arnim intended this "active behavior" to extend from the process of reading to the reader's engagement with the world around her or him.

Chapter Three
Behind the Mask of a Mentor: *Dies Buch gehört dem König* (1843)

1 This correspondence, documented in Arnim, *Bettine von Arnim und Friedrich Wilhelm IV*, ed. Geiger, continued in varying degrees of intensity for over a decade. Püschel divides the epistolary exchange between Arnim and Friedrich Wilhelm IV into four phases: "die erste in der Zeit der Hoffnungen von 1839 bis 1843, die zweite, gekennzeichnet von deren Enttäuschungen, 1844 bis 1847, die dritte in unmittelbarem Zusammenhang mit der Revolution 1848/49, die letzte ab 1850" ("Die Schriftstellerin und das Staatsoberhaupt," ...*wider die Philister* 195). In the first phase of their correspondence, before the publication of *Dies Buch*, the tone of Arnim's letters is surprisingly intimate. She writes in a postscript to a letter from April 15, 1843, for example, "O Sire! Du bist ein Bürger in den Regionen der Schönheit und Gerechtigkeit, Du mußt Dein Bürgerthum auslösen" (*Bettine von Arnim und Friedrich Wilhelm IV* 30).

2 The letter that accompanied Arnim's gift of *Dies Buch* to Friedrich Wilhelm IV in late summer of 1843 served as yet another reminder that she wrote the book for him: "Der Genius nur kann Fürst sein! Und unser König—wollte der unumschränkter Genius sein! Stieg das Ideal der Zeiten in seinem Geist uns auf! All dies ist mir durch den Kop gegangen, als ich mein Buch schreib. Wollte es Euer Majestät huldvoll aufnehmen, wie könnte ich es dankbar genug anerkennen" (Letter 6 of Arnim, *Bettine von Arnim und Friedrich Wilhelm IV* 40).

3 According to Bunzel et al., Catharina Elisabeth Goethe was invited to an audience with the queen in 1803 (*DB* 917).

4 Catharina Elisabeth Goethe died in 1808. Goethe last visited his mother in 1797.

5 As Arnim's correspondence with Pückler-Muskau and as *Ambrosia* reveal, her own life as an aging woman was not always so ideal. In one of his best known letters to Arnim, Pückler tries to distance himself from her following an intense and erotically charged relationship and accuses her of *Gehirnsinnlichkeit*. He writes in September 1833, "Wenn ich früher sagte, ich wolle mir recht gern Leidenschaftlichkeit gefallen lassen,

so habe ich darunter doch nur eine leidenschaftlich ergebene Freundschaft, wie sie mir zum Beispiel auf die schönste und angemessenste Weise eine wahrhaft hohe Frau gewidmet hat—verstanden, aber nicht die dithyrambische Raserei einer achtzehnjährigen Bacchantin mit bloßer Gehirnsinnlichkeit...die ermüdet mich, und behagt meiner Natur nicht" (Arnim and Pückler-Muskau, letter 28 of *Frauenbriefe von und an Hermann Fürsten Pückler-Muskau* 62).

6   Offering more evidence for the topicality in her text, Arnim satirizes here a poem from the wars of liberation that was popular again in the 1840s: Ernst Moritz Arndt's "Des Teutschen Vaterland." The first stanza of the poem is: "Was ist des Teutschen Vaterland? Ist's Preussenland? Ist's Schwabenland? Ist's, wo am Rhein die Rebe blüht? Ist's, wo am Belt die Möve zieht? O nein, nein, nein! Sein Vaterland muß größer sein" (*Gedichte*, vol. 2 116).

7   Another related figure is the old woman in Arnim's story that is now known as "Der Heckebeutel." See Arnim, *Werke und Briefe*, vol. 3 336–555.

8   As in all of her works, Arnim does not concern herself here with the presentation of a historically accurate chronology. When she claims that she wished Queen Louise would bear a great leader, Frau Rath is speaking in 1807, and according to the text, recalling 1804. Friedrich Wilhelm IV was already born in 1795, however. Yet perhaps the mix-up is an intentional, sly jab at the king. And perhaps Arnim is giving voice to her own frustration, which will increase throughout the 1840s, when she has Frau Rath lament: "Wir zählen jetzt: Anno Sieben! Wie wir Anno Vier zählten da hatt ich sanguinische Hoffnungen, sie sind aber gewaltig gesunken" (81).

9   Bunzel et al. note: "Während sie im *Königsbuch* Freundschaft noch als Mittel der Charakterbildung versteht, lehnt sie dann im *Frühlingskranz* Freundschaft als Schwächung des eigenen Selbst vehement ab" (*DB* 1020). As I will discuss in the following chapter, the Bettine of Arnim's fourth publication rejects friendship as Clemens defines the term, not in and of itself. Like all of Arnim's protagonists, this character insists on defining her own terms.

10 In depicting the devil as a positive figure, Arnim is working not only within a centuries-old tradition but also with a theme common in the work of the contemporaries. Ernst Osterkamp describes the positive depiction of Lucifer by English romantics. He writes of William Blake, for example, "Satan ist für Blake die Verkörperung des bewegenden Prinzips, der weitertreibenden Energie, während in Gott die Kräfte der Beharrung, der Saturiertheit im Bestehenden bedeutet sind. So wird denn Satan zum Garanten von Zukunft" (180). Within the German context of the 1840s, Jeffrey L. Sammons has pointed out in *Six Essays on the Young German Novel* that Gustav Kühne idealized evil and the devil in his 1835 novel, *Quarantäne im Irrenhause* (93).

11 For a book in the octavo format, one signature, or *Bogen*, was the equivalent of 16

pages.

12 The law did require that the author's name appear on the title page, which was not the case with Arnim's text. Yet, as Houben notes, in actuality Arnim was not breaking this law: "Der Sinn des Gesetzes aber war natürlich der, daß der Verfasser überhaupt bekannt sein müsse. In diesem Sinne war Bettinens Königsbuch nicht anonym, denn ihre Urheberschaft kannte ganz Berlin und ebenso das Ministerium" (36).

13 Montag, den 13. November 1843, *Tagebücher*, vol. 2 225.

14 "Ihre Beziehung zu Friedrich Wilhelm IV erfuhr im Lauf der Zeit beträchtliche Modifikationen, sie schillerte in vielen Farben, von Selbstgefühl über Erfolgszwang bis Eitelkeit, neben sozialem Verantwortungsbewußtsein traten Elemente von Selbstbewegung auf, vom eigentlichen Impuls abgelöst—die bindende Erklärung aber besteht nach meiner Erkenntnis darin, daß in dieser Beziehung Bettinas höchste Möglichkeit zum Handeln lag. Dieser Komplex von Handlungsmöglichkeiten, unmittelbaren wie mittelbaren, war an seiner Spitze substituiert, Bettina konnte nur einen anderen, den König, bewegen, beeinflussen, in ihrem Sinn zu handeln. Ausgedrückt in Bettinas poetischem Vokabular: statt selber der Held zu sein, mußte sie sich mit der Rolle seines Dämons begnügen" (Püschel, "Die Schriftstellerin und das Staatsoberhaupt" 191).

Chapter Four
Child Turns Woman: *Clemens Brentano's Frühlingskranz* (1844)

1 Otto-Peters first published the *Frauen-Zeitung* in April of 1849.

2 Auguste Bussmann married again in 1817 but, unable to cope with what Drewitz describes as her *Melancholie* (62), drowned herself in 1832.

3 Arnim had no patience with what she considered to be her brother's religious fanaticism. After seeing Clemens in Schlangenbad in August of 1824, she wrote to her husband, "er ist vielleicht jetzt noch eitler und inkonsequenter wie sonst; er lügt sich selbst am meisten vor, ist überzeugt, daß er durch den Umgang mit der Nonne ein halber Prophet geworden. Alles was geschehen, will er vorher gewußt haben, er hat einen ganzen Koffer voll blutiger Tücher und Binden von der Nonne, die will er jedermann zum Anrühren geben, und wer sich davor ekelt, der kriegt eine tüchtige Salve; ans Übertreiben hat er sich so gewöhnt, daß nichts wie Wunder und Wunder aus nichtsbedeutenden Dingen gemacht werden." "Bettina an Arnim," 24 August 1824, letter 265 of *Achim und Bettina in ihren Briefen* 474.

4 Steig compares these letters to the text in his 1891 edition of Arnim's works. The letters are also reprinted in the Deutscher Klassiker Verlag edition.

5 One could perhaps even argue that it was not coincidence but Arnim's ever-present

political consciousness that enabled her to shrug off the censorship of this work following its publication (Friedrich Wilhelm IV eventually lifted the ban) in order to turn to her *Armenbuch-Project*. Arnim wrote to Alexander von Humboldt on July 2, 1844, "Auch hab ich die Schlangenhaut, an der die Zensurbehörde und Polizei jetzt zerren, schon abgeworfen, und bin in etwas anderm begriffen, was mir mehr am Herzen liegt. Es ist die Beantwortung der Preisfragen, die von der Potsdamer Regierung Anno 1842 gestellt über das Zunehmen der Armut, und wie ihr zu steuern sei" (quoted in *CBF* 1000).

6   In his study of German romanticism, *Über die ethische und religiöse Bedeutung der neueren romantischen Poesie in Deutschland*, Eichendorff wrote that, while both Clemens and Bettina sought autonomy, Clemens suffered from this drive to individuation more than his sister: "Bettina jubelt noch bis heute eigensinnig fort in ihrer Eigenmacht, während Clemens, jede Eigenmacht vielmehr als eine falsche Fremdherrschaft erkennend, mit dem Phantom gerungen hat bis sein Ende." (181)

7   In her dissertation, "Textile in Texturen," Carmen Janssen focuses in her chapter on Arnim on the presentation of textile work in *Frühlingskranz*.

8   According to Schultz, "Der Großmutter blieb freilich die erotische Komponente der Geschwisterliebe nicht verborgen, und der Briefwechsel beginnt mit einer kleinen 'Zensurmaßnahme,' die vermutlich dazu dienen sollte, die schwärmerische Liebe des jungen Mädchens zu dem faszinierenden Studenten, der ihr so artverwandt war, zu dämpfen" ("Nachwort" 348–349). Hildegard Baumgart discusses the erotic aspect of this relationship in *Bettine Brentano und Achim von Arnim—Lehrjahre einer Liebe*.

9   Monika Shafi compares the experience of these Bettine figures to that of the figure Psyche, which Arnim incorporated into many of her works and especially into her Goethe monument. Shafi notes that "Brentano-von Arnim's great demands are frustrated by the social and individual limits of her various partners. Even the fictionalization of her letters cannot hide the distance their recipients maintained, either consciously or subconsciously. It seems to me that the self-centeredness expressed in the epistolary novels also reflected this fundamental lack of a 'resonance,' which the author nevertheless transformed into an even greater attention to her self" ("The Myth of Psyche as Developmental Paradigm…")

10 Quoted in Bürger, *Leben Schreiben* 135.

11 This is related to the criticism of the *Philister* that runs through Arnim's texts, for in romantic thinking the *Philister* was considered incapable of true friendship: "Zu einem tiefen, wahrhaftigen, seelischen Kontakt sind die Philister unfähig, denn sie suchen am Anderen gar nicht sein innerstes Wesen, sondern wählen ihre Freunde allein nach dem Äußern, nach bloßen Fertigkeiten, Talenten, beruflichen Erfolgen, der gesellschaftlichen Position" (Schormann, *Bettine von Arnim* 110). Although Clemens generally does not concern himself with Bettine's superficial qualities, he does maintain an inter

est in Bettine's talents and in Bettine herself as a surface upon which he can project his ideal of her.

12 In her analysis of *Günderode* and *Frühlingskranz* Goodman suggests that, in addition to Schleiermacher, both Spinoza and the Dutch philosopher Hemsterhuis influenced Arnim's conception of friendship. She writes of Hemsterhuis, "If something is capable of evoking a reaction, according to Hemsterhuis, it is active. Individuals may thus recognize and activate the otherness of nature, as they may recognize and activate the otherness of each individual…Only an active being (*être activ*), one who elicits a reaction and thereby realizes its activity, can become a guiding force in the creation of this world concept. Such beings render other beings coexistent, activate them" ("Through a Different Lens" 134). Within this framework one could say that, although Clemens strove to shape his sister's development, he gradually became incapable of "activating" her, inspiring her to activity, at least within the timeframe of *Frühlingskranz*. If one steps back, of course, it becomes clear that the correspondence with Clemens Brentano did "activate" Bettina von Arnim to write the letter book that bears his name.

13 Luise Pusch's volume, *Die Schwestern berühmter Männer*, confirms that in many brother-sister relationships into the nineteenth century sisters were dwarfed by more prominent brothers.

14 Goodman points out that Clemens uses the term "sociability" to define the ideal of domesticity that he advocates: "With the key word 'sociability' Clemens's image summons up the romantic ideal of domestic bliss, radical around 1800. According to it, the ideal woman does not merely perform household duties and remain unseen and unheard. Rather her 'feminine' nature expresses itself in her ability to promote sociable discourse and unite disparate family members and friends in harmonious interchange. The character, Clemens, thus represents ideals formulated by a generation older than the one seeking new freedoms in the 1840s" ("Through a Different Lens" 124). As with the term "friendship," Bettine's conception of sociability differs significantly from that of her brother in that it does not dictate that women serve only as mirrors but rather allows them to search for others who can mirror them.

15 These values are spelled out for women in the text *Elisa oder das Weib wie es sein soll* (attributed to Wilhelmine K. von Wobeser) and include being neither too educated nor too ignorant. That Clemens Brentano held these ideals to be his own is evident in a letter he wrote to Savigny on 9 September 1801: "Bettine war mit den beiden andern einige Tage hier und ich habe dies *Mädchen wie es sein soll* recht begriffen…Gott! ich bin Prometheus bei Bettinen geworden ohne es zu wissen. Die gestohlne Flamme, der bloße Mignon, hat Urteil, kaltes ruhiges Urteil bekommen" (*Das unsterbliche Leben* 226–230).

16 In the longest of the three extant letters from the original correspondence, Clemens Brentano's weakness is more apparent, the emphasis on female gender roles not quite

so pronounced. This evidence would support the claim that, when writing *Frühlingskranz* in the 1840s Arnim was quite aware of contemporary debates on women's role in society, and although she did not explicitly take up the issue of women's emancipation, offers her text as a contribution to the argument in favor of women's self-determination and *Mündigkeit*.

17 That Arnim did not accept predetermined gender rolls is evident from a letter she wrote to Sophie Mereau in 1805 in response to a question from the latter regarding manifestations of ideal femininity and masculinity: "indessen kann ich Deine Frage auch *ernsthaft* nicht beantworten, ich habe zu wenig Erfahrung, und dann meine ich daß um sie zu beantworten müßte ich schon eine ganz reine Erscheinung der Weiblichkeit gesehen und gefühlt haben, ich glaube aber daß diese eben so wie die der Männlichkeit selten, ja nie zum Vorschein kommen, und daß beide von jeher so gemischt waren wie ihre Vorfahren [die zweigeschlechtlichen Menschen, von denen die platonische Tradition weiß] und auch daß keine vor der andern in sich selbst, mehr Vorzug hat, soll ich Dir aber sagen wo ich denke daß der Menschliche Geist am besten und kräftigsten wirken könne…da wo Jugend sich zum ersten und letztenmal mit dem Alter vereint bis sie nach und nach sich von dem Äußeren ablöst und nun eine innige Verbindung stifftet mit ihrem inneren Geist" (quoted in *CBF* 1075–1076).

18 For a comparison of the two see Oehlke, *Bettina von Arnims Briefromane*.

19 The Deutscher Klassiker Verlag edition of the texts suggests that this section may allude to the erotic word play in Act III, Scene 2 of Shakespeare's tragedy.

20 See Krimmer for a discussion of Gachet's cross-dressing.

21 Eve Kosofky Sedgwick, *Epistemology of the Closet* 88. Here Sedgwick is referring to Adrienne Rich's concept of the "lesbian continuum" as described in the essay "Compulsory Heterosexuality and Lesbian Existence."

22 "Cette pensée…": This thought is my guide, she said, and it will accompany me through all worlds and heaven.

23 In this regard, Arnim was perhaps more progressive than the majority of women involved in the early women's movement who, as Frevert notes, distanced themselves from *Mannweibern*: "[Die Frauenbewegung] hielt nichts von der Zügellosigkeit der Leidenschaften, von der Nachahmung männlichen Verhaltens, sondern forderte, im Einklang mit den 'ewigen Gesetzen echter Weiblichkeit,' das Recht weiblicher Selbstentfaltung in Familie und Gesellschaft" (77).

24 Bäumer and Schultz hypothosize that Arnim integrated the discussion of the French Revolution into the letters while working on *Frühlingskranz* for publication (17).

25 Like Achim von Arnim and other members of the *Christliche Teutsche Tischgesellschaft*, the historical Clemens Brentano was vehemently anti-Semitic in the first decade of the nineteenth century. In a speech before the *Tischgesellschaft*, "Der

Philister vor, in und nach der Geschichte," he explains to members why they must protect themselves from both *Philister* and *Juden.*

26 "Sonntag, den 28. April 1844," *Tagebücher,* vol. 2 291.

Chapter Five
"Motherhood" and the Perils of Autonomy:
Ilius Pamphilius und die Ambrosia (1847)

1 See Bäumer, "*Ilius Pamphilius und die Ambrosia.* Bettina von Arnim als Mentorin." As Bäumer notes in this article, Arnim's interactions with these men frequently served her professional interests.

2 Fanny Lewald wrote in her review of 1849, "Pamphilius ist kein Genie; kein Genius, sondern ein Zwitterwesen voll Wollen und nicht Können, voll augenblicklichem Aufschwung des Gefühls und kleinlich nagender Speculation; ein Mensch der nie ganz den vollen Pulsschlag des Lebens empfindet" (683).

3 In her article, "Bettinas Umgang mit Außenseitern," Hoock-Demarle attributes Arnim's empathy with "others" such as Jews, Italians, and Poles in part to the author's Italian origins.

4 Here we are reminded of Bettina von Arnim the mother who used natural cures and homeopathy to nurse her seven children through their many illnesses.

5 The Prussian author Susanne von Bandemer recorded in 1802, for example, her "Zufällige Gedanken über die Bestimmung des Weibes und einige Vorschläge dieselbe zu befördern": "Ich will keine herrischen, keine stolzen, keine übermütigen Schönen bilden; nein, ich will ihnen raten, gegen euch zärtlich, nachgebend und beständig zu sein, damit sie die liebenswürdigsten Weiber, die besten Mütter und die nützlichsten Weltbürgerinnen werden" (Quoted in Lange, *Ob die Weiber Menschen sind* 16).

Chapter Six
The Genius Speaks: *Gespräche mit Dämonen* (1852)

1 Infirmity eventually forced Arnim to live with the boredom she and her characters had struggled so hard to flee. Varnhargen wrote in his diary on 9 October 1858: "Abends bei Frau Bettina von Arnim, die wir sehr mißbehaglich und verstimmt fanden, sie sagte, es gehe recht schlecht, indes versicherten später die Wärterin und die Töchter, sie habe in der Regel keine Schmerzen, esse gut, schlafe mehrere Stunden gut, fahre alle Tage aus, jedoch leide sie an Langerweile, für die es doch keine Mittel gebe, seit das Lesen aufgehört hat. Nur wenn von dem Goethedenkmal die Rede ist, zeigt sie lebhaftere Aufmerksamkeit, und wenn man ihr von dessen Ausführung spricht, einige

Befriedigung" (quoted in Härtl, *Chronik* 47).

2   Schultz has argued further that, because their form invited engagement with the ideas they espouse, *Dies Buch* and *Gespräche* were politically less acceptable than genres such as the folk song and the fairy tale, which were gaining in popularity at the time: "Die Romantik hat als fiktionale, kunstvolle Form nicht nur das Volkslied, das Volksmärchen und die Volkssage hervorgebracht, sondern eben auch das volkstümliche Gespräch. Daß politische Aufklärung sich als Hauptziel dieser Variante des Salongesprächs herauskristallisiert, läßt diese Gattung jedoch zugleich zur politischen Zweckform werden, der wegen der politischen Umstände keine Zukunft im 19. Jahrhundert bescheiden war. Während Volkslied, Volksmärchen, Volkssage unverfänglich bzw. sogar politisch erwünscht waren, ist ein Buch, in dem volksnah politische Aufklärung im Sinne einer gemäßigt-liberalen Richtung betrieben wird, nicht erwünscht" ("Euer Unglaube" 269).

3   Citing Varnhagen, Konrad suggests two other possible motivations behind Arnim's dedication: that she wished to gain the sultan's support of a poor Turkish family living in Berlin, and that she wished his financial support for her Goethe monument (490). While such assertions are certainly plausible, they are not incompatible with two other facts: 1) that Arnim was highly conscious of the influence of her works upon her reading public; 2) that she used the first pages of her book to suggest a standpoint from which her ideal reader should approach this work.

4   Goozé has written that "The 'Dämon' is not to be totally equated with Bettine, because she converses as herself with the Primas. The 'Dämon' is an independent character, who is joined in the dialogue by other spirits as well" (348). Yet the distance between the Bettine figure/narrator and the daemon is far less than Goozé claims it is, for although in the first section the narrator writes of the king's daemon as an independent being, in this section she depicts herself as transforming into this very daemon; it is actually an ethereal "Bettine" who does the talking to the king. Evidence for this claim can be found in the primate's praise for the narrator after the conversation is over.

5   Schmitz has pointed out that the *Klosterbeere* offers a structural symbol of this movement, "denn wie sie 'reift,' entwächst auch der Religions- und Gottesbegriff, der zunächst—im Kloster—kirchlich gebunden war, den 'kleinen Zellen' der 'Nönnchen' und weitet sich zur Geistreligion und zum 'Kultus des Genius'…Schließlich wird die geistige Abgrenzung, die im Begriff des Auserwählten ja mitgesetzt wurde, überwunden in dem universalen Toleranzmodell des Orientalismus, das Juden, Christen, und den Islam umfaßt—dies aber ist erst im Medium des 'Geistes' möglich. Solche *Verwandlung des Konkreten ins Geistige ist die grundlegende Strategie der Bildsprache Bettines*" ("Die freie Kultur" 144). While I agree that the transformation of the concrete into the spiritual is central to Arnim's work, I disagree with the claim that the borders of the individual are overcome in this text, or even in the dream sequences of it. A sobering aspect of this and in other works by Arnim is that the individual can

never step out of his or her boundaries.

6 While some have argued that Arnim was forced by the political climate to censor her own writing and that she used this device as a humorous means of criticizing censorship, Bäumer and Schultz write: "Zensureingriffe gab es nach 1848 nicht mehr, und Bettinas Befürchtungen zu einem neuen Pressegesetz...waren unbegründet. Möglicherweise wollte sie die Phantasie des Lesers anregen und variierte Heines satirischen Umgang mit der geistlosen Zensur" (128).

7 Staff and Baldwin discuss in detail the nineteenth-century treatment of Jews in Prussia.

8 We are reminded here that Arnim witnessed the dramatic funeral of those killed during the 1848 uprising in Berlin. In a letter to her son Siegmund, she describes a parade of revolutionaries presenting the bodies of some of the fallen to the king: "Unter den Linden begegneten wir einem Leichenzug von der imposantesten Art: Ein großer, offener Möbelwagen mit 17 Leichen, hinter diesem neun Leichen, welche einzeln mit offnen Wunden je von vier Leuten getragen wurden und mit Blumen geziert waren, eine ungeheure Masse von Volk, welches alles baarhaupt ging, und an allen Fenstern Leute, viele vom Volk weinten, wahrscheinlich warens Freunde der Gefallnen" (An ihren Sohn Siegmund, Undated, probably Berlin, 19–20 March 1848, *Werke und Briefe*, vol. 5, ed. Konrad 407).

WORKS CITED

Primary Sources

Arnim, Bettina von. *Sämtliche Schriften*. 11 vols. Berlin: Expedition des von Arnim'schen Verlags, 1853. [Ausgabe letzter Hand.]

———. *Bettina von Arnims Sämtliche Werke*. Ed. Waldemar Oehlke. 7 vols. Berlin: Propyläen Verlag, 1920–22.

———. *Werke und Briefe*. Ed. Gustav Konrad and Joachim Müller (Bd. 5). 5 vols. Frechen: Bartmann, 1959–63.

———. *Werke*. Ed. Heinz Härtl. 2 vols. Berlin: Aufbau, 1986 ff.

———. *Werke und Briefe*. Ed. Walter Schmitz and Sibylle von Steinsdorff. 3 vols. Frankfurt/Main: Deutscher Klassiker-Verlag, 1986 ff.

———. *Die Andacht zum Menschenbild: Unbekannte Briefe*. Ed. Wilhelm Schellberg and Friedrich Fuchs. Jena: Diederichs, 1942.

———. *Bettina von Arnims Armenbuch*. Ed. Werner Vordtriede. Frankfurt: Insel, 1981.

———. *Bettine von Arnim und die Polen*. Mit einer Einführung von Jürgen Kuczynski und einem Nachwort von Ruth Krenn. Berlin: Aufbau, 1949.

———. *Bettine von Arnim und Friedrich Wilhelm IV.* Ed. Ludwig Geiger. Frankfurt: Rütten und Loening, 1902.

———. *Bettina von Arnims Polenbroschüre*. Im Auftrag der Deutschen Akademie der Künste. Ed. Ursula Püschel. Berlin: Henschelverlag, 1954.

———. *Bettinas Briefwechsel mit Goethe*. Auf Grund ihres handschriftlichen Nachlasses nebst zeitgenössischen Dokumenten über ihr persönliches Verhältnis zu Goethe. Ed. Reinhold Steig. Leipzig: n.p., 1922.

———. *"Dies Buch gehört dem König!" 1842 (Auszüge)*. Vorkämpfer Deutscher Freiheit

Heft 14. Munich: Buchhandlung Nationalverein, 1910.

———. *Der Magistratsprozess der Bettina von Arnim.* Ed. Gertrud Meyer-Hepner. Weimar: Arion Verlag, 1960.

Arnim, Bettina von, and Achim von Arnim. *Achim und Bettina in ihren Briefen. Briefwechsel von Achim von Arnim und Bettina Brentano.* Ed. Werner Vordtriede and Rudolf Alexander Schröder. 2 vols. 1961. Frankfurt/Main: Insel Verlag, 1982.

———. *Briefe der Freundschaft und Liebe.* Ed. Otto Betz and Veronika Staub. 2 vols. Frankfurt/Main: Joseph Knecht, 1986–1987.

Arnim, Bettina von, and Max Prokop von Freyberg. *Der Briefwechsel zwischen Bettine Brentano und Max Prokop von Freyberg.* Ed. Sibylle von Steinsdorff. Quellen und Forschungen zur Sprach- und Kulturgeschichte der germanischen Völker. Neue Folge 48. Berlin: de Gruyter, 1972.

Arnim, Bettina von, and Jakob and Wilhelm Grimm. *Der Briefwechsel Bettine von Arnims mit den Brüdern Grimm. 1838 – 1841.* Ed. Hartwig Schulz. Frankfurt/Main: Insel Verlag, 1985.

Arnim, Bettina von, and Philipp Hössli. *Ist dir bange vor meiner Liebe? Briefe an Philipp Hössli, nebst dessen Gegenbriefen und Tagebuchnotizen.* Ed. Kurg Wanner. Frankfurt/Main: Insel, 1996.

Arnim, Bettina von, and Hermann Fürst Pückler-Muskau. "Pückler und Bettina von Arnim." *Frauenbriefe von und an Hermann Fürsten Pückler-Muskau.* Ed. Heinrich Conrad. Munich: Georg Müller, 1912. 1–218.

Secondary Sources

Abel, Elizabeth, Marianne Hirsch, and Elizabeth Langland. *The Voyage In: Fictions of Female Development.* Hanover: University Press of New England, 1983.

Adelson, Leslie A. *Making Bodies Making History: Feminism and German Identity.* Lincoln: University of Nebraska, 1993.

Alcoff, Linda. "Cultural Feminism versus Post-Structuralism: The Identity Crisis in Feminist Theory." *SIGNS* 13.3 (1988): 405–436.

Alexis, Willibald. "Göthe's Briefwechsel mit einem Kinde." *Blätter für literarische Unterhaltung* 110 (20. April 1835): 453–456.

Althusser, Louis. "Ideology and Ideological State Apparatuses (Notes towards an Investigation)." 1970. *Essays on Ideology.* London: Verso, 1984. 1–60.

Altman, Janet Gurkin. *Epistolarity: Approaches to a Form.* Columbus: Ohio State University Press, 1982.

Ametsbichler, Elizabeth G., and Hiltrud Arens. "Erzählstrategie und Geschlechtskomponente in Bettina von Arnims *Die Günderode* und Clemens Brentanos *Frühlingskranz*. Ein Vergleich." *Internationales Jahrbuch der Bettina-von-Arnim-Gesellschaft* 5 (1995): 73–89.

Apuleius. *Der goldene Esel.* Frankfurt: Insel Verlag, 1975.

Arndt, Andreas. "Geselligkeit und Gesellschaft: Die Geburt der Dialektik aus dem Geist der Konversation in Schleiermachers 'Versuch einer Theorie des geselligen Betragens.'" Schultz 45–61.

Arndt, Ernst Moritz. *Gedichte.* Vol. 2. Frankfurt/Main: P.W. Eichenberg, 1818.

Arnim, Peter-Anton von. "Der eigentliche Held in dieser Zeit, die einzige wahrhaft freie und starke Stimme. Die jüdischen Aspekte in Leben und Werk Bettina von Arnims als Herausforderung." Schultz, *"Die echte Politik muß Erfinderin sein"* 164-215.

Assing, Ludmilla, ed. "Briefwechsel zwischen Pückler und Bettina von Arnim." *Aus dem Nachlaß des Fürsten Pückler-Muskau. Briefwechsel und Tagebücher.* Vol. 1. 1873. Bern: n.p., 1971.

Aston, Louise. *Revolution und Counterrevolution.* 2 vols. Breslau: n.p., 1849.

Baldwin, Claire. "Questioning the 'Jewish Question.' Poetic Philosophy and Politics in *Conversations with Demons.*" Frederiksen and Goodman 213–243.

Bäumer, Konstanze. *"Bettine, Psyche, Mignon:" Bettina von Arnim und Goethe.* Stuttgarter Arbeiten zur Germanistik 139. Stuttgart: Heinz, 1986.

———. "Die Bettina-Siedlung in Texas. Ein kleiner historischer Exkurs zur Bettina von Arnim-Forschung." Härtl and Schultz 355–370.

———. "*Ilius Pamphilius und die Ambrosia*: Bettina von Arnim als Mentorin." *Internationales Jahrbuch der Bettina-von-Arnim-Gesellschaft* 3 (1989): 263–282.

———. "Interdependenzen zwischen mündlicher und schriftlicher Expressivität: Bettina von Arnims Berliner Salon." Schmitz and Steinsdorff 154–173.

———. "Margaret Fuller (1810–1850) and Bettina von Arnim: An Encounter between American Transcendentalism and German Romanticism." *Internationales Jahrbuch der Bettina-von-Arnim-Gesellschaft* 4 (1990): 47–70.

———. "Die Rezeption Bettina von Arnims in der Berliner Kultur und Literaturgeschichte." *Internationales Jahrbuch der Bettina-von-Arnim-Gesellschaft* 1 (1987): 39–52.

Bäumer, Konstanze, and Hartwig Schultz. *Bettina von Arnim.* Stuttgart: Metzler, 1995.

Baumgart, Hildegard. *Bettine Brentano und Achim von Arnim: Lehrjahre einer Liebe.* Berlin: Verlin Verlag, 1999.

Bakhtin, M.M. *The Dialogic Imagination*. Ed. Michael Holquist. Trans. Caryl Emerson and Michael Holquist. Austin: Texas University Press, 1992.

Balzac, Honoré de. *Modest Mignon*. 1844. Trans. Friedrich Sieburg. Zurich: Diogenes, 1977.

Barrett, Michèle. "Ideology and the Cultural Production of Gender." *Feminist Criticism and Social Change: Sex, Class and Race in Literature and Culture*. Ed. Judith Newton and Deborah Rosenfelt. New York and London: Methuen, 1985. 65–85.

Barthes, Roland. "The Death of the Author." 1968. *Image. Music. Text*. Trans. and ed. Stephen Heath. London: Fontana, 1977.

———. *S/Z*. 1970. Trans. Jürgen Hoch. Frankfurt: Suhrkamp, 1976.

Becker-Cantarino, Barbara. "'Feminismus' und 'Emanzipation?' Zum Geschlechterdiskurs der deutschen Romantik am Beispiel der *Lucinde* und ihrer Rezeption." Schultz, *Salons der Romantik* 21–44.

———. "Priesterin und Lichtbringerin. Zur Ideologie des weiblichen Charakters in der Frühromantik." *Die Frau als Heldin und Autorin. Neue kritische Ansätze zur deutschen Literatur*. Ed. Wolfgang Paulsen. Munich: Francke, 1979. 111–124.

Bellos, David. "Balzac and Goethe's Bettina." *Literary Communication and Reception*. Proceedings of the IXth Congress of the International Comparative Literature Association. Ed. Rédigés Par. Innsbruck: Innsbrucker Gesellschaft zur Pflege der Geisteswissenschaften, 1980. 359–369.

Bode, Wilhelm, ed. *Goethe in vertraulichen Briefen seiner Zeitgenossen*. Munich: Beck, 1982.

Börne, Ludwig. "Goethes Briefwechsel mit einem Kinde." 1835. *Sämtliche Schriften*. Ed. Inge and Peter Rippmann. Vol. 2. Düsseldorf: Metzler, 1964. 854–869.

Bossinade, Johanna. "Bettina von Arnim: Identifikationen des Ich. Entwurf für eine Lesart." *Romantisches Erzählen*. Ed. Gerhard Neumann. Stiftung für Romantikforschung 1. Würzburg: Königshausen und Neumann, 1995. 85–106.

Brentano, Clemens. *Godwi*. 1800. *Werke*. Vol. 2. Ed. Friedhelm Kemp. Munich: Carl Hanser Verlag, 1963.

———. "Der Philister vor, in und nach der Geschichte." *Werke*. Vol. 2. Ed. Wolfgang Frühwald and Friedhelm Kemp. 1963. Munich: Hanser, 1980.

———. *Das unsterbliche Leben: Unbekannte Briefe von Clemens Brentano*. Ed. Wilhelm Schellberg und Friedrich Fuchs. Jena: Diederichs, 1939.

Büchner, Georg. *Sämtliche Briefe und Dokumente*. Vol. 1. Ed. Henri Poschmann. Frankfurt: Deutscher Klassiker Verlag, 1992.

Bürger, Christa. *Leben Schreiben: Die Klassik, die Romantik und der Ort der Frauen.* Stuttgart: Metzler, 1990.

Bürger, Christa, and Birgitt Diefenbach, eds. *Bettina von Arnim: Ein Lesebuch.* Stuttgart: Reclam, 1987.

Bunzel, Wolfgang. "'Phantasie ist die freie Kunst der Wahrheit.' Bettine von Arnims poetisches Verfahren in *Goethes Briefwechsel mit einem Kinde*." *Internationales Jahrbuch der Bettina-von-Arnim-Gesellschaft* 1 (1987): 7–28.

Burwick, Roswitha. "Bettina von Arnims *Die Günderode*: Zum Selbstverständnis der Frau in der Romantik." Schöne, Stephan, and Pietzcker 62–67.

Carriere, Moriz. "Bettina von Arnim." *Nord und Süd. Eine deutsche Monatsschrift.* Ed. Paul Lindau 40.118 (January 1887): 65–103.

Cixous, Hélène. *Die unendliche Zirkulation des Begehrens.* Trans. Eva Meyer and Jutta Kranz. Berlin: Merve, 1977.

"The Combahee River Collective Statement." *Capitalist Patriarchy and the Case for a Socialist Feminism.* Ed. Zillah Eisenstein. New York: Monthly Review Press, 1979. 362–372.

Daley, Margaretmary. "Corresponding Artists: Self and Genre in the Letters of Goethe, Schiller, Schlegel-Schelling, Varnhagen, and Von Arnim." Diss. Yale University, 1994.

———. *Women of Letters: A Study of Self and Genre in the Personal Writing of Caroline Schlegel-Schelling, Rahel Levin Varnhagen, and Bettina von Arnim.* Columbia, South Carolina: Camden House, 1998.

Daumer, Georg Friedrich. *Bettina. Gedichte aus Goethes Briefwechsel mit einem Kinde. Nebst erläuternden und vergleichenden Anmerkungen.* Nürnberg: Bauer und Raspe, 1837.

Diamond, Irene, and Lee Quinby, eds. *Feminism and Foucault. Reflections on Resistance.* Boston: Northeastern University Press, 1988.

Dischner, Gisela. *Bettina von Arnim: Eine weibliche Sozialbiographie aus dem neunzehnten Jahrhundert kommentiert und zusammengestellt aus Briefromanen und Dokumenten.* Berlin: Wagenbach, 1977.

Dohm, Hedwig. *Schicksale einer Seele.* Ed. Ruth-Ellen Boetcher Joeres. Munich: Frauenoffensive, 1988.

Drewitz, Ingeborg. *Bettine von Arnim. Romantik-Revolution-Utopie.* 1969. Hildesheim: Classen, 1992.

Duden, Barbara. "Das schöne Eigentum. Zur Herausbildung des bürgerlichen Frauenbildes an der Wende vom 18. Zum 19. Jahrhundert." *Kursbuch* 47 (1977): 125–140.

"Der echte und der unechte Briefwechsel zwischen Goethe und Bettine von Arnim." Teil II. *Beilage zur Allgemeinen Zeitung* 201 (20. Juli 1865): 3275.

Edler, Erich. *Die Anfänge des sozialen Romans und der sozialen Novelle in Deutschland.* Studien zur Philosophie und Literatur des neunzehnten Jahrhunderts 34. Frankfurt/ Main: Klostermann, 1977.

Egloffstein, Hermann Freiherr von. *Alt-Weimars Abend. Briefe und Aufzeichnungen aus dem Nachlasse der Gräfinnen Egloffstein.* Munich: Beck, 1923.

Eichendorff, Joseph von. "Über die ethische und religiöse Bedeutung der neueren romantischen Poesie in Deutschland." *Joseph von Eichendorff Werke in sechs Bänden.* Vol. 6. Ed. Hartwig Schultz. Frankfurt/Main: Deutscher Klassiker Verlag, 1990. 61–280.

The Encyclopedia of Islam. New Edition. Vol. I. London: Luzcac & Co., 1960.

The Encyclopedia of Islam. Vol. VI. Leiden: E.J. Brill, 1991.

Fichte, Johann Gottlieb. *Die Bestimmung des Menschen.* 1799/1800. *Schriften zur Wissenschaftslehre. Werke.* Vol. 1. Ed. Wilhelm G. Jacobs. Frankfurt: Deutscher Klassiker Verlag, 1997.

Fish, Stanley. *Doing What Comes Naturally: Change, Rhetoric, and the Practice of Theory in Literary and Legal Studies.* Durham: Duke University Press, 1989.

———. *Is There a Text in this Class? The Authority of Interpretive Communities.* Cambridge, MA: Harvard University Press, 1980.

Foucault, Michel. "Nietzsche, Genealogy and History." *Language, Counter-Memory, Practice.* Ithaca: Cornell, 1977.

———. "The Order of Discourse." 1970. Trans. Ian McLeod. *Language and Politics.* Ed. Michael Shapiro. New York: New York University Press, 1984. 108–137.

———. "What is an Author?" *Textual Strategies. Perspectives in Post-Structuralist Criticism.* Ed. and Trans. Josué V. Haran. Ithaca: Cornell University Press, 1979. 141–160.

Frederiksen, Elke, and Katherine Goodman, eds. *Bettina Brentano-von Arnim: Gender and Politics.* Detroit: Wayne State University Press, 1995.

Frederiksen, Elke, and Monika Shafi. "'Sich im Unbekannten suchen gehen': Bettina von Arnims *Die Günderode* als weibliche Utopie." Schöne, Stephan, and Pietzker 54–61.

French, Lorely Elsa. "Bettina von Arnim: Toward a Women's Epistolary Aesthetics and Poetics." Diss. University of California, Los Angeles, 1986.

———. "Strategies of Female Persuasion: The Political Letters of Bettina Brentano-von Arnim." Frederiksen and Goodman 71–94.

Frevert, Ute. *Frauen-Geschichte zwischen bürgerlicher Verbesserung und neuer Weiblichkeit*. Frankfurt/Main: Suhrkamp, 1986.

Fromm, Leberecht. *Ruchlosigkeit der Schrift "Dies Buch gehört dem König." Ein unterthäniger Fingerzeig*. Bern: Jenni, 1844.

Fuss, Diana. *Essentially Speaking: Feminism, Nature & Difference*. New York: Routledge, 1989.

Gajek, Bernhard. "Bettine von Arnim und die bayerische Erweckungsbewegung." Härtl and Schultz 215–230.

Gajek, Enid Margarete. "Die Bedeutung des Fürsten Hermann Pückler für Bettine." Perels 253–260.

———. "'Das gefährliche Spiel meiner Sinne,' Gedanken zu Bettine und Pückler." *Jahrbuch der Bettina-von-Arnim-Gesellschaft* 3 (1989): 249–261.

Geiger, Ludwig. "Goethe, Bettine und die Frankfurter Juden." *Allgemeine Zeitung des Judentums* 67.40 (2. Oktober 1903): 474–477.

Geist, Johann Friedrich and Klaus Kürvers. *Das Berliner Mietshaus 1740–1862*. Munich: Prestel, 1980.

Gersdorff, Dagmar von. *Bettina und Achim von Arnim. Eine fast romantische Ehe*. Berlin: Rowohlt, 1997.

Gille, Klaus F. "'Der anmutige Scheinknabe,' Bettina von Arnim und Goethes Mignon." Härtl and Schultz 271–285.

Goethe, Johann Wolfgang von. *Briefe Goethes an Sophie La Roche und Bettina Brentano nebst dichterischen Beilagen*. Ed. Gustav von Loeper. Berlin: Wilhelm Hertz, 1879.

———. *Goethes Werke. Hamburger Ausgabe in 14 Bänden*. Ed. Erich Trunz. 13th ed. Munich: Beck, 1982.

Goodman, Katherine. *Dis/Closures: Women's Autobiography in Germany between 1790 and 1914*. New York University Ottendorfer Series 24. New York: Peter Lang, 1986.

———. "Through a Different Lens: Bettina Brentano-von Arnim's Views on Gender." Frederiksen and Goodman 115–141.

Goodman, Katherine, and Edith Waldstein, eds. *In the Shadow of Olympus: German Women Writers around 1800*. Albany: State University of New York Press, 1992.

Goozé, Marjanne. "Bettine von Arnim, the Writer." Diss. Berkeley, 1984.

———. "The Reception of Bettina Brentano-von Arnim as Author and Historical Figure."

Frederiksen and Goodman 349–420.

Grass, Günter. *Der Butt.* Darmstadt und Neuwied: Luchterhand, 1977.

Greiner, Bernhard. "Echo-Rede und 'Lesen' Ruths. Die Begründung von Autorschaft in Bettina von Arnims Roman *Goethe's Briefwechsel mit einem Kinde.*" *Deutsche Vierteljahrsschrift* 70.1 (1996): 48–66.

Grimm, Herman. "Bettina von Arnim." *Goethe-Jahrbuch.* Vol. 1. Ed. Ludwig Geiger. Frankfurt/Main: Rütten & Loening, 1880.

Grimm, Jakob, and Wilhelm Grimm. *Deutsches Wörterbuch.* Leipzig: S. Hirzel, 1897.

Gutzkow, Karl. "Bettinens *Königsbuch.*" *Berliner Erinnerungen und Erlebnisse.* Ed. Paul Friedländer. Berlin: Das Neue Berlin, 1960. 430–439.

———. "Silhouetten literarischer Notabilitäten, Bettina von Arnim." *Telegraph für Deutschland* 137 (August 1838): 1092–1096.

———. *Wally, die Zweiflerin.* 1835. Ed. Günter Heinz. Stuttgart: Reclam, 1979.

Häberlin, Karl Ludwig [under the pseudonym of H.E.R. Belani], *Reaktionäre und Demokraten. Geschichtlich-politischer Roman aus der neuesten Zeit.* 2 vols. Leipzig: C.L. Fritzsche, 1850.

———. *Die armen Weber und andere Novellen aus den Mysterien einer neueren und älteren Zeit.* Leipzig: C.L. Fritzsche, 1845.

Härtl, Heinz. "Bettina Brentano-von Arnim's Relations to the Young Hegelians." Frederiksen and Goodman 145–184.

———. *Bettina von Arnim. 1785–1859. Eine Chronik.* Weimar: Otto Schöpfel, 1984.

———. "Übereuropäisches bei Arnim und Bettina." Härtl and Schultz 215–230.

———. "'Dies Völkchen mit der vorkämpfenden Alten.' Bettina von Arnim und die Junghegelianer." *Jahrbuch des Freien Deutschen Hochstifts* (1992): 213–254.

———. "Zur zeitgenössischen publizistischen Rezeption des Königsbuches." Schmitz and Steinsdorff 208–235.

Härtl, Heinz, and Hartwig Schultz, eds. *"Die Erfahrung anderer Länder:" Beiträge eines Wiepersdorfer Kolloquiums zu Achim und Bettina von Arnim.* New York: de Gruyter, 1994.

Hahn, Karl-Heinz. *Bettina von Arnim in ihrem Verhältnis zu Staat und Politik.* Weimar: Hermann Böhlaus Nachfolger, 1959.

Hausen, Karin. "Die Polarisierung der 'Geschlechtscharaktere'—Eine Spiegelung der Dissoziation von Erwerbs und Familienleben." *Sozialgeschichte der Familie in der Neuzeit Europas.* Ed. Werner Cunze. Stuttgart: Klett, 1976. 363–393.

Hesekiel, Georg. *Die Bastardbrüder oder Geheimnisse von Altenburg. Roman aus dem Nachlaß eines Criminalbeamten*. 2 vols. Altenburg: Julius Helbig, 1845.

Heuberger, Rachel, and Helga Krohn. *Hinaus aus dem Ghetto...Juden in Frankfurt am Main 1800–1950*. Frankfurt: Fischer, 1988.

Heukenkamp, Marianne. "Den 'Willen zum Ideal' ins Leben verwandeln: Bettina von Arnims *Die Günderode* im Spannungsfeld von Leben, Philosophie und Poesie. Untersuchungen zum ideellem Gehalt, Textaufbau und Wirkung des Briefromans." Diss. Halle, 1989.

Hirsch, Helmut. "Jüdische Aspekte im Leben und Werk Bettina von Arnims." *Internationales Jahrbuch der Bettina-von-Arnim-Gesellschaft* 1 (1987): 61–76.

———. "Zur Dichotomie von Theorie und Praxis in Bettines Äußerungen über Judentum und Juden." *Internationales Jahrbuch der Bettina-von-Arnim-Gesellschaft* 3 (1989): 153–172.

Hock, Lisabeth. "'Sonderbare,' 'heißhungrige' und 'edle' Gestalten: Bettina von Arnims Darstellung von Juden und Judentum im Kontext ihrer Zeit und ihres Werkes." Schultz, *Salons der Romantik* 317–341.

Hölderlin, Friedrich. *Hyperion oder der Eremit in Griechenland*. *Sämtliche Werke und Briefe*. Vol. 1. Ed. Michael Knaupp. Munich: Hanser, 1992. 483–760.

Hoock-Demarle, Marie-Claire. "Bettinas Umgang mit Außenseitern." *Internationales Jahrbuch der Bettina-von-Arnim-Gesellschaft* 2 (1988): 76–91.

———. *Die Frauen der Goethezeit*. Trans. Renate Hörisch-Helligrath. Munich: Fink, 1990.

———. "The Nineteenth Century: Insights of Contemporary Women Writers." *Woman as Mediatrix. Essays on Nineteenth-Century European Women Writers*. Ed. Avriel H. Goldberger. Contributions in Women's Studies 73. New York: Greenwood Press, 1987.

Houben, Heinrich Hubert. "Bettina von Arnim." *Verbotene Literatur von der klassischen Zeit bis zur Gegenwart*. Vol. 1. 1924. 2. Nachdruck. Hildesheim: Olms, 1992. 30–41.

Iser, Wolfgang. *Der Akt des Lesens. Theorie ästhetischer Wirkung*. Munich: Fink, 1976.

Janssen, Carmen Viktoria. "Textile in Texturen: Lesestrategien und Intertextualität bei Goethe und Bettina Brentano-von Arnim." Diss. University of Maryland at College Park, 1997.

Jauss, Hans R. *Literaturgeschichte als Provokation*. Frankfurt/Main: Suhrkamp, 1979.

———. *Toward an Aesthetic of Reception*. Trans. T. Bahti. Harvester Press: Brighton, 1982.

Joeres, Ruth-Ellen Boetcher. *Respectability and Deviance. Nineteenth-Century German*

Women Writers and the Ambiguity of Representation. Chicago: University of Chicago Press, 1998.

———. "'We are adjacent to human society': German Women Writers, the Homosocial Experience, and a Challenge to the Public/Domestic Dichotomy." *The Women in German Yearbook* 10 (1995): 39–57.

Kant, Immanuel. "Beantwortung der Frage: Was ist Aufklärung?" 1784. *Was ist Aufklärung? Aufsätze zur Geschichte und Philosophie.* Ed. Jürgen Zehbe. Göttingen: Vandenhoeck & Ruprecht, 1967.

———. *The Conflict of the Faculties. Der Streit der Fakultäten.* 1798. Trans. Mary J. Gregor. New York: Abaris, 1979.

Kirsch, Sarah. "Wiepersdorf." *Rückenwind.* Ebenhäusen bei München: Langewiesche-Brandt, 1977. 18–29.

Kittler, Friedrich. "In den Wind schreibend, Bettina." *Dichter, Mutter Kind.* Munich: Fink, 1991. 219–255.

Krieger, Leonard. *The German Idea of Freedom. History of a Political Tradition.* Boston: Beacon Press, 1957.

Krimmer, Elisabeth. "Offizier und Amazone: Frauen in Männerkleidung in der deutschen Literatur um 1800." Diss. University of Massachusetts Amherst, 1998.

Kristeva, Julia. "Word, Dialogue and Novel." *The Kristeva Reader.* Ed. Toril Moi. New York: Columbia University Press, 1986. 34–61.

———. *Revolution in Poetic Language.* 1974. Trans. Margaret Waller. New York: Columbia University Press, 1984.

Kundera, Milan. *Immortality.* 1990. Trans. Peter Kussi. New York: Grove Weidenfeld, 1991.

Landfester, Ulrike. "'Da, wo ich duldend mich unterwerfen sollte, da werde ich mich rächen.' Mignon auf dem Weg zur Revolte, Stationen einer Rezeptionsgeschichte." *Internationales Jahrbuch der Bettina-von-Arnim-Gesellschaft* 4 (1990): 71–98.

Lange, Sigrid, ed. *Ob die Weiber Menschen sind. Geschlechterdebatten um 1800.* Leipzig: Reclam, 1992.

La Roche, Sophie von. *Geschichte des Fräuleins von Sternheim.* 1771. Ed. Barbara Becker-Cantarino. Stuttgart: Reclam, 1983.

Lauer, Gerhard. "Der 'rothe Sattel der Armuth.' Talmudische Gelehrsamkeit oder die Grenzen der poetischen Technik bei Bettine von Arnim." *Schnittpunkt Romantik. Text- und Quellenstudien zur Literatur des 19. Jahrhunderts. Festschrift für Sibylle von Steinsdorff.* Ed. Wolfgang Bunzel, Konrad Feilchenfeldt, and Walter Schmitz.

Tübingen: Niemeyer, 1997. 289–320.

Lauretis, Teresa de. *Alice Doesn't: Feminism, Semiotics, Cinema*. Bloomington: Indiana University Press, 1984.

———. *Technologies of Gender: Essays on Theory, Film, and Fiction*. Bloomington: Indiana University Press, 1987.

Leitner, Ingrid, and Sibylle von Steinsdorff, "'…wunderliche Bilder… Gedanken in tönenden Strömen…' Überlegungen zu Bettine von Arnims romantischem Stil anhand der russischen und der französischen Übersetzung von *Goethes Briefwechsel mit einem Kinde*." Schmitz and Steinsdorff 174–207.

Lemke, Ann Willison. "Bettine's Song: The Musical Voice of Bettine von Arnim." Diss. Indiana University, 1998.

Lewald, Fanny. *Adele*. Braunschweig: Friedrich Bieweg und Sohn, 1855.

———. "Der Cultus des Genius." Serialized in *Blätter für literarische Unterhaltung*. 171 (18 Juli 1849): 681–683; 172 (19 Juli 1849): 685–687; 173 (20 Juli 1849): 689–690); 174 (21 Juli 1849): 693–694.

———. *Meine Lebensgeschichte*. Ed. Ulrike Helmer. 3 vols. Frankfurt/Main: Helmer, 1988–1998.

Liebertz-Grün, Ursula. "Bettine Brentano-von Arnim: *Dies Buch gehört dem König*." *Internationales Jahrbuch der Bettina-von-Arnim-Gesellschaft* 3 (1989): 59–80.

———. *Ordnung im Chaos: Studien zur Poetik der Bettine Brentano-von Arnim*. Heidelberg: Winter, 1989.

Loeper, Gustav von. "Bettina." *Allgemeine Deutsche Biographie*. Vol. 2. Leipzig: Duncker & Humblot, 1875. 578–582.

Maierhofer, Waltraud. "Einfühlen, Einvernahme und Mißverstehen. Rilke und Bettine von Arnim." *Internationales Jahrbuch der Bettina-von-Arnim-Gesellschaft* 4 (1990): 125–150.

Mallon, Otto. "Bettina-Bibliographie." *Imprimatur* 4 (1933): 141–156.

Martin, Biddy. "Feminism, Criticism, and Foucault." Diamond and Quinby 3–19.

———. "Lesbian Identity and Autobiographical Difference[s]." *Life/Lines: Theorizing Women's Biography*. Ed. Bella Brodzki and Celeste Schenck. Ithaca: Cornell University Press, 1988. 77–103.

———. *Woman and Modernity: The Life-Styles of Lou Andreas-Salomé*. Ithaca: Cornell University Press, 1991.

Meyer-Hepner, Gertrud. "Bettina in Ost und West." *Neue Deutsche Literatur* 7.1 (1959):

152–154.

———. "Das Bettina von Arnim Archiv." *Sinn und Form* 6 (1954): 594–611.

———. "Die Differenz. Nach Bettinas Tod." *Neue Deutsche Literatur* 12.3 (1964): 188–190.

———. "Neues über Bettina." *Neue Deutsche Literatur* 7.1 (1959): 148–151.

Meysenbug, Malwida von. *Memoiren einer Idealistin*. 1875. 9th edition. Vol. 1. Berlin: Schuster & Lieffler, 1905.

Mickel, Karl. "Halsgericht. Erster Teil: Bettina Vampira." *Volks Entscheid. 7 Stücke*. Leipzig: Reclam, 1987. 221–242.

Möhrmann, Renate. *Die andere Frau. Emanzipationsansätze deutscher Schriftstellerinnen im Vorfeld der Achtundvierziger-Revolution*. Stuttgart: Metzler, 1977.

———. "'Die Teilnahme der weiblichen Welt am Staatsleben ist eine Pflicht!' Vormärzautorinnen ergreifen das Wort." *Frauen-Literatur-Geschichte*. Ed. Hiltrud Gnug and Renate Möhrmann. 2nd ed. Stuttgart: Metzler, 1999. 377–386.

———, ed. *Frauenemanzipation im deutschen Vormärz*. Stuttgart: Reclam, 1978.

Montgomery-Silverstolpe, Malla. *Das romantische Deutschland. Reisejournal einer Schwedin (1825–1826)*. Mit einer Einleitung von Ellen Rey. Leipzig: Albert Bonnier, 1912.

Mühlbach, Luise. (Pseudonym for Clara Mundt). *Ein Roman in Berlin*. Berlin: Mylius, 1846.

Mundt, Theodor. *Carmela oder die Wiedertaufe*. Hannover: C.F. Kius, 1844.

———. "Goethe und das Kind." *Literarischer Zodiacus* 11 (Mai 1835): 418.

Neuhaus-Koch, Ariane. "Bettine von Arnim im Dialog mit Rahel Varnhagen, Amalie von Helwig, Fanny Tarnow und Fanny Lewald." *"Stets wird die Wahrheit hadern mit dem Schönen": Festschrift für Manfred Windfuhr zum 60. Geburtstag*. Ed. Gertrude Cepl-Kaufmann. Cologne: Böhlau, 1990. 103–119.

Novalis. *Werke*. Ed. Gerhard Schulz. 2nd ed. Munich: Beck, 1981.

Nussbaum, Felicity A. *The Autobiographical Subject. Gender and Ideology in Eighteenth-Century England*. Baltimore: Johns Hopkins University Press, 1989.

Oehlke, Waldemar. *Bettina von Arnims Briefromane*. Ed. Alois Randle, Gustav Roethe, and Erich Schmidt. Palaestra Untersuchungen und Texte aus der deutschen und englischen Philologie 41. Berlin: Mayer und Müller, 1905.

Oesterle, Günter. "Juden, Philister und romantische Intellektuelle: Überlegungen zum Antisemitismus in der Romantik." *Athenäum* 2 (1992): 55–89.

Osterkamp, Ernst. *Lucifer. Stationen eines Motivs.* Berlin: de Gruyter, 1979.

Perels, Christoph. "Bettines Gegenwärtigkeit in der Poesie des 20. Jahrhunderts." Perels 281–292.

Perels, Christoph, ed. *"Herzhaft in die Dornen der Zeit Greifen..." Bettine von Arnim 1785–1859.* Frankfurt/Main: Freies Deutsches Hochstift, 1985.

Plato, *Symposium.* Trans. Benjamin Jowett. Intr. Fulton H. Anderson. Indianapolis: Bobbs-Merrill Educational Publishing, 1980.

Poovey, Mary. *Uneven Developments: The Ideological Work of Gender in Mid-Victorian England.* Chicago: University of Chicago Press, 1988.

Püschel, Ursula. "Bettina von Arnims September-Briefe an Friedrich Wilhelm IV. aus dem Jahr 1848." Härtl and Schultz 313–353.

———. "Weibliches und Unweibliches der Bettina von Arnim." *Mit allen Sinnen. Frauen in der Literatur. Essays.* Halle-Leipzig: Mitteldeutscher Verlag, 1980.

———. *"...wider die Philister und die bleierne Zeit." Untersuchungen, Essays, Aufsätze über Bettina von Arnim.* Berlin: Altberliner Bücherstube, 1996.

Pusch, Luise. *Schwestern berühmter Männer. Zwölf biographische Portraits.* Frankfurt: Insel, 1985.

Rich, Adrienne. "Compulsory Heterosexuality and Lesbian Existence." *Feminist Frontiers III.* Ed. Laurel Richardson and Verta Taylor. New York: McGraw-Hill, 1993. 159–179.

Riley, Denise. *War in the Nursery: Theories of the Child and Mother.* London: Virago, 1983.

Rilke, Rainer Maria. *Die Aufzeichnungen des Malte Laurids Brigge.* 1910. *Werke in drei Bänden.* Vol. 2. Frankfurt/Main: Insel, 1991. 107–346.

Roetzel, Lisa. "Acting Out: Bettine as Performer of Feminine Genius." *The Women in German Yearbook* 14 (1999): 109–125.

Sammons, Jeffrey L. *Six Essays on the Young German Novel.* Chapel Hill: The University of North Carolina Press, 1972.

Schiller, Friedrich. *Über die ästhetische Erziehung des Menschen in einer Reihe von Briefen.* Stuttgart: Reclam, 1965.

Schlegel, Friedrich. "Gespräch über die Poesie." *Charakteristiken und Kritiken I.* Ed. Hans Eichner. *Kritische Friedrich-Schlegel-Ausgabe.* Vol. 2. Munich: Schöningh, 1967. 284–351.

———. *Lucinde.* 1799. *Dichtungen.* Ed. Hans Eichner. *Kritische Friedrich-Schlegel-*

Ausgabe. Vol. 5. Munich: Schöningh, 1962. 1–92.

Schlegel-Schelling, Caroline. *"Lieber Freund, ich komme weit her schon an diesem frühen Morgen." Briefe.* Ed. Sigrid Damm. 4th ed. Darmstadt: Luchterhand, 1988.

Schleiermacher, Friedrich. "Versuch einer Theorie des geselligen Betragens." 1799. *Schriften.* Ed. Andreas Arndt. Frankfurt: Deutscher Klassiker Verlag, 1996. 65–91.

Schmitz, Walter. "'...die freie Kultur eines idealischen Sinnes.' Bettine von Arnims Alterswerk *Gespräche mit Dämonen.*" *Internationales Jahrbuch der Bettina-von-Arnim-Gesellschaft* 3 (1989): 137–152.

Schmitz, Walter, and Sibylle von Steinsdorff. "Kindheit und Jugend." Perels 7–17.

Schmitz, Walter, and Sibylle von Steinsdorff, eds. *"Der Geist muß Freiheit genießen...!" Studien zu Werk und Bildungsprogramm Bettine von Arnims. Bettine-Kolloquium vom 6. bis 9. Juli 1989 in München.* Bettina von Arnim-Studien 2. Berlin: Saint Albin Verlag, 1992.

Schöne, Albrecht, Inge Stephan, and Carl Pietzcker, eds. *Kontroversen, alte und neue, VI: Frauensprache-Frauenliteratur? Für und wider eine Psychoanalyse literarischer Werke.* Akten des VIII. Internationalen Germanisten-Kongresses, Göttingen 1985. Tübingen: Niemeyer, 1986.

Schormann, Sabine. *Bettine von Arnim: Die Bedeutung Schleiermachers für ihr Leben und Werk.* Tübingen: Niemeyer, 1993.

———. "Bettines Rezeption der frühromantischen Philosophie." *Internationales Jahrbuch der Bettina-von-Arnim-Gesellschaft* 3 (1989): 33.

———. "'Was ich nur ahndete, das machte er mir zur Gewißheit:' Zur Freundschaft Bettines mit Friedrich Schleiermacher." Schmitz and Steinsdorff 106–127.

Schorn, Adelheid von. *Das nachklassische Weimar.* Vol. 2. Weimar: Kiepenheuer, 1912.

Schultz, Hartwig. "Bettines Auseinandersetzung mit Friedrich Karl von Savigny um die Einstellung der Brüder Grimm in Berlin." Perels 261–268.

———, ed. *"Die echte Politik muß Erfinderin sein." Beiträge eines Wiepersdorfer Kolloquiums zu Bettina von Arnim.* Wiepersdorfer Kolloquium 3. Berlin: Saint Albin Verlag, 1999.

———. "'Euer Unglaube an die Naturstimme erzeugt den Aberglauben an eine falsche Politik.' Fiktive Salongespräche in Bettines *Königsbuch.*" Schultz, ed. 251–270.

———. "'Ich bin nicht zahm und knien mag ich nicht.' Das Bettine-Verständnis von Joseph von Eichendorff und Annette von Droste-Hülshoff." *Internationales Jahrbuch der Bettina-von-Arnim-Gesellschaft* 3 (1989): 291–308.

———. "Nachwort." *Clemens Brentanos Frühlingskranz.* By Bettine von Arnim. Frankfurt:

Insel, 1985. 344–358.

———, ed. *Salons der Romantik. Beiträge eines Wiepersdorfer Kolloquiums zu Theorie und Geschichte des Salons.* Wiepersdorfer Kolloquium 2. Berlin: de Gruyter, 1997.

Schwaneflugel, Susan C. "Modes of Performance: Women's Musico-Literary Masquerade in Early Nineteenth-Century Germany." Diss. University of Pennsylvania, 1997.

Sedgwick, Eve Kosofsky. *Epistemology of the Closet.* Berkeley: University of California Press, 1990.

Shafi, Monika. "The Myth of Psyche as Developmental Paradigm in Bettina Brentano-von Arnim's Epistolary Novels." Frederiksen and Goodman 95–114.

———. *Utopische Entwürfe in der Literatur von Frauen.* Utah Studies in Literature and Linguistics 30. New York: Peter Lang, 1990.

Shakespeare, William. *Hamlet.* Ed. Harold Jenkins. The Arden Shakespeare. Walton-on-Thames Surrey: Thomas Nelson & Sons Ltd., 1997.

Simpson, Patricia Anne. "Letters in Sufferance and Deliverance: The Correspondence of Bettina Brentano-von Arnim and Karoline von Günderrode." Frederiksen and Goodman 247–277.

Sonnenfels, Anna. "Die Erhebung der Frau in ihrem Zusammenhang mit der Literatur." *Monatsblätter für deutsche Literatur* 9 (1904/05): 313–322, 486–500.

Staff, Ilse. "Einführung." *Bettina von Arnim. Dies Buch gehört dem König.* Frankfurt/Main: Insel, 1982. 9–58.

Stahr, Adolph. *Bettina und ihr Königsbuch.* Hamburg: Verlags-Comptoir, 1844.

Steig, Reinhold. "Bettina." *Deutsche Rundschau* 18.11 (August 1892): 262–274.

Stoll, H.W. *Die Götter und Heroen des classischen Alterthums. Populäre Mythologie der Griechen und Römer.* Vol. 1. Leipzig: Teubner, 1879.

Susman, Margarete. "Bettina." *Frauen der Romantik.* Jena: Diederichs, 1931.

Tatlock, Lynne. "The Young Germans in Praise of Famous Women: Ambivalent Advocates." *German Life and Letters* 39 (1986): 193–209.

Toegel, Edith. "Margaret Fuller, Bettina von Arnim, Karoline von Günderrode: A Kinship of Souls." *Yearbook of German-American Studies* 23 (1988): 141–151.

Varnhagen, Rahel. *Jeder Wunsch wird Frivolität genannt. Briefe und Tagebücher.* Ed. Marlis Gerhardt. 6th ed. Darmstadt: Luchterhand, 1989.

Varnhagen von Ense, Karl August. *Tagebücher von Karl August Varnhagen von Ense.* 2nd ed. Leipzig: Brockhaus, 1863.

Vogel, Stanley M. *German Literary Influences on the American Transcendentalists.* 1955. Hamden, Connecticut: Archon Books, 1970.

Waldstein, Edith. *Bettine von Arnim and the Politics of Romantic Conversation.* Studies in German Literature, Linguistics, and Culture 3. Columbia, South Carolina: Camden House, 1988.

——. "Goethe and Beyond: Bettine von Arnim's *Correspondence with a Child* and *Günderode.*" Goodman and Waldstein 95–113.

Walker, Cheryl. "Persona Criticism and the Death of the Author." *Contesting the Subject. Essays in the Postmodern Theory and Practice of Biography and Biographical Criticism.* Ed. William Epstein. West Lafayette: Purdue University Press, 1991. 109–121.

Weissenborn, Birgit. *Bettina von Arnim und Goethe. Topographie einer Beziehung als Beispiel weiblicher Emanzipation zu Beginn des 19. Jahrhunderts.* Frankfurt: Peter Lang, 1987.

White, Hayden. "The Historical Text as Literary Artifact." *Tropics of Discourse. Essays in Cultural Criticism.* Baltimore: Johns Hopkins University Press, 1978. 81–100.

Wobeser, Wilhelmine Karoline von. *Elisa oder das Weib wie es sein sollte.* 1799. Ed. Lydia Schieth. Frühe Frauenliteratur in Deutschland 8. Hildesheim: Olms, 1990.

Wolf, Christa. *Im Dialog.* Frankfurt: Luchterhand, 1990.

——, ed. *Karoline von Günderode. Der Schatten eines Traumes.* 1979. Darmstadt: Luchterhand, 1988.

——. "Nun ja! Das nächste Leben geht aber heute an. Ein Brief über die Bettina." *Ins Ungebundene gehet eine Sehnsucht. Gesprächsraum Romantik.* Ed. Christa Wolf and Gerhard Wolf. Berlin: Aufbau, 1985. 318–354.

Wülfing, Wulf. "Zur Mythisierung der Frau im Jungen Deutschland." *Zeitschrift für deutsche Philologie* 99.4 (1980): 559–581.

Wuthenow, Ralph-Rainer. "Das Hölderlin-Bild im Briefroman *Die Günderode.*" *Homburg von der Höhe in der deutschen Geistesgeschichte. Studien zum Freundeskreis um Hegel und Hölderlin.* Ed. Christoph Jamme und Otto Pöggeler. Stuttgart: Klett-Cotta, 1981.

Wyss, Hilde. *Bettina von Arnims Stellung zur deutschen Romantik und dem Jungen Deutschland.* Diss. Bern, 1935. Nendeln: Kraus, 1970.

INDEX

Abd al–Madjîd I, Ottoman Sultan, 184
Abel, Elizabeth, 13–14
Adelson, Leslie, 18–19, 51, 127
Africa, 106
agency, 18, 21, 28, 45, 50, 63, 64, 178, 209, 211, 213, 214, 223n.12
Alcoff, Linda, 18–19
Alexis, Willibald, 7, 53
allegory, 93
Allgemeine Landrecht für die Preußischen Staaten, 107, 119
Althusser, Louis, 11
Altman, Janet, 10, 15, 37, 50, 55, 91, 130, 223n.8, 225n.18 (*see also* epistolary writing)
androgyny, 33, 35, 68, 69
Anneke, Mathilde Franziska, 126
Apuleius, 38
Arndt, Ernst Moritz, 226n.6
Arnim, Achim von 1, 2, 3, 9, 110, 126, 128, 133, 157, 216n.6, 216n.8, 223n.10, 227n.3, 228n.8, 230n.25; Works: *Des Knaben Wunderhorn*, 5
Arnim, Armgardt von, 182
Arnim, Bettina von, Goethe Monument, xiii, 6, 22, 26, 38, 42, 47, 184, 228n.9, 232n. 3; Works: "An die aufgelöste Preußische National–Versammlung. Stimmen aus Paris" (*Die Polenbroschüre*), 182, 217n.12; *Das Armenbuch*, 216n.12, 227–228n.5; *Clemens Brentano's Frühlingskranz*, xiii, xvii, xviii, xix, 4, 5, 7, 9, 12, 14, 34, 93, 123, 125–156, 160, 163, 165, 166, 172, 178, 195, 211, 216n.2, 220n.19, 226n.9, 228n.7, 229n.12, 229–230n.16, 230n.24; *Dies Buch gehört dem König*, xix, 1, 4, 6, 31, 41, 78, 87–124, 127, 129, 131, 137, 151, 152, 154, 157, 158, 162, 163, 165, 166, 169, 171, 172, 173, 175, 181, 183, 184, 187, 192, 194, 195, 196, 200, 203, 208, 212, 213, 215n.2, 225n.1, 225n.2, 232n.2; *Gespräche mit Dämonen*, xvii, xix, 1, 6, 90, 103, 116, 129, 151, 154, 163, 166, 171, 172, 173, 178, 181–210, 212, 213, 215n.2, 217n.15; *Goethe's Briefwechsel mit einem Kinde*, xvi, xvii, xviii, xix, 4–7, 9, 12, 14, 21–52, 61, 63, 65–68, 72–73, 84, 87–89, 91, 94–95, 99, 102, 104, 114, 115, 118, 122, 128–130, 134–136, 140, 146, 157, 159, 161, 163, 165, 166, 167, 168, 172–173, 174, 178, 181, 185–187, 192–193, 195, 199, 211, 212, 215n.2, 217n.14, 218n.1, 219n.4, 220n.14, 220n.19, 221n.24, 223n.12; *Goethes Correspondence*

with a Child (Arnim's English translation of *Briefwechsel*), 6, 163, 167, 168; *Die Günderode*, xiii, xv, xvii, xviii, xix, 2, 4, 5, 7, 9, 12, 14, 30, 31, 35, 40, 51, 53–86, 87, 88, 89, 91, 94, 99, 102, 104, 109, 113, 114, 115, 118, 129, 130, 132, 134, 135, 136, 140, 145, 146, 147, 148, 150, 158, 161, 164, 166, 168, 173, 174, 185, 192, 195, 204, 211, 212, 215n.1, 223n.10, 223n.12, 229n.12; "Der Heckebeutel," 226n.7; *Ilius Pamphilius und die Ambrosia*, xvii, xviii, xix, 4, 5, 21, 22, 40, 59, 139, 157–180, 196, 209, 212, 213, 215n.2, 218n.1, 225n.5, 231n.1; *Der Magistratsprozeß*, 216–217n.12; Arnim's Bettine Personae: Bettine, Introduction through Conclusion, *passim*; Frau Rath, xviii, xix, 25, 27, 29, 30, 31, 32, 34, 37, 38, 40, 41, 43, 45, 50, 88, 89, 90, 91, 92, 93–109, 111–120, 122, 124, 127, 130, 137, 140, 162, 163, 166, 173, 184, 195, 213, 226n.8; French magpie, 88, 96, 97, 98, 104, 105, 113, 115, 116, 117, 118, 119, 120, 122, 195; Swiss educator, 97–99, 113, 117–122; Ambrosia, 5, 8, 159–178, 181, 212; Narrator of *Dämonen*, 166, 173, 184–190, 192, 193, 195–197, 199, 200, 203

Arnim, Gisela von, 182
Arnim, Maximiliane von, 131, 182
Arnim, Peter-Anton von, 217n.15
Arnim, Siegmund, 233, n.8
Arnim-Bärwalde, Achim von, xiv
Arnim-Boitzenburg, Adolf Heinrich von, 121
Assing, Ludmilla, 219n.4
Aston, Louise, 34, 72, 126; Works: *Revolution und Counterrevolution*, xvi
Atzel, See magpie
Austria, 22, 93, 121, 123, 219n.9

autobiography, xviii, xix, 5, 7, 8, 10, 12–14, 16, 23, 45, 47, 129, 140, 218n.19; *kontinuierliche Partnerautobiographie*, 13, 16, 208 (*see also* Bäumer); radical, 12, 16 (*see also* Goodman); referential model, 6, 7, 8, 23; textual model, 6, 7, 8; traditional, 8, 23, 218n.19

Bäumer, Konstanze, xvii, 4, 13, 15, 29, 46, 68, 158, 159, 217n.15, 218n.1, 219n.4, 220n.12, 221n.23, 221n.28, 222n.2, 222n.4, 222n.6, 230n.24, 231n.1, 233n.6 (*see also* Autobiography)
Bakhtin, M. M., 11
Baldwin, Claire, 183, 201, 208, 233n.7
Balzac, Honoré de, *Modeste Mignon*, xvi
Bandemer, Susanne von, 231n.5
Barrett, Michèle, 11, 218n.21
Barthes, Roland, 11, 12
Bauer, Bruno, 216n.8
Bauer, Edgar, 111, 131, 154, 216n.8
Baumgart, Hildegard, 223n.10
Bavaria, 22, 26, 93, 121, 123, 219n.9, 220n.20
Becker-Cantarino, Barbara, 31, 220n.16
becoming (*werden*), 32, 35, 57, 64, 79, 116, 120, 130, 150, 152, 199, 203, 211, 220–221n.20 (*see also* individual development)
Beethoven, Ludwig van, 22, 50, 163, 216n.8
Benkert, Karl Maria, 182
Berlin, 2, 3, 5, 6, 53, 56, 87–89, 92, 97, 99, 107, 109, 117–120, 122, 131, 154, 157, 158, 169, 181, 208, 222n.3, 222n.4, 227n.12, 232n.3, 233n.8; Academy of Sciences, 89; University, 53, 89, 118; *Vogtland*, 88, 97, 99, 107, 117, 118

Bildungsroman, See novel of development
biologism, 12
Blake, William, 226n.10
Blechen, Carl, 53
Börne, Ludwig, 7, 217n.14
Brentano, Bettina, 2, 5, 6, 21, 22, 23, 34, 54, 94, 127, 129, 217n.13, 219n.11, 220n.20, 221–222n.28 (*see also* Bettina von Arnim)
Brentano, Clemens, xvi, 25, 29, 54, 110, 127–128, 130, 134, 135, 139, 142, 145, 157, 158, 216n.8, 220 n.13, 223n.10, 229n.12, 229n.15, 229n.16, 230n.25; Works: *Godwi*, 129, 220n.13; *Des Knaben Wunderhorn*, 5; Clemens figure in Arnim's texts, xiii, 5, 57–59, 84, 127–158, 165, 178, 112, 183, 184, 195, 205, 227n.9, 229n.12, 229n.14
Brentano, Franz, 54
Brentano, Gunda, 57, 142
Brentano, Maximiliane, 21, 215n.3
Brentano, Sophie, 127
Brentano, Peter Anton, 127
Brentano-Mereau, Sophie, 125, 127, 128, 139, 223n.10, 230n.17
Büchner, Georg, *Leonce und Lena*, 61
Bürger, Christa, 8, 217n.18, 228n.10
Bunzel, Wolfgang, 28, 116, 225n.3, 226n.9
Burwick, Roswitha, 60, 61, 224n.14
Bussmann, Auguste, 128, 227n.2

canon, 9, 11, 32, 208
Carl, King of Württemberg, 91
Carlsbad Decrees, 89, 90, 120
Carriere, Moriz, 8, 87, 158, 216n.8, 217n.17, 222n.4
Catholicism, 105, 128, 163
censorship, 87, 90, 93, 120–122, 131, 154, 169, 195, 227–228n.5, 233n.6

cholera epidemic, 5, 6, 118, 169, 216n.10
Christliche Teutsche Tischgesellschaft, 230–231n.25
Cixous, Hélène, 13, 16, 68
colonialism, 106
Congress of Vienna, 89
Creuzer, Georg Friedrich, 221n.24, 223n.12
criminals, treatment of, 96, 98, 106, 107, 108, 109, 119
cross-dressing, 33, 34, 230n.20
cult of personality, xvii, 10, 158

Dahlmann, Friedrich, 111
Dalberg, Karl Theodor von, 48, 54, 114, 186, 188
Daley, Margaretmary, xvii, 167
Daumer, Georg Friedrich, 53
Demagogenverfolgung, 88, 120
Demeter, 196
devil, 115, 116, 226n.10
Diamond, Irene, 218n.23
Dickinson, Emily, 93
digression, 94–96
Dischner, Gisela, 68, 74, 220n.17, 221n.22, 222n.5
discourse, 11, 12, 16, 17, 19, 20, 29, 42, 51, 79, 145, 146, 211
Döring, Julius, 4, 122, 158, 171
Dohm, Hedwig, *Schicksale einer Seele*, xvi
Doktorenklub, 54, 56, 158
Doppelgänger, 181
Drewitz, Ingeborg, 2, 3, 88, 111, 131, 160, 215n.1, 227n.2
Duden, Barbara, 220n.16

Eberhard, Wilhelmine, 125
echo, 43, 66, 81, 106, 137, 166, 174, 177, 205, 224n.14

Eco, Umberto
Edler, Erich, 119
education, 15, 24, 34, 37–39, 41, 46, 48, 65, 72, 96, 102, 104, 108, 109, 126, 133, 134, 142, 143, 145, 149, 150, 151, 154, 163, 166, 173, 184, 189, 197, 203, 206, 207
Egloffstein, Caroline von, 222n.1
Eichendorff, Joseph von, 228n.6
Emmerich, Anna Katharina, 128
Ephraim, 7, 54, 57, 58, 69, 72–74, 80–82, 118, 150, 217n.15
epistolary writing, 2, 5, 8, 10, 13–16, 21, 37, 39, 43, 50, 51, 53, 55, 65, 66, 68, 73, 75, 85, 90, 91, 127, 128, 130, 141, 172, 183, 213, 215n.2, 220n.15, 223n.8, 225n.18, 225n.1, 228n.9
essentialism, 12, 13, 16, 18, 69, 103, 214
experience, xviii, 1, 4, 5, 6, 10, 12, 17–20, 24, 26, 29, 30, 35, 37–39, 40, 54, 55, 58, 69, 78, 79, 82, 85, 95, 98, 99, 101, 102, 118, 125, 140, 142, 161, 162, 169, 175, 188, 209, 211, 212, 214, 228n.9

Fallersleben, Hoffmann von, 122, 216n.8
feminism, 11, 69, 218n.21, 218n.23
feminist scholarship, 7, 10, 11, 16, 18, 68, 69, 125
Fichte, Johann Gottlieb, 44, 77, 220n.14
fiction, approaches to reading Arnim's texts, 9, 10, 13, 15 (*see also* autobiography; novel of development)
Fish, Stanley, 11
five-mark bill, xiii, xv
Foucault, Michel, xx, 11, 12, 16
Frankfurt am Main, 22, 25, 47, 48, 59, 88, 89, 95, 96, 97, 98, 105, 111, 112, 186, 188, 189, 217n.14, 222n.29; *Freie Reichsstadt*, 95, 98, 111
Frederiksen, Elke, 17, 68, 217n.16, 218n.24
Freiburg, Max Prokop von, 23
French, Lorely, 26, 139, 167, 215n.2, 222n.6
French Revolution, 22, 71, 117, 129, 131, 133, 143, 151, 152, 153, 154, 230n.24
Frevert, Ute, 126, 230n.33
Friedrich Wilhelm III (King of Prussia), 89, 109
Friedrich Wilhelm IV (King of Prussia), 109, 121, 122, 131, 154, 157, 182, 183, 184, 193, 206, 225n.1, 225n.2, 226n.8, 227n.14, 227–228n.5
friendship, 7, 22, 30, 55, 58, 65, 67, 68, 83, 96, 98, 103–105, 110, 132, 136–139, 144, 151, 159, 176–178, 189, 191, 194–196, 205, 207, 226n.9, 228n.14, 229n.12, 229n.14
Fromm, Leberecht, 123
Fuss, Diana, 218n.23

Gachet, Madame de (Princess Bourbon-Conti), 34, 133, 138, 142, 143, 146–151, 165, 230n.16
Gajek, Bernhard, 220–221n.20
Gajek, Enid Margarete, 219n.4
Geiger, Ludwig, 7, 217n.14, 223n.1
Geist, Johann Friedrich, 97, 118, 119
Gersdorff, Dagmar von, 2, 3, 216n.10, 223n.10
Gille, Klaus, 221n.21, 221n.23
Goethe, Catharina Elisabeth, xix, 21, 22, 51, 89, 98, 99, 118, 223n.10, 225n.3, 225n.4; Frau Rath figure and Bettine persona in Arnim's Texts, Frau Rath, xviii, xix, 25, 27, 29–34, 37, 38, 40, 41, 43, 45, 50,

Index 255

88, 89–124, 127, 130, 137, 140, 162, 163, 166, 173, 184, 195, 213, 226n.8
Goethe, Christiane Vulpius, 22
Goethe, Johann Wolfgang von, xiii, 1, 3, 4, 7, 9, 21–26, 34, 36, 46–48, 51, 78, 98, 184, 215n.2, 216n.8, 216n.11, 217n.13, 217n.14, 218n.20, 218n.1, 219n.8, 220n.14, 221–222n.28, 223n. 10, 225n.3, 225n.4; Works: *Dichtung und Wahrheit*, 22; *Die Leiden des jungen Werthers* 26, 30, 34, 35; *Die Wahlverwandtschaften*, 26, 33, 35, 36, 48, 63; *West-östlicher Divan*, 24, 26; *Wilhelm Meisters Lehrjahre*, 14, 21, 25, 34–36, 62, 63, 67, 174, 221, n.21, 221n.23, 229n.15; "Urworte, Orphisch," 46, 66; Goethe figure in Arnim's texts: 14, 25, 26–38, 40–51, 62, 66, 68, 84, 88, 89, 94, 97, 101, 102, 114, 128, 149, 159, 161, 165, 170, 171, 18, 184, 186, 193, 213;
Göttingen Seven, trial of, 53, 89, 111, 158, 169
Goodman, Katherine, 11, 12, 13, 15, 16, 17, 218n.21, 218n.22, 218n.24, 220n.17, 229n.12, 229n.14; radical autobiography, 12, 16
Goozé, Marjanne, 139, 218n.1, 220n.17, 232n.4
Grass, Günter, *Der Butt*, xvi
Greiner, Bernd, 30
Grimm, Jakob and Wilhelm, 53, 89, 118, 157, 158, 169, 216n.8, 222n.3
Grimm, Ludwig, xiv
Grunholzer, Heinrich (Swiss educator), 97–99, 113, 117–120, 122
Günderrode, Karoline von, xix, 1, 4, 21, 22, 24, 51, 54, 56, 58, 61, 74, 98, 125, 126, 128, 157, 158, 215n.2, 223n.10, 223n.12, 224n.14; Günderode figure in Arnim's texts: xiii, xv, xix, 5, 15, 25, 29, 30, 31, 32, 35–43, 45, 50, 53, 54–83, 101, 104, 132, 133, 134, 137, 138, 142, 145–152, 163, 164, 168, 175, 186, 195, 198, 213
Gutzkow, Karl, 53, 91, 92, 96, 108; Works: *Wally, die Zweiflerin*, xvi

Häberlin, Karl Ludwig, *Reaktionäre und Demokraten*, xvi, 119
Härtl, Heinz, 22, 110, 215n.1, 215n.3, 222n.5, 231–232n.1
Hahn, Karl-Heinz, 110, 123, 208, 222n.5
Hahn-Hahn, Ida, 126
Hausen, Karin, 220n.16
Hegel, Georg Willhelm Friedrich, 220n.14
Hemsterhius, 229n.12
Herder, Johann Gottfried, 38
Herwegh, Emma, 34
Heuberger, Rachel, 217n.14
Heukenkamp, Marianne, 224n.16, 225n.18
Hirsch, Helmut, 7, 217n.14
Hirsch, Marianne, 13, 14
Hock, Lisabeth, xvii, 217n.15
Hölderlin, Friedrich, 54, 61, 72, 80–82, 166, 220n.13, 224n.17
homoeroticism, 146, 148
Hoock-Demarle, Marie-Claire, 7, 217n.15, 231n.3
Hössli, Philipp, 3
Houben, Heinrich, 93, 120, 121, 227n.12
Huch, Ricarda, xvii
Humboldt, Alexander von, 92, 93, 120, 216n.8, 228n.5
Hungary, 91, 181, 182, 191

immortality (*Unsterblichkeit*), xiii, xv, 57, 91, 103, 161, 192, 196

individual development (individuation), 26, 37, 88, 116, 123, 129, 134, 137, 141, 174, 183, 187, 188, 228n.6
inquisition, 105, 108
Iser, Wolfgang, 11
isolation, 68, 98, 130, 134, 141, 166, 213
Italy, xiv, 148, 149, 162, 163, 164, 175, 176
Janssen, Carmen Viktoria, xvii, 228n.7
Jauss, Hans Robert, 11
Jews: anti-Semitism, 7; depiction of, 231n.3; education of, 48; in Frankfurt, 25, 47, 200; rights of, 7, 233n.7
Joeres, Ruth-Ellen Boetcher, 65, 219n.10
July Revolution (1830), 23

Kant, Immanuel, 77, 205, 207, 208, 220n.14; Works: "Was ist Aufklärung?" 205, 208
Kertbeny, Karl Maria (Benkert), 91
Kinkel, Gottfried, 182
Kirsch, Sarah, xvi
Kittler, Friedrich, 219n.6
Kleist, Ulrike von, 34
Klopstock, Friedrich Gottlieb, 97
Krieger, Leonard, 110, 111
Krimmer, Elisabeth, xvii, 220n.19, 230n.20
Kristeva, Julia, 11
Krohn, Helga, 217n.14
Kügelgen, Helene von, 219n.3
Kühne, Gustav, 226n.10
Kürvers, Klaus, 97, 118, 119

Landfester, Ulrike, 221n.23
Langland, Elizabeth, 13–14
La Roche, Sophie von, 2, 21, 54, 73, 133, 142, 216n.8, 217n.13, 220n.15,
223n.10; Grandmother figure in Arnim's texts, 38, 57, 63, 72, 73, 84, 133, 140, 142, 148, 151, 152
Lauer, Gerhard, 217n.15
Lauretis, Teresa de, xviii, 16–20, 51, 127, 161
Leitner, Ingrid, 221n.25
Lemke, Ann Willison, xvii, 215n.5, 216n.9, 224n.17
Lessing, Gotthold Ephraim, *Nathan der Weise*, 187, 188
Levysohn, Wilhelm, 158
Lewald, Fanny, 4, 72, 126, 173, 216n.7, 231n.2; Works: *Adele*, xvi
Liebertz-Grün, Ursula, 10, 31, 41, 90, 95, 133, 228n.14
Locke, John, 198, 202
Loeper, Gustav von, 7, 8, 215n.1, 217n.13, 217n.17, 218n.4
Lombardian, 191
Louise, Queen of Prussia, 94, 95, 102, 109, 226n.8
love, 6, 21, 24–26, 37–47, 58, 62, 66, 67, 71, 78, 81, 82, 88, 115, 132, 136, 138, 151, 174, 176, 187, 188, 191, 207, 221n.25

magpie, French (*Atzel*), 88, 96, 97, 98, 104, 105, 113, 115–119, 120, 122, 195
Martin, Biddy, 6, 11, 12, 218n.21
Marx, Karl, 182, 216n.8; Works: *Communist Manifesto*, 183
medium, 38, 56, 66, 72, 81, 83, 84, 115, 165, 171, 199
memory, 31, 55, 56, 68, 74, 77, 84, 140, 182, 187
menopause, 160
Meyer-Hepner, Gertrud, xvii, 216–217n.12
Meysenbug, Malwida von, 72, 126; Works: *Memoiren einer Idealisten*, xvi

Mickel, Karl, *Halsgericht*, xvi
Mignon, 34, 35, 36, 62, 63, 67, 174, 217n.15, 221n.21, 221n.23, 229n.15
Mirabeau, Gabriel de Riqueti, Count, 151, 152
mirror motif, xiii, xiv, xvi, xx, 26, 29, 31, 36, 43–45, 49, 60, 66, 80–83, 101, 114, 132, 134, 136, 138, 141, 151, 159, 172, 174, 176, 179, 191, 204, 205, 207, 211, 212
Möhrmann, Renate, 125, 126, 127, 154
Molitor, Joseph, 48, 54, 222n.29
monarchy, 111, 112, 123, 124, 197, 198, 205, 206, 207; constitutional, xix, 53, 90, 98, 112, 113, 123, 206, 212
Montgomery-Silverstolpe, Mala, 3
motherhood, xix, 20, 31, 36, 40, 45, 81, 94, 96, 98, 99, 101–105, 108, 114, 115, 157, 159, 166, 170, 171, 173, 176, 190, 193, 194, 196, 197, 198, 207–209, 212, 231n.4
Mühlbach, Luise (pseud. for Clara Mundt), 126–127
Müller, Friedrich von, 22, 25
Mundt, Clara, 126–127
Mundt, Theodor, 53; Works: *Carmela oder die Wiedertaufe*, xvi

Napoleon, 75, 76, 98, 103, 219n.9
Napoleonic Wars, 22, 34, 102, 111
narcissism, 45, 174, 176–177
Nathusius, Philipp, 1, 4, 6, 98, 122, 157–159, 162, 178; Pamphilius figure in Arnim's texts, 5, 159, 160–178, 212, 213, 231n.2
Novalis, 29, 110, 197
Novalis: *Glauben und Liebe*, 110, 197, 205

novel of development (*Bildungsroman*), xix, 9, 10, 14, 15, 16, 36, 199; female, 13, 14, 15, 16, 24
Nussbaum, Felicity, 12, 13, 218n.19

Oehlke, Waldemar, 215n.2, 218n.1, 230n.18
Oppenheim, Bernhard, 158, 216n.8, 222n.4
Osterkamp, Ernst, 226n.10
Ottilie, 35, 36, 63
Otto-Peters, Louise, 126, 227n.1
outsider, 81, 82, 102, 150, 151, 187

pantheism, 79, 199
pedagogical eros, 159, 165, 173
Peirce, Charles Sanders, 17
Petöfi, Sandor, 182
philistinism, 28, 29, 60–64, 78, 116, 117, 205, 208, 223n.13
Piautaz, Claudine, 2, 82, 215n.3
Plato, Works: *Politeia*, 90; *Symposium*, 37
Poland, 181, 182, 191, 204, 217n.12
positionality, xix, 16, 18, 19, 51, 64, 161
poverty, 12, 96, 97, 98, 106, 108–110, 118–120, 126, 182, 216n.12
Prussia, 6, 53, 87, 88, 89, 90, 93, 96, 101, 105, 106, 107, 120, 121, 122, 123, 169, 184, 200, 216n.12, 233n.7
Psyche, 22, 38, 39, 216n.11, 221n.23, 228n.9
Pückler, Hermann von, 22, 24, 26, 98, 122, 171, 216n.8, 219n.4, 219n.7, 225n.5
Püschel, Ursula, xvii, 122, 123, 205, 208
Pusch, Luise, 229n.13

Quinby, Lee, 218n.23

Rauch, Christian, 22
responsibility, 36, 63, 80, 87, 178, 197, 198, 200, 201, 204, 205, 212
Revelations, Book of, 197
Revolution of 1848, 6, 123, 125, 181, 182, 225n.1, 233n.6, 233n.8
Rich, Adrienne, 230n.21
Rilke, Rainer Maria, *Die Aufzeichnungen des Malte Laurids Brigge,* xvi
Ring, Max, 158, 222n.4
Roetzel, Lisa, 223n.9
role playing, 1, 11, 15, 19, 20, 26–30, 32, 36, 37, 46, 47, 49, 51, 56, 58, 59, 61, 70, 72, 82, 97–99, 102–105, 108, 113–115, 120, 122, 129, 134, 135, 137, 142, 144, 151, 157–171, 173, 176, 181, 187, 190, 192, 193, 194, 196, 197, 198, 199, 207, 209, 211, 212; Roles played by Arnim's Bettine personae: activist, xvi, xvii, 134, 151, 166, 169; child (das Kind), xiv, xvi, xix, 14, 20, 21, 23, 26–32, 35–38, 41, 46, 49, 51, 55, 58, 59, 60, 83, 90, 92, 93, 98, 100, 102, 103, 107, 113, 114, 119, 122, 125, 129, 130, 134, 135, 137, 138, 142, 149, 161, 162, 165, 166, 167, 170, 171–176, 181, 186, 187, 193, 194, 196, 198, 208, 209, 212, 217n.14, 219n.11, 220n.12, 220n.13; daemon, xviii, 46, 47, 49, 59, 71, 79, 80, 81, 84, 99, 115, 116, 117, 120, 171, 176, 181–185, 186, 188–209, 212, 213, 232n.4, 227n.14; friend, xv, xix, 20, 40, 43, 44, 53, 58, 60, 64–68, 72, 77, 81, 88, 97, 98, 99, 103, 108, 112, 113, 131, 134–138, 166, 176, 193, 194, 196, 208, 212; genius, xix, 22, 26–31, 41–44, 46, 47, 49, 50, 51, 58, 59, 66, 79, 80, 81, 84, 94, 102, 104, 146, 159, 161, 165, 166, 168, 171, 172, 175, 176, 181, 184, 186, 191, 196, 197, 199, 202, 206, 209, 212, 223n.9, 224n.16, 225n.2, 231n.2, 232n.5; lover, xvi, xix, 20, 26, 35–38, 45, 46, 49, 58, 134, 136, 139, 165, 166, 171, 173, 175, 176, 208, 212; mother, xix, 20, 36, 40, 96, 98, 99, 102, 103, 104, 108, 114, 115, 166, 170, 171, 172, 173, 176, 190, 193, 194, 196, 197, 198, 207, 208, 209, 212, 231n.4; old woman, 99, 101, 117, 212; sister, 25, 31, 130, 133, 134, 135, 136, 137, 138, 140, 143; writer, xv, xvii, xix, 1, 4, 26, 31, 49, 50, 51, 57, 58, 72, 82, 83, 84, 89, 92, 101, 115, 122, 128, 130, 134, 139, 142, 166, 167, 169, 193, 195, 196, 209; youth, 30, 53, 55, 59, 60–67, 81, 83, 84, 99, 114, 159, 170, 193
romantic sociability, 37, 47, 55, 57, 59, 65–67, 73, 90, 110, 124, 136, 141, 144, 160, 165, 166, 172, 173, 175–178, 189, 212, 213, 229n.14
romanticism, xvii, 222n.5, 228n.6
Rücksichtslosigkeit, 122, 140, 162
Ruge, Arnold, 111

salon, xvi, 53, 54, 60, 87, 90, 91, 122, 131, 157, 158, 182, 222n.10, 232n.2
Sammons, Jeffrey, 226n.10
Sand, George, 34,
Savigny, Friedrich Karl von, 3, 23, 54, 57, 58, 69, 134, 135, 169, 215n.4, 216n.8, 222n.3, 223n.12, 229n.15
Sedgwick, Eve Kosofky, 230n.16
Shafi, Monika, 68, 217n.16, 221n.23, 228n.9
Schiller, Friedrich von, 78, 143, 144, 220n.14
Schlegel, Dorothea, 32, 125, 126

Schlegel, Friedrich, 29, 31, 37, 41, 44, 91, 135; *Universalpoesie*, 91; Works: *Lucinde*, 31, 41, 44, 45, 49, 51, 135, 142
Schlegel-Schelling, Caroline, 2, 32
Schleiermacher, Friedrich Daniel Ernst, 37, 38, 46, 54, 56, 77, 87, 150, 175, 186
Schmitz, Walter, 134, 183, 206, 208, 219n.8, 232n.5
Schopenhauer, Johanna, 32, 125
Schormann, Sabine, 37, 38, 78, 216n.8, 219n.5, 222n.5, 223n.11
Schorn, Adelheid von, 216n.11
Schultz, Hartwig, xvii, 4, 13, 68, 90, 128, 130, 138, 139, 159, 208, 219n.4, 222n.3, 222n.6, 228n.8, 230n.24, 232n.2, 233n.6
Schwaneflugel, Susan C., xvii
Schwebereligion, 56, 78, 79
Shakespeare, William, 32, 230n.16; Works: *Hamlet*, 146; *The Merchant of Venice*, 200
Simpson, Patricia Anne, xix
Socrates, 46, 91, 105, 120
Sonnenfels, Anna, 217n.17
Spinoza, Baruch, 229n.12
Spontini, Gasparo, 87, 118, 122
Staff, Ilse, 106, 107, 123, 204, 208, 233n.7
Stahr, Adolph, 113, 121, 123
Steig, Reinhold, 8, 217n.17, 218n.1, 227n.4
Steinhäuser, Karl, xiii
Steinsdorff, Sibylle von, 134, 219n.8, 221n.25
Strauss, David Friedrich, 87, 224n.16
subjectivity, 10, 11, 12, 15, 16, 17, 19, 205, 209
subjectivity: fragmented, 12, 13, 15, 16, 117, 120
subjectivity: subject positions, 18, 20, 27, 98
Susman, Margarete, 217n.14

Swiss educator, 97, 98, 99, 113, 117, 118, 119, 120, 122 (*see also* Heinrich Grunholzer)

Tarnow, Fanny, 125
Teplitz fragments, 22, 42, 218n.2
Trunz, Erich, 219n.8
Tyrolean uprising (1809), 23, 26, 33, 35, 36, 48, 118, 181, 219n.9

Varnhagen, Karl August von, 4, 121, 129, 154, 216n.8, 217n.15, 232n.3
Varnhagen, Rahel, 2, 32, 125, 126, , 223n.10
Veilchen, 7, 133, 138, 142, 151, 152, 153, 163
Vogtland, See Berlin
Vormärz, 61, 93, 110, 126, 181

Waldstein, Edith, 66, 68, 92, 123, 172, 217n.16, 218n.22, 220n.17, 222n.6, 222n.7
Waldemar, Prince of Prussia, 130, 131, 154
Walker, Cheryl: persona, xviii
White, Hayden, 75
Wiepersdorf, xvi, 2
Wildermeth, Karl Ludwig von, 3
Wilhelm, King of Prussia, 130
Wobeser Wilhelmine K. von, 229n.15
Wolf, Christa, xvi, xvii, 3, 17, 91, 218n.20; Works: *Kein Ort. Nirgends*, xvi
Wolzogen, Karoline von, 125
women's movement, 6, 125, 126, 127, 154, 230n.23
Wuthenow, Ralph-Rainer, 224n.17
Wyss, Hilde, 110, 208, 222n.5

Young Germany movement, xvi, 6, 23,
  54, 87, 112, 125, 223–224n.13,
  226n.12
Young Hegelian movement, xvi, 6, 23,
  54, 87, 110, 125, 154

OHIO UNIVERSITY LIBRARY

Please return this book as soon as you have finished with it. In order to avoid a fine it must be returned by the latest date stamped below. All books are subject to recall after two weeks or immediately if needed for reserve.

CF